Writing My Wrongs

A Memoir by
Shaka Senghor

ISBN 978-0-9794606-9-2

Additional copies of this book are available by contacting the publisher directly.
Send correspondence to:

Drop a Gem Publishing, LLC
P.O. Box 23176
Detroit, MI 48223
(313) 720-5546

Or visit www.shakasenghor.com

Printed in the U.S.A. by
Drop a Gem Publishing
P.O. Box 23176
Detroit, MI 48223

Dedication

To Ebony, you are my everything.

To my children Lakeisha Todd, James Angelo White II, and Sekou
Senghor,
I love you more than words can express.

To my parents James and Marie White and Ronald (RIP) and Arlene
Howard, thank you for your love and support.

To my brothers on lockdown who are working hard to make a difference
and transform their lives, you inspire and motivate me.

To the victims of crimes throughout the world,
your pain will never be forgotten.

Acknowledgements

I want to acknowledge all of the amazing people I have worked with and been inspired by. The list is much too long to include everyone so if by some chance I forgot you, trust that I have you on a special list in my heart. Ebony Roberts, James White, Marie White, Alan Neal, Arthur Neal, Tamica Neal, Will Redd III, Vanessa Redd, Nakia White, Shamica White, Sherrod Redd, all of my nephews and nieces, Malik Yakini, Clement Fame Brown, Jr., Carmen Brown, Yusef Bunchy Shakur, Virgil Taylor, MIT Media Lab, BMe, IDEO, Joi Ito, Jess Sousa, Colin Rainey, Sean Bonner, Lisa Katayama, Stacie Slotnick, Trabian Shorter, Katrina Storm, Joel Fluent Greene, Toni Jennings, Melissa Deshields, Marcus Little, Shuntez, O'neal, Jerrel O'neal, all of the students at Cody High School and Tri County Educational Center. To all of my guys on lockdown, much love and respect to you.

Peace,

Shaka

Foreword

On July 1, 2012, the MIT Media Lab announced that we would be creating an Innovators Guild–a team of scholars, executives, and designers that would go to communities around the world using the power of innovation to help people. Our first focus for this was Detroit.

Three weeks later the Knight Foundation, which was funding our trip, organized a meeting with Detroit community leaders. We gave presentations about MIT and the Media Lab and about how we had come to Detroit to explore how we could create innovative solutions to long-standing problems.

Then, during the Q&A, a tough-looking black man with dreadlocks stood up and spoke. "Many well-meaning people come to Detroit with a missionary mentality. Then they get discouraged when they realize how just how tough our problems are. If you want to make a real impact you have to go out among the people in the communities and not buy into the romanticized view of Detroit based on Midtown and Downtown." Although there were other comments expressing skepticism, this one stood out. We realized, for the first time, that we were looking into the face of reality–The Truth.

After the formal part of the meeting, the man came up to us and introduced himself as Shaka. He said that if we were willing he would show us the real Detroit. We immediately accepted the offer. On the next trip we avoided downtown altogether and went straight to Brightmoor on Detroit's West Side, a neighborhood full of burned-out, vacant homes and liquor stores fronted with bulletproof glass. Shaka told us stories that had none of the romance, but they were real.

We quickly realized that we couldn't just fly in, do good, and go home. We needed to introduce ourselves to the community, learn about the people who live there, and build trust. If we wanted to have a positive impact on Detroit we had to be there for the long haul.

In the following weeks, my team from the Media Lab and creatives from the design firm IDEO flew to Detroit, working with Shaka and others to come up with a plan for how we might be able to join the community and work together. We then invited Shaka and the Detroit team to the MIT Media Lab to meet students and faculty and see and learn about what we do. Bonds began forming between the Lab and the Detroiters.

In October, we all converged on Detroit–setting up a base at the headquarters of OmniCorpDetroit, a vital, local organization. We were a team of community leaders, chief innovation officers, students, and designers. Each of the teams started working on projects ranging from solving the streetlight issue to urban farming. Shaka emerged as our natural leader, keeping the energy high and the teams working together.

By the end of an insanely productive three days, I had a plan. I would make Shaka a MIT Media Lab Fellow and he'd be our man in Detroit–our connection to the incredibly important world he represents. Since then, Shaka and the Media Lab team have started to work together extensively, and Shaka continues to inspire and challenge us.

In December, Shaka emailed me that he had a rough draft of his memoirs and asked if I was interested in reading it. I read the entire book in two sittings, riveted. Shaka is, among his other talents, an amazing storyteller. The book is funny and moving and astute and by the end I felt as if I had been the one convicted of murder, as if I'd spent seven years in the hole, and gone through the dramatic transformation from angry, scared young boy, to enlightened teacher and leader.

And by the end, I could begin to see how a generation of bright children full of promise are channeled into a system that sees them as little more than felons-in-waiting. Yet again, Shaka has inspired me to help right the wrongs by, in this instance, helping him write the wrongs.

The book may be about Shaka's past, but it points to a future in which we all take the next step to build a more just society.

Joi Ito

Director, MIT Media Lab
January 2013

Prologue

I stared at the mirror watching the tears roll slowly down my face, each drop carrying the pain of my childhood. It was my deepest moment of reflection, a sacred moment in time where I came face-to-face with true forgiveness.

I stared at my battle-scarred image and began the long, tedious process of forgiving. I forgave all of the people who had teased me in my childhood, making fun of my jack-o-lantern-sized head, which earned me the nickname, Pumpkin. I forgave everyone who had made fun of my gap-toothed smile. While I still have my issues with the chasm between my teeth, I have learned to smile when I see other successful owners of the gap. Whether it is watching Michael Strahan analyze football on Fox Sports or reminiscing about the days when "Uncle Luke" and the 2 Live Crew reigned supreme, I find solace in knowing that they made it although they didn't have picture perfect smiles.

In forgiving, I opened up deep wounds that I had stuffed with the gauze of self-hatred and low self-esteem. The words from my past ricocheted off the walls of my mind like an errant bullet fired from an AK 47. As each word whizzed by in a blur, my instincts told me to duck. However, I knew I had to trust the Kevlar vest of self-love to protect me as I stood in the line of fire. Bravely, I faced the fusillade of thoughts from my past.

I forgave everyone who ever called me nappy-headed, making me feel insecure about the royal crown that the Creator had bestowed upon me. I ran my hands through my long locs, which cascaded over my shoulders like velvet.

I forgave my mother for all of the ass whoopings she gave me as I reflected back on the fire of the belt cutting into my tender flesh. I also forgave her for all of the moments she wasn't there when I needed her most.

I forgave my siblings and homies for abandoning me when I was at the lowest point in my life. I also forgave the guy who shot me and made me feel like I had to carry a gun. The levees broke and the tears flowed with the turbulence of the Mississippi in the spring as I inhaled and exhaled, breathing in a deep, abiding peace and exhaling the toxic hatred from my past.

I had heard a lot about the healing power of forgiveness, but it took me several years to fully appreciate the power of forgiving others. I didn't forgive them to let them off the hook or to free them of their culpability. This was about me. I had to free myself from the anger, fear and hurt of my past, so I had to forgive them. But more importantly, I had to forgive myself.

It was one of the hardest things I had ever done, because I didn't feel I was worthy of forgiveness. Guilt from all of the hurt, destruction and disappointment that I had caused others clung to me like a sweaty T-shirt on a humid summer day, but I knew in my heart that it was a necessary part of my atonement process. If I wanted to make it right with others, I had to make it right with myself first. In order to feel like I was worthy of their forgiveness and capable of forgiving them, I had to forgive myself for all the hurt I had brought into my own life.

It was in this moment that I realized no one could make me feel anything I didn't want to feel. I was ultimately responsible for my anger and the actions that I took in response to it. Thus began my eight-year journey to forgiveness, which culminated with me writing a letter of forgiveness to the victim of my crime.

During one of my group therapy sessions I wrote the following letter. Out of respect to my victim's family and their privacy I have omitted his named. The letter reads as follows:

Dear Mr. *****,

I am writing this letter to share with you what has been on my mind and in my heart for several years now. For the last few nights, I have stayed awake writing this letter in my head, and each time, I found myself mentally balling up the pages because I couldn't find the right words to convey how deeply sorry I am for causing your death. Somehow saying I am sorry for robbing you and your family of your life seems too small of a gesture.

Every time I think back to that fateful night, I often find myself asking the question, "Why didn't I just walk away?" When I finally found the answer, I understood for the first time the true meaning of the words 'weakness' and 'strength.' See, all along I had twisted their meaning around in my head. I thought walking away from an argument would make me appear weak and make me a loser. But in reality, it takes strength to walk away from conflict, and back then that was something I was lacking.

Instead of being as strong and powerful as I imagined myself to be, I was the epitome of weakness; I was afraid and I allowed my fears to dictate my actions. See, I was wearing a mask of 'hood toughness, but underneath that façade were deep-rooted fears and insecurities.

Sixteen months prior to me shooting you, I was shot in a similar incident. I allowed the fear from my shooting to consume me. Instead of seeing it as an isolated incident, I programmed myself to think that it could happen again at any given moment. I became desperately angry because anger was the only emotion that could conceal the fear I had inside of me. Anger became my mask and carrying a gun with me everywhere I went became my shield.

So when we encountered each other, I was already programmed to kill. I had convinced myself that it was better to shoot than to be shot. In my mind at the time, it was easier to shoot than to walk away, and sadly, it took me years to understand how wrong I was.

For years, I blamed you for making me mad enough to shoot, but I realize now that no on can make me feel anything I don't want to feel. I blamed your death on the fact that we were both intoxicated, but now I recognize that the thought to shoot anyone I perceived as a threat had been planted long before we met. I blamed everything and everyone but myself, even though I pled guilty. Pleading guilty was easy because I knew I had violated the law, but it didn't mean I was taking full responsibility for causing your death.

It wasn't until I was ten years into serving my sentence that I began taking responsibility for causing your death. It started with a letter I received from my son. His letter made me face up to the fact that it was

3

my thinking and the choices I made that caused your death and led to me being incarcerated.

Today when I look back, I wish I could change the past. I wish I could restore your life so that your children could have enjoyed the safety and security of having a father in the house. I wish I could bring you back to life so that your wife could enjoy the presence of her husband and your parents could see you reach your dreams and goals.

I know saying I am sorry can never restore your life. However, I believe in the power of atonement, and I have taken responsibility for taking your life by dedicating my life and talents to atoning. For the last five years, I have been actively involved with anti-violence organizations that work with at-risk youth. I have used my talent as a writer to share our story so that others may learn from it and make wiser choices than I did as a teenager. If nothing else, know that your life and the time I am serving in prison hasn't and will not be in vain.

Lastly, I hope at some point that you can find it in your spirit to forgive me. I learned about the power of forgiveness from your godmother, Mrs. Weaver. She started writing me five years into my sentence. She wanted to know what occurred that night to cause me to shoot and kill you. That was one of the hardest questions I've ever had to answer, however I knew that I owed your family closure. I responded and told them about our dispute; however, I chose to leave out the fact that it was a drug transaction. I didn't feel that it was necessary for them to be exposed to that part of your life. When she told me that she forgave me and encouraged me to seek God's forgiveness, I took her words to heart. It took years before I was able to finally forgive myself, but it has helped. It helped me to see that even though I forgave myself, I still had a lot of work to do, and each day I am blessed with, I have the will to live with meaning and purpose.

Sincerely,

Shaka

Chapter 1

The piercing sound of sirens blaring burst through the quiet morning air and startled me from my restless slumber. I crawled from beneath the thin, scratchy, wool blanket and approached the cold, grey cell bars. I watched a chubby roach navigate its way across the bars before I hollered down the tier.

"Yo, Satan, what the fuck they hit the siren for," I asked as I wiped the crust from the corner of my eyes.

Satan was from Inkster and one of the few cats I spoke to on a regular basis. Though we were from different cities, we had a lot in common and had formed a bond during the time I was in county jail.

"I don't know, homie," he responded from a few cells down. "You know how they do around here. They probably hate that they ass can't get no sleep, so they fucking with us," he continued, causing a few other inmates to laugh.

Satan's statement expressed the sentiment of most of the cats on lockdown; the deputies would do anything they could to make our stay as unbearable as possible. While their theory worked in the movies, it rarely, if ever, worked in real life. Most of us had come from environments where abuse, violence and disrespect were the norm. It went against common sense to think that you could change a person for the better by treating him or her like an animal. The way I see it, you get out of people what you put into them.

"They might be coming to get y'all and take y'all to different county jails," another inmate called from further down the tier.

"Come get us for what?" Satan asked, a bit irritated.

"Man, they take that escape shit serious. Ain't nobody tried to pull off that shit y'all just tried," he said, alluding to the escape attempt that Satan and I were in the hole for.

"Bitch ass nigga, mind your business 'cause you speaking on shit you don't even know about. You working with the police or something, saying some shit like that? You don't know if them brothers tried to escape or not. You trying to get niggas indicted around this bitch," another brother hollered from my end of the tier, causing everyone to burst into laughter.

"Man, I was just saying," the first inmate stammered.

"That's the problem now, so shut the fuck up!" the brother responded, leading to more laughter.

I sat on the corner of my bunk and listened to them argue back and forth as the siren continued blaring. It felt weird listening to two guys I didn't know speak with so much authority about something I was accused of doing. It had been a week since me, Satan, Gee, White Boy, and Jabo were placed in the hole. We were charged with attempting to escape from the sixth floor of the Wayne County Jail. With no evidence other than a confidential statement made by another inmate, we were found guilty and sentenced to 15 days in the hole.

Two days after being thrown in the hole, we were each called out by an officer from the Internal Affairs division. He threatened each of us with lengthy sentences and promised us the world if we snitched on one another. One by one, we refused to answer any questions regarding the escape attempt and the matter was dropped as far as Internal Affairs was concerned. However, the Wayne County Hearing Officer, who was basically an internal, autonomous judge and jury, found us guilty and sentenced us to 15 days in the hole. It was an irony that vexed us to no end. In jail and in prison, when a confidential informant makes a statement against an inmate, it is enough to find him or her guilty of any charge. However, when we have witnesses who are capable of exonerating us, their testimony is ruled no good.

Understanding the embarrassment that the Wayne County Sherriff's Office had suffered as a result of the almost-successful escape attempt, it was feasible that they could be coming to get us and ship us off to different county jails. We would quickly learn, however, that what we were accused of was minor in comparison to what led the siren to be sounded.

After nearly half an hour of blaring, the siren suddenly grew quiet, leaving in its wake an eerie silence. Within moments, we could hear

6

the sounds of keys jingling and the urgent crackling of deputies' radios. Little did we know, it would quickly become the soundtrack of chaos.

Minutes after the siren stopped, a team of deputies, better known as the goon squad, rushed our tier and began snatching us out of our cells, one at a time. They wore an assortment of looks on their faces, from astonishment to sadness and anger. The officer who came and removed me was one of the few who we considered cool. He usually came to work cracking jokes and talking shit to lighten the mood. He understood, for the most part, that we were all miserable. Most of us were facing serious charges and it was likely that we would be spending the bulk, if not all, of our lives in prison. Unlike most officers who thought it was their personal duty to add to our misery, he did what he could to make our day a little brighter. Most days, he would leave the entrance door to our tier cracked and turn on the radio. It was a small gesture that went a long way as the sounds of FM 98 broke up the monotony of the hole.

When the officer came to my cell, he had a look of total disbelief on his face. I could sense that there was something seriously wrong when he ordered me to step out of the cell. As he escorted me around the corner to another cell, I asked him what was going on. He hesitated before he spoke.

"Somebody shot and killed Sergeant Dickerson," he responded solemnly.

"Do they think we had something to do with it?" I asked, trying to fit the pieces of the puzzle together in my head.

"No, they're just taking precautions," he whispered as another officer approached with handcuffs in tow.

It wasn't until later on that day that we would find out what happened. The details of that fateful September morning astounded us as much as it did the officers. It was an ingenious escape plot made for Hollywood. An inmate who shall remain nameless was accused of smuggling a gun into the county jail. Allegedly, he threw a hand-made rope out of the window and had someone tie a gun to it. According to the allegations, he was on his way to court when he pulled out the gun in

7

an attempt to liberate himself. A scuffle ensued, and when the dust settled, Officer Dickerson lay dead.

Two days later, I was on a van heading upstate. It was a somber exclamation point that marked the end of my stay in Wayne County Jail. In the two months I was there, I had witnessed the worst that exists in humans who live lives filled with desperation. From rape and robbery to murder, I had seen it all, and it reminded me of my twisted life on the streets. Little did I know, the violent tug-of-war between inmates and officers was just beginning.

Chapter 2

"Wayne County Jail" were three words that every hustler and street thug in the Metro Detroit area feared hearing. The stories of violence, corruption and desperation were legendary. In the tall, inconspicuous building that looked as though it had been stuffed down into the earth where it stood on St. Antoine was a sub-culture that could only be described as primitive. All signs of civility were recklessly discarded at the door like a used tampon. The only law was the law of the jungle – survival of the fittest.

In the early eighties during the heyday of Young Boys Incorporated, the infamous drug ring of street lore, the county jail's reputation for violence skyrocketed. With tiers named after characters from the popular cartoon Transformers, few were safe from unprovoked attacks organized by other inmates. From robberies, beatings and rape, anyone entering was subject to a violent attack.

I sat in a dingy cell on 1300 Beaubien at police headquarters. The stories I had heard over the years about the county jail bounced around in my head like a pinball. It was my second arrest as a young adult and by far the most serious in my short career as a hustler. The days of going to the precinct or youth home, only to be let right back out, were over. One month into my nineteenth birthday, I had officially graduated to the big leagues. The consequences I faced were serious. There would be no more slaps on the wrist or warnings from an irate judge. There would be no bailouts from a counselor who could see my potential. If I lost this one, it could possibly cost me the rest of my life in prison. It was a sobering reality that my young mind wasn't quite ready to accept.

I was snapped out of my thoughts by the sound of the bars rattling. I removed the shirt that covered my head and looked up with a scowl on my face. A light-skinned officer with a no-nonsense expression on his face stood at the cell bars.

"Get up and get dressed. You're being transferred to the county jail," he barked, then turned and walked down the tier. He repeated the same order to some other unfortunate souls. I pulled myself up from the small, cramped bunk, slipped into my shoes and walked over to the bars. I looked out onto the dusty tier as I put on the wrinkled shirt I had been wearing for the last three days. My body and clothes smelled like I had been sleeping inside of a garbage dumpster behind one of Detroit's famed Coney Island restaurants.

I rinsed my mouth and splashed my face with the tepid, rust-colored water that drizzled from the sink. As I waited for the officer to return to my cell, my stomach fluttered like a charm of hummingbirds. The clanging sounds of metal against metal rung out as cell doors were opened and banged shut. A handful of inmates were herded down the tier and into a holding cell in preparation for the transfer to the county jail.

My heart began beating like a drum when the officer returned to get me. I shuffled down the hallway slowly, barely holding my shorts up and doing my best not to lose my shoes. They had taken my belt and shoe laces when I entered the precinct. It was their way of making sure we didn't hang ourselves or choke someone else. When I reached the intake desk, they returned my shoelaces, belt, and the knot of money that I had in my pocket when they arrested me. When I grabbed the thick wad of hundred and twenty dollar bills, a small current of excitement shot through my body. The ill-gotten currency was a brief reminder of the city streets I had left behind. But just as quickly as the excitement hit me, it disappeared as the thought that I might never see the streets of Detroit hit me with the force of an 18-wheeler Mack truck.

I was stuffed into the bullpen where a dozen or so other inmates were waiting to go to the county jail. Most of them were in their early- to mid-twenties, and from the looks on their faces, it was clear that they were thinking the same thing I was thinking despite their efforts to conceal it. We all wanted to know how our lives had come to this and what lay ahead of us.

I flashed back to my childhood. I thought about the first time my mother asked me what I wanted to be when I grew up. I told her I wanted to be a doctor. I wanted to help people recover from their illness and mend their broken bones. I wanted to be the one to give children balloons and lollipops as my way of saying sorry for giving them shots.

The thoughts of me in a white lab coat with a stethoscope around my neck quickly faded to black as I returned my thoughts to the present. I stood with my back against the wall, lost in thought about my current situation. All I needed was one more shot at freedom and I would turn my life around, I thought to myself. It wasn't the first time I had told myself that. There was the time I caught the felonious assault and drug possession case that led to me being sent to the Wayne County Youth Home. I promised my father that I would turn my life around when I got out, and for a few months, I did okay. I went off to Job Corps in Prestonburg, Kentucky, got my GED, and was doing well in my trade as a carpenter. But I hadn't completely relinquished my old ways. The entire time I was at Job Corps, I was involved in every kind of illegal activity you could imagine. I sold six-dollar joints and ran a loan-sharking ring, which culminated in me getting kicked out. I was sent back home to Detroit on the next Greyhound, to my father's great disappointment.

Then there was the case I had just beaten in Monroe County. I was on my way back from one of my many trips to Ohio with a car full of cash and a trunk full of guns. We were pulled over and arrested for receiving and concealing stolen property. As I sat in the holding cell with my co-defendants, I told myself that was it. I was tired of the streets and all that came with it. At least that's what I told myself as I sat in the cell sober, with plenty of time to think about my life. On some levels, I was really tired, but not tired enough to completely leave the streets alone.

As soon as we beat the case and returned to the 'hood, it was business as usual. That was the routine I had established for myself. As long as there was a threat to my freedom, I acted like I was ready to change. It wasn't until nearly a decade later that I would understand the work it requires to turn a life around. Real change comes only at that point in which you are completely and thoroughly disgusted with your actions and the consequences they produce. As the Honorable Elijah Muhammad once said, "One hundred percent dissatisfaction brings about one hundred percent change." In 1991, I was only about forty percent dissatisfied, so I continued to do the same thing as soon as the opportunity presented itself. I was a bullshit artist par excellence. It was easy for me to fool people into thinking I was going to turn my life around, even myself. We all knew that I had the potential and the intelligence to do anything I put my mind to, but it wasn't until years later that I realized I had to truly desire change in my life if I wanted to change. Back then, I wasn't ready or willing to do the work necessary to turn my life around.

I loved living in the streets. I loved the fast money, fast cars and fast women. Above all that, I loved the reputation I had earned in the 'hood. I was known as a crazy motherfucker who wouldn't hesitate to shoot anyone I felt posed a threat to me and my crew. It was the one thing that made me feel like I was somebody. It gave me a false sense of power, and what I felt was control, over my life. When I drove or walked around the 'hood, people acknowledged me out of fear or respect and that was the greatest feeling in the world to me at the time. When I look back, it is really sad to see how insecure I was. I didn't like or respect myself, and I sought validation from people who were just as insecure and distorted in their thinking as I was. It is this vicious cycle that gave birth to my hyper-violent behavior. As noted Black psychologist Amos Wilson argued, the young Black male has perfected the art of being the best at being the worse, and that was me; I was becoming one of the best at being one of the worst predators in our community.

I was pulled out of my train of thought by the feeling that I was being watched. When I looked up, I noticed a tall, slim guy staring at me. I returned his glare before I walked over to him and asked him why he was staring at me. The way I saw it, if there was going to be a problem, I may as well get it out of the way; I didn't want to spend the rest of my day worrying about whether there was going to be a problem between us. It was one of those unwritten laws of the 'hood, jail and prison yard. When you encountered another male and you exchanged glances, you had to be up to the challenge or you would be considered weak. In our world, being weak meant being preyed upon, and I wasn't about to be anyone's prey.

A smile creased his face as he told me he remembered me from over on a street named Savannah, which was on the city's eastside. It was a street my sister had lived on back in the day. Listening to him speak, I realized that he was a guy named Jimmy who lived around the corner from my sister. I barely recognized him because he had grown several inches since the last time I had seen him, which was when we were about 13 or 14. We kicked it about the old neighborhood for a minute before I asked him what he was being charged with. He told me he had been charged with armed robbery and felony firearm, and before I could tell him what I had been charged with, he began telling me what he had overheard the officers talking about regarding my charges. Apparently, they were disturbed by the violent act that I had committed at such a young age. Back then, I didn't realize that some of the officers had sons my age. Understanding the statistics for young Black males, they saw their sons in my face.

I was so disconnected from my humanity that I didn't possess the ability to feel sorry for myself. A few of the older brothers who were standing nearby gathered around as they overheard snippets of our conversation. They were intrigued by my youthfulness and the callous manner in which I discussed how I was going to beat a murder rap. It was youthful ignorance and arrogance. The gravity of my situation hadn't fully sunk in. I was in survival mode and all that mattered to me was getting back out. That's how it always worked in my distorted world.

In a psychologically twisted way, I felt like a celebrity. This pathological thinking is common among Black and Latino males. These are the young brothers who have been marginalized because of their race and lack of education. These are the young males who hang out in front of liquor stores and Bodegas with their version of the American dream stashed in plastic bags that they've stuffed in their boxers alongside the semi-automatic tools of freedom snuggly tucked in their waistbands. In the 'hood, the villain is the hero and someone that others look up to.

It wasn't until nearly a decade later that I would come face-to-face with the truth. Like many young brothers, I was suffering from an untreated mental illness as a result of being shot. I had been living with Post Traumatic Stress Disorder (PTSD). What's more disturbing is that people in the 'hood idolized guys like me. They knew I would go to any extreme to prove myself and make sure that my reputation as a "crazy nigga" remained intact. Sadly, it is this mentality that has our community drowning in the murk and mire of gun violence and other self-destructive behavior.

I continued to talk with Jimmy about the old days until two deputies came and got us. We were herded into a white Wayne County Sheriff's van with a gold and brown badge on the side. Most of us grew quiet as we sat lost in our own thoughts, our heads hung low like a sapling branch covered with the ice.

The ride was relatively short and uneventful. With the exception of one annoying inmate who had obviously made the trip several times, everyone was quiet. For some odd reason, he felt compelled to give us a dissertation on his trips to prison. In every prison or jail I've been in, there was always that one loquacious person that annoyed everyone. Amidst the soundtrack of his grating voice, the Wayne County Jail emerged. The towering building that sat on St. Antoine didn't look as imposing as the super-sized stories of violence and pain that were associated with it. As we exited the van, I could feel the nervous energy that passed from one inmate to another as we stole glances at each other.

We all wore the same stoic masks that we had worn standing on the corners in our respective 'hoods. From the violence-filled streets of Detroit to the organized crime families of Chicago, from the dirty South to the gang-infested streets of LA and the five boroughs of New York City, we all wear the masks. It is the mask that far too many young, Black males are forced to wear at far too early an age. It is the mask that says, "I am fearless, I don't care, and I will destroy anything in my path, including myself." But all of us know that just beneath the surface exists an uncovered truth. Indeed, beneath this mask of 'hood savvy and toughness exists a small, vulnerable young boy whose heart has been turned cold by the emotional neglect and physical violence of his daily existence. Earth, Wind and Fire wrote about it in a song, "A child is born with a heart of gold, ways of the world make his heart turn cold." That was us, a huddled crowd of scared little boys forced to act like street-wisened, hard-hearted veterans in an urban war movie. Sadly for us, there would be no Academy Awards or Emmys to place on our mantels, only dark and lonely prison cells and freshly dug graves. Despite this morbid reality, I vowed to play my role until the end credits rolled.

Once we enter the building, we are hustled through the bowels of the jail over to another bullpen where processing was underway.

✒ ✒ ✒

The nauseating smell of spoiled ass, super-funky armpits, and crusty toes that had been stuffed inside of musty socks for days punched me in the nose as soon as I stepped into the cramped bullpen. The antiquated central air system did nothing to alleviate the stench, which made my eyes water. As I entered, I scanned the room, observing the rest of the lost souls that were waiting to be processed into the county jail. The hodge-podge of inmates was from all walks of life. There were the veterans of lockdown who had grown accustomed to the dehumanizing existence of jail. There were a few heroin addicts bestrewn across the hardwood benches and urine- and spit-soaked floors. They lay curled in a fetal position, shaking like scared puppies as they fought the pain of withdrawal. Then there were a few young brothers like myself who were experiencing the criminal version of the major leagues for the first time.

Every ten minutes or so the deputy sheriffs would call about five to ten names. When our names were called, we were ordered into a room where we were dressed out. We exchanged our street clothes for the drab, vomit green county jail uniforms. I leaned against the wall in the back of the bullpen and listened to the various war stories being exchanged between other inmates. In each story, the storyteller was the hero. This is one of the things I find disturbing to this day when I think about prison culture. Most guys are slow to expose their vulnerabilities. No one wants to admit they're a drug addict or victim of violence, but everyone is quick to say they were drug lords and perpetrators of violence. Over the years, I have discovered that in ninety percent of the cases, guys are a mixture of both. If more would only admit this, real healing in our community would begin; however, as long as we continue to lie to ourselves and glorify pathological behavior, we will continue to suffer. Despite this, I do recognize why so many use embellished storytelling as a coping tool.

Being in prison and stripped of your freedom is a very painful and degrading experience. Every day in there was a fight to maintain my sanity. In order to escape from that brutal reality, there are inmates who will make up a whole different life. They will say anything in order to be seen as different or above the rest of us poor, wretched souls. There are some who are so good at lying, they no longer know where reality begins and fantasy ends. Some are so outrageous in their storytelling that everyone knows they are lying, but because they are such artful storytellers, we sit around and listen to them anyway. Then there are those who have perfected the art of lying to the point that they could probably convince former President G.W. Bush that he was Black and he only made it through college because of Affirmative Action.

As I sat listening to their tales, I started thinking about what I would rather be doing. In that very moment, I would have traded anything to be back in the 'hood hustling and drinking with my homeboys. My nostalgic longings were interrupted by the sound of my name being called along with a few more inmates. It was our turn to get dressed out in Wayne County's finest. We stepped into the hallway and followed the deputy around the corner to the dress-out room. A few inmates from the last group were just slipping into their county greens when we entered the room, which smelled like an ass had just exploded. The stench nearly caused me to buckle as I did my best to hold my breath.

We were all placed in line and told to strip. As we removed our clothing, we were ordered to hand them to the deputies one article at a time. They shook each item out methodically as they searched for contraband. This lengthy search would be the first in a long line of humiliating experiences I would be subjected to.

Once we were stripped of our personal clothing, we were ordered to raise our hands above our heads, lift up our nut sack, then turn around and spread our ass cheeks. It was then that I understood why the room smelled as if an ass had exploded. That room must have been subject to thousands of unwashed assholes over the years, and I'm not speaking of the foul officers. As I followed the instructions to lift my

16

hands above my head and lift up my nut sack, I knew in my head that the first of my many troubles was about to begin. At that point, I decided I was not going to spread my ass cheeks for anyone so I turned around and half-squatted down. It was something I had learned in the youth home. Most officers didn't care to be looking up our rectum, but there was always one who seemed to take some type of sick pleasure in this dehumanizing act. Squatting down was an unwritten compromise of sorts. Fortunately, the deputy shaking me down didn't seem to care. When I turned back around, he asked me what size I wore, handed me my county greens and returned my underwear and socks. Underwear and socks were the only personal clothing items we were allowed to keep. I felt real trifling putting back on a pair of dirty socks and drawers that I had been wearing for the last few days. It was a harsh reminder of how much of my life I had forfeited. Little did I know, the chipping away at my humanity had just begun. Like Dante journeying through the inferno, my life would forever be altered by the abuses, violence, and desperation that characterize prison life – oppressed against oppressor, predator against prey, the insane against the criminally insane, and the hopeful against the hopeless.

The sound of the steel doors banging shut was a sign that the iron monster had once again been fed, and thus my journey began.

Chapter 3

"Come up off all that shit, lil' nigga!" Tiny said desperately as he held the nickel-plated pistol to my head.

My heart fluttered erratically like the broken wings of a baby bird. I was terrified. The cold, steel barrel pressing into my juvenile flesh pressed into my consciousness a colder reality – I could die at fourteen. The toxic stench of the streets poured from Tiny's body mingled with the sickly sweet smell of Wild Irish Rose. I struggled to breathe as Tone, Tiny's partner-in-crime, wrapped his crusty arm around my neck. The dirt beneath his chipped fingernails and the scars where abscesses had attempted to heal imbedded themselves in my mind. Tiny gripped the gun with his right hand, which was bloated with open sores containing pools of festering, greenish-brown pus. He was a heroin addict and a crack fiend, one of the worst combinations in a stick-up man.

It was known in the streets that dope fiends wouldn't hesitate to kill in order to get their next fix. Adding crack to the mixture gave birth to the super-predators that roamed inner city jungles. The fact that I was young enough to be their son didn't matter to them. All they cared about were the small, white crack rocks that were concealed in my underwear. It was like the late-great rapper Notorious B.I.G. once said in a song, "Don't you know niggas will kidnap kids, fuck 'em in the ass, throw 'em over the bridge. That's how it is." This characterized the streets of Detroit during the apex of the crack epidemic. Murdering a child would have been all in a day's work if that's what it took for them to feed their addiction.

In my short career as a drug dealer, I had made several crucial mistakes that nearly cost me my life. For one, I had trusted someone who was one of many victims of the most potently addictive drug at the time. I hadn't paid attention to my gut instinct, which whispered danger, danger, danger. I had allowed Tiny and Tone to see too much, and now I was at their mercy. I was too numb with fear to scream or plead for my life.

When the initial shock passed, I went into survival mode. I retrieved the plastic bag from my underwear and handed it over to Tiny. He then reached into one of my pockets and retrieved a small knot of cash, nearly ripping my pocket off in the process. He stuffed the crack and money into his pocket and gave Tone the signal to let me go. I knew in that moment that they were going to shoot me and push me down the basement steps where a tenant would find my decomposed body days later when the smell became too strong to ignore. Instead, he pushed me toward the door of the building, prodding me forward with the pistol.

"Get your punk ass away from here," Tiny ordered as he shoved me out of the door onto the cracked sidewalk on Chalmers.

A flood of emotions overtook me. I was relieved that they hadn't killed me. My thin, teenaged body trembled with fear as I walked to the Coney Island that sat on the corner of Chalmers and Jefferson. I was a bit disoriented and unclear about what to do. When I stepped into the Coney Island, I felt like everyone inside knew what had just happened to me. I looked from one unfriendly face to the next, hoping that someone would see the fragile child I was. Instead, all they saw was a designer-clad youth trying to be grown before his time. As I look back, I wonder if what I had interpreted as angry glares were really puzzled faces wondering why I didn't have my ass in school with the rest of the children my age.

I calmed down, then turned and walked out of the restaurant. As I walked, a deep feeling of shame and loneliness overcame me. When I walked into the restaurant, I wanted someone to rescue me from the streets. I wanted someone to see a lovable, smart little boy who was hurting inside. I wanted to cry out, but I knew I couldn't because I had made a promise to never allow anyone to make me cry or see me cry again. Deep down, I was ashamed of feeling afraid. I was supposed to be brave and ready to die, but the truth was, I wasn't.

I walked a couple of blocks before I came to a phone booth on Kercherval. By the time I dialed my boss's pager number, anger was the only emotion I was feeling, or at least that's how I acted. There was no way I was going to tell Miko that I was scared. I couldn't let anyone in our crew know that the prospect of dying in a urine-soaked hallway didn't appeal to my young mind. See, death wasn't something I had bargained for when I decided to sell dope. I thought about the money I would make to buy the clothes that I wanted. I thought about being able to buy a Honda Elite 150. I thought about being able to buy happiness, love and a safe place to lay my head. I hadn't given any serious thought to the fact that I could possibly forfeit my freedom or life over a bag of rocks that were only worth a thousand dollars. Sadly, this is a reality that exists to this day. Young brothers and sisters are willing to risk their lives in a never-ending quest for the ghetto dream.

Miko returned my call and told me to meet him back at the spot on Marlborough and Jefferson. I walked the short distance back to the large, white house that I had been lured out of. The paint was peeling and the roof sagged as though it was ready cave in. The front door was ajar and the smell of decay poured out of every crack. The inside of the house made me uncomfortable, which made it easy for me to leave when Larry told me that he had a better spot around the corner on Chalmers. I had served Larry a few times and he appeared cool, so when he offered his apartment as a new spot to roll from, I didn't hesitate. Adding to the allure of a new spot was the fact that the spot on Marlborough was hot as hell. The narcotics unit boldly parked a couple of houses down almost every day, and sometimes they pulled directly in front of the spot. It was one of the many reasons I had never liked the Marlborough spot. That and the fact that it was unfit for human habitation.

The bathtub was full of shit, piss and dirty clothes. The toilet overflowed with wrappers from the nearby Coney Island and roaches crawled across the floors and walls in droves. The smell of cheap insecticide mixed with the unmistakable smell of human despair. The whole scene was depressing and the thick aroma made me nauseous. In many ways, the house on Marlborough reflected the mentality of the people in the streets. Little did I know, this same sickness was soaking into my pores.

I was on edge as I sat on the porch waiting for Miko to arrive. The rustling of garbage in the overgrown grass lot next door caused me to jump nervously. I turned around quickly, only to find a stray mutt foraging through the garbage looking for something to eat. I calmed my nerves as a deep burning anger began simmering inside of me. I reflected back to the day that I left my mother's house and the events that led to the dissolution of our family. My heart throbbed with a longing for things that used to be.

My parents' marriage deteriorated in stages like an arthritic knee. Piece by piece, things fell apart. And that's what made their divorce so hard for me to accept. They would separate and then get back together, giving me a glimmer of hope that things would go back to how they used to be. But that day never came. Instead, over the course of a five-year period, our family experienced the valleys and peaks of a young couple trying to keep their family together while battling external factors that slowly pulled them apart.

I remember the first time my parents separated. They called us into the kitchen in our nicely kept brick home on Detroit's east side on Camden Street. I knew something was amiss, but my 11-year-old mind was not prepared for the devastating news that would come.

My parents argued like I imagine any other couple did, but they never berated each other and they never physically fought. So when they announced that they were separating, it shocked us into silence.

"You know things haven't been going that good between me and your father," I recall my mother saying. "So we have decided it's best for us to separate," she continued, her voice cracking as she spoke.

I looked at my father for an answer. The corner of his mouth trembled and his eyes watered as he began speaking.

"Even though things aren't working out between me and your mother, I will always be y'all father," he said as he fought back tears.

I was lost. I didn't understand what they were talking about. Did separation mean he would be sleeping on the couch like he did sometimes after they argued? Did it mean he would go and spend a couple of nights at his best friend Clark's house? Or would he come and live upstairs with us? Never did I consider the alternative – my father living in a house separate from us. When he finally explained that he would be moving to Highland Park that coming weekend, my once cozy home existence became alarmingly frightful. All kinds of thoughts about what my father meant to our household began flowing through my young mind. I thought about the holidays and how he would organize my siblings and me so that we could put up the Christmas tree. I thought about him giving us an allowance every other Saturday morning so that we could go skating at Royal Skateland. I thought about the sound of him pulling into the driveway each night at approximately 11:45 p.m. when he got off of work.

It was as though everything that symbolized family stability had been sucked out of the room by their news. As they went on to explain that my father would live in the first floor flat of a duplex on Pasadena, my young heart went numb. I listened as my mother explained to me and my three sisters that we would spend the summer, winter break, holiday vacations and weekends at my father's, and we would go to school from her house. In my mind, that's just what our once happy home on Camden became – her house. Without my father and her husband residing with us full-time, her house could never be the warm, loving home we once shared as a family.

I tried to process all they had shared with us as my father called me to join him in the basement. I slunk down the stairs trying to be brave and strong because he told me that I would be the man of the house. It was hard for me to accept his words considering my puny chest and string bean arms, but I made a silent vow not to let my father down. As I descended the stairs and entered the first room of our basement, I started having flashbacks of how our home had developed over the years. I remembered watching my father and uncles hang paneling on the walls while my mother and aunts painted each room, the sounds of Parliament Funkadelic blaring throughout the house. Our home was family central and every one of my aunts, uncles and cousins had lived with us at some point. But after that fateful day, our family would never be the same again.

When we began packing, my father outlined what my responsibilities would be now that he was leaving. He told me that I would have to cut the grass and wash the car for my mother. He told me that I was responsible for my two younger sisters who were 3 and 8 at the time, and that I had to maintain my honor roll status at school. He continued to talk as we packed some of his albums in orange and blue milk crates. The images of each album cover conjured up visions of the house parties that my parents had thrown in our basement. As he rifled through the albums by The Isley Brothers, The Ohio Players, The O'Jay's and Marvin Gaye, I took in the Afros, platform shoes, and scantily clad women. I thought about my uncle John rousing me from my sleep so that I could come and dance to the sounds of '70s funk as my aunts and uncles cheered me on. The taste of Schlitz Malt Liquor came creeping back as I thought about my uncle Chris or uncle Keith sneaking me a lil' sip to ensure that I went right back to sleep when the dancing was over.

I looked at my father as he stared at one of his many albums, and I could sense that he was experiencing the same feeling I was. When he looked up at me, his eyes were red and the tears began flowing freely. He hugged me tight and cried from deep within. His scruffy beard scratched my face and the smell of his cologne drifted up my nose as his body heaved with the pain of seeing his family torn apart. In an instant, we were both crying and hugging each other. Thinking back, my father's tears are the best gifts he's ever given me. He showed me that real men cry, especially when they love deeply, and there is no deeper love than the love that my father has for his family.

We packed and cried, and packed and cried until we finally began laughing and joking with each other. When we were done in the basement, he assured me that he would always be there for me no matter what, and to this day, he has never let me down.

Over the course of the weekend, we moved my father's belongings to his new home on Pasadena Street in Highland Park. Little did I know, that weekend would mark the beginning of an emotional roller coaster ride for our family. After being separated for a little over a year, my parents got back together. Their reconciliation lasted for a short period before they separated for the second time a couple years later.

When my parents decided to get back together, I was overjoyed. I imagined our family coming back together and things returning to normal, but it wasn't long before my quixotic notions were shattered. After a few months, I noticed my father sleeping on the couch. My parents would go days without speaking to each other and the tender kisses and affection that they once displayed were replaced with empty stares. My nights became restless as I stayed awake late into the night waiting for my father to come home from work. I would listen intently when he entered the house, and sometimes I would crawl from my bedroom into the hallway and peak down the stairs into our living room. I held my breath hoping that instead of seeing my father asleep on the couch, the couch would be empty. But night after night, I was disappointed when I saw him curled up in a ball on the couch. In my mind, I knew it was only a matter of time before they would be breaking the bad news.

I felt betrayed by my parents. I wanted them to stay together forever. I didn't want my mother to love another man, and I didn't want my father to love another woman. I learned to distrust them on the days that things were going smoothly between them. Every time I thought things were returning to normal, I was dealt a blow by my father's presence on the couch. Finally, the day came when they decided to separate for the second time. It had been nearly two years since the first split. I had seen all of the signs, but a part of me was still in denial until my mother called me into the house to break the news.

I was a few houses down the block playing touch football in the middle of the street with my childhood friends when my mother stepped onto our front porch and called my name. I took a two-step drop-back and hurled the ball into the air as I yelled out Terry Bradshaw. I watched in awe as the ball spiraled down into the outstretched hands on my best friend Steve. He cradled the cracked, leather hide to his chest, ignoring the stinging in his hands as he hollered out Lynn Swann and slammed the ball into the ground. Like other kids on the playground, we always summoned the names of the greats in hopes that it would make us better. We were innocent and still held dreams of making or throwing the game-winning touchdown in the Super Bowl. In our eyes, we were destined for greatness.

I walked the short distance to my house, sulking a bit at having my football game interrupted. How was I ever going to make it to the NFL if she kept breaking up my games to have me run errands? Didn't she realize I needed to practice? These were the questions that danced through my little head as I climbed the porch stairs. Then, a little smile crept across my face when I realized that she had seen me throw a perfect spiral.

When I entered the house, my mother was on her way upstairs where my bedroom was located. My focus then shifted from my football exploits to my mother's movements. Maybe I was in trouble for leaving my room in a mess, or maybe the bathroom I shared with my sisters wasn't cleaned to her liking.

Her voice cascaded down the stairs in a gentle stream as she called my named again. I immediately sensed something was wrong. The melodious voice that she used was usually reserved for special occasions like when I brought home a good report card or during a holiday celebration when we had a house full of company.

When I reached my room, she was standing with her back to me, looking at the walls where pictures of my sports heroes and dream cars were taped haphazardly. For the briefest moment, I thought she was about to tell me to dismantle my fiscally responsible interior decorations. I couldn't bear the thought of having to remove my posters of Tony Dorsett or the '69 Cutlass 442 that I was deeply in love with. When she turned to face me, tears clung to the corners of her eyes like little diamonds. She pulled me close to her, embracing me in a warm hug, and then inhaled deeply before she began speaking.

"Pumpkin," she said, using the nickname that my Aunt Bebe had given me. "I want you to know I will always love you no matter what happens. As you know, me and your father have been going through some problems and we have decided it's best for us to separate again," she said before pausing.

As her words barreled into my ears, my heart began crumbling into pieces like stale crackers. I didn't want to believe that they were separating again. They promised us that they had fixed things. Although I didn't want her words to be true, the signs were obvious. I nodded my pumpkin head letting her know that I understood.

As she continued speaking, I could see her inner turmoil. Her words cartwheeled around inside of her mouth before leaping out. Each word attacked me in a flurry, hitting me indiscriminately. I stumbled

25

around in an emotional fog, grasping for something to hold onto, but her words staggered me like a punch from Mike Tyson.

"You will have to move in with your father this time. I can no longer raise you. You are a young man now and you will be better off living with your father," she explained before suddenly turning away from me.

Her words shredded my heart like a cheese grater. I didn't have a problem living with my father. The problem was the deep feeling of rejection that I felt. How could a mother give up her child? What was wrong with me to make her not want to keep me? Was I a bad person? Why was I the only one going away? Who would love me like only a mother could? In that moment, I began erecting an emotional wall that I felt would protect me from my parents and any other intruder. I was tired of being hurt and confused by two people who I loved more than anyone.

Soon after, my relationship with my mother became very antagonistic and a chasm slowly developed between us. By the time my parents reconciled for the second time a year later, our disconnect was evident. When my father and I moved back home, there was a great deal of tension between my mother and me. We clashed over any and every thing. I had grown accustomed to the liberal way that my father raised me, and at the age of fourteen, I was not ready to conform to her strict rules. I had begun smoking cigarettes and had taken a keen interest in girls. I was used to being on my own and doing what I wanted to do because my father worked all day. I had had a taste of what it felt like to be an only child and no longer wanted to share with my younger sisters or spend much time with them.

I resented my sisters because I felt like my mother had chosen them over me. I also resented my mother because I felt like she was rejecting me. Every chance I got, I defied her authority. My father tried to rein me in and support her in her efforts to bring me under control, but it was too late. I had developed an "I don't give a fuck attitude." Little did I know, it was a protective shell that a lot of Black males wear. The way I saw it, if I don't care about anything, nothing can hurt me.

My mother responded to my recalcitrant behavior by physically beating me. It wasn't long before I reached my breaking point. At fourteen, I felt I was too old to accept another ass whooping, and having grown physically stronger, I knew it was time for me to leave before I reacted to her physical assaults. She reminded me often that I could leave if I didn't want to abide by her rules, so I said fuck it and left.

Deep inside, I wanted her to stay up worrying about me like mothers do. I wanted her to search for me with tears in her eyes. I wanted her to be concerned about my safety and well-being. I wanted her to hurt the way that I hurt. But more than anything, I wanted to be validated by her love. That never happened, so I turned to the streets for love.

I lived the life of a transient for two weeks. I slept and ate in the basements and garages of my childhood friends Tommie Seymour and Ernie. They did their best to conceal me and help me out, but they were only able to hide me for so long before their parents were on to us. One day while deciding what my next move would be, an older guy from the neighborhood came riding down the street. He stopped and asked us if we knew anyone willing to work in one of his drug houses. After listening to his sales pitch, which included a place to lay my head and money to buy food, I took him up on his offer. I didn't know what I was getting myself into, and it wasn't long before I realized that I was in way over my head.

Chapter 4

"I thought you were getting transferred back upstate," I heard a voice call out from the day room as my cell door slid open.

"They canceled the transfer," my bunky said over his shoulder as he entered the small, cramped cell.

I watched him as he reorganized his toiletries and commissary on the metal desk that was attached to the back wall of the cell.

"Man, you ain't gonna believe this shit," he turned to me as he hand-rolled a cigarette.

"What happened?" I asked, leaned up against the wall watching his methodical movements.

"This nigga in the bullpen raped a white boy this morning," he said with a puzzled expression on his face. It was as though he was still trying to make sense of what he had witnessed.

"Who got raped?" Satan asked as he approached our cell door.

"Come on, I'll tell y'all what went down," my bunky replied as he exited the cell. He lit up a cigarette and sat on the table in front of our cell. He inhaled deeply, sucking in the bitter smoke of the cigarette, then exhaled as though he was forcing the painful memory up from his lungs along with the acrid smoke. "This morning when we went down to the bullpen to transfer, this nigga named Seven gave this white boy his cereal and donut. We didn't think nothing of it until we seen him talking to him in the back of the bullpen," he explained as he took another drag of his cigarette.

"What happened, dog?" a guy named Twin said as he walked up.

"Nigga got fucked in the butt in the bullpen," someone said, causing a trickle of nervous laughter to travel around the room.

It was the first time many of us had come face-to-face with one of the most brutal and violent aspects of prison life. I could sense that the men in the room were asking themselves questions. Some wondered if they would ever be the victims of such a vicious attack on their manhood. Others questioned whether they would ever become so

28

sexually desperate that they'd resort to raping another man. Still others wondered what they would do if they were a witness to such an attack. Before we could fully process the questions in our heads, my bunky continued, "First, the nigga Seven asked the white boy how he was going to pay him back for the cereal and donut he had eaten. The white boy told him he thought he had given him the food because he wasn't hungry and couldn't take it with him. He said it half-jokingly, which seemed to give Seven some kind of sick thrill. He moved in close to the white boy massaging his dick, and then told him he knew how he could repay him."

I could see my bunky struggling with the image in his head as he continued telling us what happened. "A few motherfuckers started making jokes about how nothing in prison was free. I don't think they realized how serious Seven was until he put the White boy in a choke hold," he recounted as he took the last puff of his cigarette, then thumped the butt across the day room. The butt hit the wall and caused sparks to fly before it landed in a pool of fetid water by the shower.

"He choked the White boy for about a minute before his face started turning blue, then he passed out. I never thought he would take it further than that," he said with a distant look in his eyes. "But he wasn't finished. It looked like he had snapped. He dropped the white boy on the floor, and then rolled him onto his stomach. He pulled the white boy's pants down, spread his ass cheeks apart and spit in his ass. He didn't give a fuck that we were all sitting there. He pulled his pants down and started fucking the guy in his ass like he was with a woman," he continued as he shook his head.

"That's fucked up," Satan said.

"Did the white guy wake up?" Twin asked.

"Yeah, he woke up while that nigga was fucking him and started screaming. That shit made the nigga Seven go crazy and he started fucking him harder until the deputies rushed to the bullpen to see what was going on."

"Why y'all ain't stop the nigga?" someone asked.

"What the fuck you mean, why we didn't stop him? Nigga, you know the rules to this shit," my bunky responded angrily.

"Yeah fool, you know the rules to this shit. Mind your motherfucking business," Satan said in defense of my bunky.

"What the deputies do to Seven?"

"I think they were just as shocked as we were. They couldn't believe he was raping the guy in front of us like there was nothing wrong with what he was doing. And the worst part of it all is the white boy was only going to boot camp."

"That's fucked up," Twin said. "He should sue these slimy motherfuckers for putting him in the bullpen with that crazy nigga in the first place."

"I don't know if he'll get any money, but he should. The deputies didn't really do shit but tell Seven to let him up. When he was finished, he got up laughing as he pulled up his pants. The white boy laid in the middle of the floor crying until someone helped him up. They put Seven in a bullpen by himself, and they took the white boy to the hospital," my bunky replied before lighting up another cigarette.

I listened for a little bit longer before I returned to my cell to think about all he had shared and the response of the other men. I had only been in the county jail for two weeks and had learned a great deal about jail and prison life. I thought about what it would feel like to live the rest of my life around men who were capable of raping and killing another human over something as insignificant as a bowl of cereal or a cigarette. I thought about the human breaking point, the fragmenting of the human psyche. What kind of mental pressure would it take for me to become a complete savage capable of the most reprehensible acts of violence and depravity?

In that very moment, I promised myself I would not leave prison worse than I entered. I understood the serious nature of my crime; however, I knew there were some things I would never be capable of, and raping another human being was one of them. Nor would I ever become a snitch in order to get out of prison early. I was a firm believer that a man must step up and accept the consequences of the decisions he makes. Sadly, I would soon learn that not many had the same philosophy when it came to doing time.

During the first two weeks of my stay in the county jail, I got an uncensored glimpse into prison and jail culture. This was not MSNBC Lockdown, however. This was real life. There was a clear pecking order and the laws of the jungle governed all behavior from staff to inmates. It was truly survival of the fittest.

As I stepped through the sliding glass doors onto 6 NW, the room grew silent. The only sound I could hear was the drone of the raggedy television that sat atop a metal table. The door groaned as it closed, banging shut with the same finality as a judge's gavel. I scanned the room, taking stock of the black and brown faces that were present. I processed each face rapidly like a computer on steroids. I was on the lookout for any potential enemies from the streets or familiar faces from the 'hood. I was hoping for the latter and felt a sense of trepidation about the former.

I proceeded to my cell after taking stock of the room and concluded that there was no one there I knew. I could feel the heat from the unfamiliar eyes that bore into me. Out of my peripheral, I saw a bald-headed, dark-skinned inmate talking to a brown-skinned inmate with a long scar on his face. They whispered to each other as they watched me. My street senses kicked in and I knew immediately that if I were going to have a problem, it would originate with them. It was clear from how the other inmates reacted to them that they were at the top of the food chain, and I could sense the rest of the guys in the room waiting to see what they would do. This behavior was symptomatic of guys who where used to following instead of leading and was a constant in jails, prisons and on the streets. Very few of the men I have encountered over the years have the courage to stand on their own.

I knew I was being sized up from the moment I stepped onto the rock. It was evident from the inmates' behavior that they were waiting to see what the Alpha males would do in response to my presence. I returned their glares, sending a clear message that I wouldn't hesitate to fight to the death if need be, but I didn't allow my stare to linger. It was my way of letting them know that I wasn't a shit starter either. It was one of the many rules of human engagement that I had learned on the streets of Detroit where staring at someone could get you shot or killed. It was

31

important to let people know that you weren't a pushover, but equally important to let them know that you weren't trying to punk them either. It was a delicate balance of life and death in an environment where getting killed over stepping on someone's shoe was a far too common occurrence. Unfortunately for us, prisons and jails have become an extension of the 'hood. Due to the growing rate of incarceration, the streets and prisons were now interchangeable, including the laws that governed both.

I entered the cell I was assigned to and tossed my bedroll on the top bunk before checking out the cell. The only thing that I wanted more than my freedom was sleep and a hot shower. I looked around the cell and my heart started beating rapidly. It felt like the walls were closing in on me. I couldn't believe that my life had been reduced to a two-man cell with a toilet in it. I knew in that moment as I looked at the metal toilet that I was going to figure out how to escape as soon as I could. My train of thought was interrupted by the cell door opening up.

I could feel my anger beginning to rise as the dark-skinned, bald-headed guy approached the door. I clenched my fist tightly and prepared to deliver the first blow as soon as he got into arm's reach. I had heard enough about the county jail to know that the guys on the tier would beat your ass for recreation if there was something they didn't like about you, and from the whispers that were exchanged, I figured there was something about me that they didn't like.

I didn't know how I would fair against a multi-pronged attack, but I knew I wasn't going to be the only one hurting or bleeding. I could feel the adrenaline coursing through my veins as the bald-headed guy stepped into the cell.

"You smoke?" he asked as he walked past me to the desk in the back of the cell.

"Yeah," I said, a bit confused.

"You might want to roll one of these up before they lock us down for the night," he replied, passing me a pack of Bugler brand, hand-rolled cigarettes as though it was the most natural thing in the world.

I took the pack without knowing what to do with it. I had never rolled my own cigarettes, and up to that point, all I had smoked was

Newports. I looked at the pack and then back at him. He rolled a thick wad of tobacco into the cigarette paper and left the cell. I followed suit, but my rolling skills were unrefined so my cigarette came out looking like a lopsided joint. I didn't care though because all I could think about was the rush of nicotine that would satisfy my craving.

I stepped out on the rock and got a light from the automatic lighter attached to the wall. I inhaled deeply and began choking immediately. The pungent smoke felt like it was ripping my throat to shreds as I sucked it deep into my lungs. Everyone on the rock started laughing as they watched me struggle with the cigarette. Despite being the worst taste I had experienced, I continued to smoke until I had satiated my nicotine appetite. Moments later, a voice came over the PA system telling us that it was time for lockdown.

"They call me S," my bunky said by way of introduction as we returned to the cell.

"Jay," I replied with a nod.

"What they got you for," he asked as he leaned back on his bunk.

"Open murder," I said as I studied his face.

"Damn homie, I hope you beat that motherfucker," he said as he leaned forward. I could see his mind working like the mechanism of a Rolex as he thought back to his own experience. "They hit me on a murder and sentenced me to natural life," he continued. "But I'm about to give this time back," he continued with a confidence that made me believe him.

At the time, I didn't know the difference between natural life and a paroleable life sentence. Nor did I have a clue about how the judicial system worked. Natural life meant that my bunky would never be granted a parole, and if his sentence weren't overturned, he would die in prison. A paroleable life sentence meant that he could be paroled after serving twenty years or more.

We talked deep into the night about his case and prison. He had been locked up for over a year and was back on a writ fighting another case. He told me what prison life was like and gave me some basic rules to apply in the event I came to prison. He also told me that he thought I would beat my case. I didn't know what he was basing his opinion on, but in that moment, it was what I needed to hear. It gave me hope, and at that time, hope was the one thing keeping me alive. It wouldn't be until years later that I truly learned how important hope is for anyone going through a tough time in their life.

I washed my face and upper torso in the sink before hopping on the bunk. I couldn't wait for the morning so I could take a shower and get something to eat in my system. I laid back on the bunk and that's when my worst enemy – my own thoughts – hit me in the head. My whole life began running through my head in a stream of consciousness that flowed violently like the current of the Nile. I thought about some of the things I hadn't thought about for years. I had to make some sense out of my situation. I couldn't believe I was sitting in a cell with a stranger discussing the possibility of me spending the rest of my life in prison.

My reality didn't feel real. It felt like I was living in a twisted urban nightmare and I would wake up at any moment. I had to wake up because my life wasn't meant to turn out this way. I was supposed to be on my way to college to follow my dream of becoming a doctor. I was supposed to be a healer of the people, not a destroyer. I shook my head from side to side in an effort to awaken. I didn't want to see what I had become, but my thoughts wouldn't let me off the hook. They continued to hit me like a flurry of quick jabs from Floyd Mayweather. They punched indiscriminately; no area was off limits.

I laid up for hours thinking and thinking about what my life had become. I thought about what I had done and what I had to do to make it right. The hardest thoughts for me to deal with were the thoughts of my live-in girlfriend, Brenda. A deep sadness engulfed me as I thought about the life growing inside of her womb. I thought about the conversation we had the night before I was arrested. I looked into her eyes and told her that everything would be alright, that we would get away from Detroit and get a fresh start with our unborn child. We would give him or her the life that we dreamed of as children. She laid her head on my chest and looked up at me with tear-filled eyes. I rubbed her belly where our precious baby was growing and being nurtured.

"Can you feel it?" she asked as she guided my hand to the region of her stomach where our baby rested. The warmth of her belly coupled with the warmth I felt in my heart made me believe everything would be alright, but I couldn't have been more wrong.

I thought about the embarrassment and disappointment my father was experiencing as he dealt with my arrest. Up to that point, I hadn't spoken with him, my stepmother or my mother. I didn't want to call them. I had made a decision to live the street life and felt like I had to deal with the consequences of the decisions I made. I had grown accustomed to dealing with people whose love was conditional, so I had no expectations for either of my parents to be there for me. I realize now that I didn't know the true meaning of love and had no idea what it meant to be a parent who was hurting because their child was hurting. It wasn't until years later that I would learn about the many sleepless and tearful nights that my father had as a result of my incarceration.

The thoughts continued to flow like water. I thought of all the betrayals I had experienced. From being turned in by someone I thought was my best friend to having people I knew make statements against me. I could feel a small ball of anger forming in the core of my soul.

Everyone I thought of as friends had turned their back on me. I wasn't gone a week and people had begun stealing my clothes and playing on the little money I had left. The ultimate betrayal, however, and the hardest thing for me to deal with, was my own betrayal. I had turned my back on myself the first time I picked up drugs, alcohol and guns. I had given up on myself. In fact, I had never even given myself a chance to succeed. I thought about every teacher and parent who had asked me why I was wasting my potential. They believed in me more than I believed in myself.

The officers who arrested me also asked me why I was wasting my life. I was intelligent, articulate, and capable of doing something meaningful with my life; but I chose to squander it.

It can't end like this, I thought to myself as I drifted off to sleep. I didn't have any idea how I was going to write a different chapter, but one thing I was certain of, it wouldn't end like this.

Over the span of a few weeks, I was given a crash course in jailing. I learned everything about the barter system when it came to exchanging food or cigarettes for services like making phone calls or writing a letter for someone who couldn't write. I learned jail wasn't that different from the streets; it was a power-based environment and the only two things that were respected were violence and money. It was an unwritten rule that every inmate would have to prove himself at some point, and if you had money, you had to prove that you could keep it or find someone who had your back to be sure you could keep it.

The fact that I had been charged with murder was evidence to the other inmates that I was willing to defend myself. Yet I knew there would come a time when I would have to prove without a doubt that I was a lion.

Once I was settled in, I got on the phone and called a lady named Georgia who lived down the street from me. She was like a big sister and was real cool people. She took my call and I could hear concern in her voice. It was through her that I talked to all of the people that I needed to talk to. She would make three-way calls and have people that I needed to talk to come by the house. She was one of few people that I can say was truly a friend at a time when I needed a friend. She never complained and did anything she could to help me out, something I have never forgotten.

The first day I called, she went and got Brenda for me. When Brenda answered the phone, I could tell that she had been worried about me. There was a child-like vulnerability in her voice that made me want to hug her. I felt a surge of guilt shoot through my body that caused me to buckle. I had never thought about the fact that by getting locked up, I was also imprisoning everyone who loved or cared about me.

For the first few minutes, Brenda and I talked about what was going on in the 'hood. We talked about my defense strategy and what I thought needed to be done in order for me to beat the case. We also talked about some of the money issues that she was facing. I gave her a few suggestions and told her that I would talk to a few people to help her out. I gave her the date of my next court appearance, and before I could say anything else, she started crying.

"My stomach is growing, and the baby is kicking," she cried softly.

"I'll be home before the baby is born," I responded in a whisper.

"I need you here with me right now," she continued.

"I know," I said shamefully.

"Why does God take everybody I love away from me?" she asked as she continued to cry.

"I don't know baby, but I'm coming home," I said as I thought about getting out.

"You betta get your ass home," she said with a smile in her voice that nearly melted my heart.

Brenda was a tough girl who grew up in tougher circumstances, yet she had the most beautiful laugh that I had ever known. Even though we had been living together, we were still getting to know each other when I got arrested. My feelings for her confused me because I had vowed to never fall in love with a woman; however, as I listened to her on the other end of the phone, I realized that I really loved and cared about her and there was no way I could leave her out there to fend for herself and our child. She deserved to be taken care of, and she deserved to have the father of her child by her side to help raise him or her. In that moment, I vowed I would get out or die trying. I didn't know how I was going to make it happen, but I knew that I would do whatever was in my power to get back to Brenda and our baby.

When we got off of the phone, I was emotionally and mentally drained, and the last thing I wanted to do was talk to anyone on the rock. I hung the phone up and was on my way back to my cell when a guy named Twin commented on my phone call.

"That nigga Jay just got off the phone sucker stroking," he said with a laugh.

A few guys laughed at his joke. It was something guys said about guys who showed any emotions toward their girlfriends while they were on lockdown. Openly showing emotions on the streets or in jail was considered a weakness, so whenever someone showed any emotions toward a female, be it love or anger, they would say he was sucker stroking. Twin's statement was said in a joking manner, but I wasn't in the mood for joking, so I checked him and set the stage for me to show and prove that I could handle my business.

"Stay out my business, bitch ass nigga," I said as I turned toward him.

"Damn, nigga. I was just bullshitting," he responded as everyone grew silent.

"You don't know me like that to be playing, so stay the fuck out my business," I continued as my anger began growing.

I could see that he was at a loss for words and I was a bit disappointed that he didn't take the bait. I was fighting mad, and because I had not learned a healthy way of processing my emotions, I was ready to let off some of my frustration with a good fight.

"Come on, homeboy, let that go," an older cat named L said as he guided me towards my cell.

He was from the Cass Corridor and was one of the older guys on the rock. All of the guys on the rock respected him and he was the go-to-guy for advice. He would sit and talk to us about life, the Bible and prison. He was very insightful, articulate, and genuine in his concern for us. He had been to prison before and was a prisoner to his crack addiction. Like many of the guys who come through the revolving doors of prison, he was at his best in an institutional setting where he was away from the temptation of drugs.

When we reached my cell, he came inside and asked me what was going on. I gave him the rundown before a guy from Inkster named Gigolo joined us. We sat around kicking it about life and the time we were facing. Gigolo had just had a son before he got locked up and could relate to what I was going through. My anger began subsiding as we smoked a few cigarettes and kicked it. After about half an hour, Twin showed up at the door. He apologized for his comments and I apologized for snapping on him. We were all going through some tough times and trying to find ways to cope with our fucked up situation.

After my dispute with Twin, guys on the rock started looking at me differently. They often sought me out for advice and I slowly emerged as a leader on the rock. At the age of 19, I was helping older inmates solve their problems, and they had no problem deferring to me. L took this all in and gave me counsel along the way. He later told me that I reminded him of himself when he was growing up. He told me that he had always been smart, but could never pull himself away from the allure of the streets and drugs.

I developed the strongest bond with Gigolo out of all the young guys. We were a lot alike, except Gigolo liked to fight far more than I did and that made a lot of the guys on the rock distance themselves from him. For the most part, they were scared of him because he was unpredictable. It didn't take much for him to be provoked to fight.

I could sense that the other guys on the rock wanted to see me and Gigolo fight each other. It all started on the basketball court. Prior to my arrival on the rock, Gigolo was the man on the court, not because he was best player, but because he was the most aggressive and volatile. He would foul other players and intimidate them from coming to the hole. On the flip side, they were afraid to play too physical with him because he was notorious for wanting to fight after he got fouled.

The first time we went to the gym, we were on opposite teams. We were checking each other and there was a lot of shit talking coming from the sidelines. The game was very competitive and we both played very aggressively. The more intense the game got, the more the guys on the sidelines tried to incite us. However, we both knew what was going on. While we were both competitive and wanted to win, we never let it get out of control. Once guys saw that we weren't feeding into their bullshit, they sat back and enjoyed watching us go at it. My team came out victorious, but our bond was the true victor. We ended up being on the same squad the rest of the time I was there, and together, we basically ran the gym.

The way I competed against Gigolo on the court increased the respect I had amongst the other guys on the rock. They gravitated to me even more. Unlike Gigolo, I never tried to intimidate any of them; however, I always stood my ground no matter who I dealt with, something they all respected, including Gigolo. As the weeks went on, the dynamics of our rock began changing as guys left and other guys arrived.

My bunky was finally sent back upstate and I got a new bunky who I didn't talk to that often. He was the complete opposite of all the guys I dealt with. He was kind of feminine and too high maintenance. He stayed in the cell drawing most of the day or reading. In addition to my new bunky, there were a few more arrivals. Another inmate named Butterball had come back on a writ. He gravitated to us along with two cats named Jabo and G. On a daily basis, we would sit in my cell or Twin's cell and kick it about life and all the things we missed. Sometimes we would take turns peeking out of the windows where the paint had peeled away trying to steal a sliver of freedom.

Like clockwork, Twin's girlfriend came and stood outside everyday at approximately one o'clock with a sign declaring her love for him. During that time, we allowed Twin to have the window to himself. Our respect for her eventually led to one of the first physical conflicts I experienced.

A tall, slim, brown-skinned brother from the east side moved on the rock with us. He appeared to be cool, so we allowed him to play cards and shoot ball with us. Over the course of the next week, he started coming to our little counseling sessions where we talked about the things that mattered to us in life. Most of the time, we sat in my cell or in L's cell and kicked it, but sometimes we kicked it in Twin's cell.

One Saturday morning, we were all sitting around in Twin's cell smoking squares and kicking it. Some of our court dates were getting close and we were talking about our options. L knew more about the law than most of us because he had been in and out of prison several times. We had all gone to the law library, but most of the books were torn up or outdated so we relied heavily on his advice and the advice from our attorneys. After talking to us about the pros and cons of taking a plea deal, we all got ready to lock down for the afternoon count. As we exited Twin's cell, Twin noticed that a picture of his girl was missing. He asked a few of us if we had seen it. Me, Gigolo, and L told him that we hadn't seen it and let him know that we would never take a picture of his girl. As we were talking and helping him look for the picture, we realized that the new guy was gone. I immediately shot out of Twin's cell and raced down to the guy's cell where I found his door closed and a towel hanging on the window so no one could see inside.

I told him to open the door and he told me to hold on. By this time, Twin, Gigolo and L had come down to the cell. We demanded he open the door and he told us he was using the bathroom. By now, the rest of the guys on the rock had come to see what all the commotion was about.

I told Gigolo to grab the sheet we used to pop cell doors open so that we could get in and check the guy's cell. By the time we popped the door open, he was flushing the toilet. Unfortunately for him, there were remnants of the picture floating in the water. I pointed to the torn picture and Twin recognized the dress that the woman was wearing, confirming that the guy had taken the picture of Twin's girl from his cell. Before the guy could get his explanation out, I punched him in the jaw. He staggered against the door and tried to cover up as I delivered another punch, knocking him out of the door. Before he could hit the ground, Gigolo and Twin started punching him in the head and face. Then, the guy scrambled to his feet, rushed toward the door and started beating on the glass, begging a deputy to rescue him.

His face was bloody and swollen and L told us to let him be until the deputies came and got him. A deputy we called Tyson came and got him and asked him what happened. The guy told him that we beat his ass. We looked at each other and started laughing. Twin explained to the deputy what really happened. He started laughing too, and then told the guy, "I should send you back in there so they can beat your ass again."

Tyson was one of the few deputies that understood and respected the code we lived by. He knew we had one of the more laid back rocks and we didn't start shit, which meant his shift went smoothly. No one respected a thief, and what made matters worse, it turned out that the guy was being charged with rape.

The following week, things on the rock took a somber turn. G was the first one of our circle to be found guilty on the charges he was facing. He was convicted of posing as a police officer and robbing a couple of drug dealers, who came to court and testified against him. The night before G went for sentencing, we stayed up talking about the possibilities and what he hoped for. He knew the charge carried a life sentence, but thought the judge would give him no more than ten years. When he returned from sentencing and told us he had been given 85 years, we were stunned into silence. The system had changed dramatically and we all began thinking about the time we were facing. If they gave him 85 years for robbery, I was convinced they would give me life.

The feeling of desperation that I felt after talking to Brenda had increased tenfold. Everyone on the rock was feeling it, and we did our best to rally around G. Instead of being sent straight upstate, as was the custom, he stayed on the rock because he was facing another case and still had more court appearances.

During that week, they moved two more guys on the rock. It was apparent from their interaction that they knew each other prior to moving on the rock. From day one, they gave off a negative vibe. Whenever they played cards, it typically led to an argument with someone on the rock. They attempted to intimidate a few of the more laid back guys and rubbed us the wrong way. We had seen the game before and recognized their attempts to establish their dominance. I didn't see them as posing a threat, so I didn't pay them much attention. I knew they were cowards because they were selective in who they targeted for their arguments and beefs; however, Gigolo took their behavior very personal. He didn't take kindly to their presence, and the tension boiled over after a few days.

We were sitting around playing cards when things escalated. Earlier, Gigolo and one of the guys had exchanged words over Gigolo staring at him. While they were sitting down playing cards, Gigolo tried to make light of the situation, but the guy had it in his mind to fight. While they were talking, I noticed his partner come and stand up next to the table where we were sitting. He told his partner to take care of his business, which told me they had planned their attack on Gigolo earlier.

The guy stood up from the table and asked Gigolo why he had been staring at him earlier. Gigolo responded, "'Cause you a funny-looking motherfucker." That was all it took to set it off.

One of the guys took a wild swing at Gigolo, who was still sitting down. Gigolo slipped the punch, popped up on his feet and started delivering a flurry of blows to the guy before he could regain his balance. When the guy threw the punch and missed, Gigolo took advantage of his miscalculation and started punching him in the face. Gigolo had everything under control until the guy's partner grabbed him from the back of the neck. That's when I sprung up from the table and fired on him.

I hit the guy in the eye, which caused him to release his grip on Gigolo. My punch staggered him and I followed through with a few more punches that caused him to fall into the door. By this time, L had rushed out of his cell and started punching the first guy who had swung on Gigolo. Gigolo then rushed over to me and delivered some blows to the guy, who I had penned against the door. We continued to beat their ass until they started screaming for the deputy.

Tyson rushed around to the rock and opened the door, letting them out. They immediately told him that we jumped them even though they had started the shit. They started talking smack like they wanted to fight us again one-on-one, so Tyson was like, "If I open this door back up, you better go in there and fight." They didn't want any more so they told him they were straight. Tyson started laughing and talking shit about them coming on our rock starting shit.

After the two guys left, we sat around laughing and talking shit as we recounted how we had dealt with them. At the same time, I was thinking about the guys who hadn't come to Gigolo's assistance. It was proof that some of them still wanted him to get fucked up. Later on, Gigolo came to my cell and told me he appreciated me coming to his aid. He asked me why I had helped him and I told him I was a loyal guy. There was no way I could sit with him everyday talking about life, and then watch some guys I didn't know beat his ass. We laughed as we talked about all of the guys who faked like they were cool with him, but who secretly wanted to see him lose.

That incident was a reminder of some of the things we had experienced coming up in the 'hood. The definition of friendship was lost on a lot of guys. Most had become cynical and distrustful of others, and some were parasitic opportunists who wouldn't hesitate to turn their back on you when it benefitted them. I became very careful where I placed my loyalties after that experience. At the end of the day, I knew that I would never be able to count on anyone as much as I counted on myself.

Later that night, I was in my cell kicking it with Gigolo and L when G came to the door and told me that he needed to speak with me for a minute. Gigolo and L got up and left the cell so that we could talk in private. G had a serious look on his face and I could sense something was troubling him. After he was sentenced to 85 years, we gave him space to process his emotions out of respect. Each day, I would go down and check on him and see how he was holding up. Some days he wanted to kick it and talk about some of the things he was feeling, and on other days, he didn't say much but I could tell he appreciated having someone to talk to.

After L and Gigolo left, he pulled the door closed and said he had something he wanted to talk to me about. I asked him what was on his mind and he responded by lifting up his shirt, revealing a steal pipe he had concealed in his waistband.

"I know how we can get out of here," G said as he removed the pipe from his waistband and handed it to me.

I didn't know what he had planned, but I was all ears. As I held the heavy lead pipe in my hands, I thought about Brenda. I thought about the look she'd have on her face when I showed up at the door of our house. A smile crept across my face as I thought about what it would mean to be free again. When I looked up at G, he was smiling because he knew without a doubt that I would back his play. I pulled out a Newport and fired it up as we plotted our great return to freedom.

Chapter 5

The smell coming from my armpits reminded me of the onions that I generously garnished my Coney Island hotdogs with. Every time the wind blew, the stench from my body wafted up to my nose, causing my eyes to burn. I looked down at the dusty red Levi's and grungy T-shirt that I had been wearing for a few days and felt a deep sense of shame. My hair was dirty from sleeping on the floor of Ernie's basement and my teeth felt gritty from the plaque that had accumulated. I hadn't showered or brushed my teeth in days, and it was obvious.

My eyes darted around as I watched a short, light-skinned woman leaving Harper Food's Grocery Store, which sat on the corner of Harper and Newport. Her basket was full of bags and I knew it would be my chance to get something to eat. My stomach had passed the stage of growling and was now barking like a full-grown dog. Up to that point, the only thing I had eaten that day was a piece of toast with a pat of butter that my friend Ernie had smuggled out to me early that morning. Their refrigerator was basically on E so it wasn't much he could do, so I walked a few blocks up to the grocery store to hustle up on something to eat.

I had been out in the hot sun for nearly an hour trying to hustle up on a few dollars, but no one seemed interested in allowing me to make an honest buck. The woman coming out of the store was my last hope. When she stepped out, I approached her swiftly while her back was turned. Before she could protest, I retrieved two of the bags from her grocery cart.

"Allow me to help with these, ma'am," I said, mustering as much charm as I could.

She turned around, clutching her purse, and looked as though she was ready to scream. I revealed my yellow, gap-toothed smile and proceeded to her car where I waited for her to open the trunk. She relaxed and popped the trunk. I took each bag from the cart and put them in her car. When I was done, she reached into her purse and took her wallet out.

"I don't have much," she said as she pulled two shiny quarters from her purse.

I took them and stuffed them in my pocket, prepared to walk away. I guess she could sense my disappointment because she called me back.

"Here, take this and get you something to eat," she said as she handed me a food stamp that was worth a dollar.

I took it with a smile and rushed inside the grocery store. I grabbed a grape Faygo soda, a bag of Better Made Hot Chips, and a pack of cookies. When I came out of the store, I looked around, then darted into the alley behind the grocery store. I kneeled down on the side of the dumpster and ripped the bag of chips open. I stuffed them in my mouth greedily before sucking down the sweet, purple soda. The stench of rotted food coming from the dumpster wasn't enough to spoil my appetite, nor were the maggots that were feasting on a pool of reddish liquid next to me. I was so hungry that it felt like my stomach was about to start eating my spine if I didn't get the food down fast enough.

Once my stomach started filling up, I stood up and exited the alley. I knew Ernie would enjoy some of the cookies and the rest of the chips I had in the bag, but I wanted to make sure I was good before sharing my rations.

I started walking down Newport toward Wade. The Fila's I had on were on their last leg and I had to walk with my toe curled in order to avoid it dragging on the ground through the hole in the bottom of my shoes. As I walked past each street, nearing my own, my palms started sweating. It had been nearly two weeks since I left home and the last thing I wanted was for my mother to see me in my current condition. I didn't want to hear her saying "I told you so." So far, she had proven to be right when it came to being out on my own. I hadn't thought my exit strategy through, and by the time I realized it was extremely hard for a child to make it in an adult world, it was too late. My pride and stubbornness wouldn't allow me to go back nor did I have a desire to return to a place where I felt unwanted.

It was still early and there weren't many people out on my block. I breathed a sigh of relief when I reached Camden and didn't see anyone I knew. I looked down toward my mother's house and saw her Monte Carlo sitting in the driveway. A twinge of sadness shot through my body as I thought about how life used to be. I stuffed it back down where I concealed the rest of the emotions that made me feel vulnerable and kept walking until I reached Wade, which was the next street.

Before I made it to the corner, I could see everyone was out at Kurt's house, which was the corner house next door to Ernie's. I groaned inside when I noticed a few of the older guys from my neighborhood hanging out on the porch. They were laughing and joking around with each other when I approached. It was a 'hood custom for us to crack jokes on each other and nothing was off limits. The more uncomfortable the person who was the butt of the joke became, the more the crowd laughed. Looking down at my attire, I knew I was walking into the line of fire when I approached. For the last week or so, I had been on the receiving end of jokes about my clothes and hygiene, but the most painful jokes came at the end of the day when some of the older guys cracked jokes about me not having anywhere to go. I felt like a bum. There was nothing like being homeless. I tried to laugh along with them like their words didn't faze me, but underneath, my feelings were being torn to shreds. There were even moments when I was so angry that I wanted to fight, which made everyone laugh even harder because I wasn't big enough to beat any of them.

Before I made it up to the porch, I could hear them snickering. When I saw that Ernie wasn't outside, I went next door and they immediately started cracking on my shoes and dirty pants. I held back the tears that were beginning to fight their way to the surface. In that moment, I wanted to cut through the alley and go home. I didn't know how much more I could take being the neighborhood joke.

Moments later, Ernie came to the door and let me in. I handed him the rest of the chips and cookies and went straight down into the basement where I listened to a mixed tape that Ernie was playing on his boom box. A few minutes later, another one of my friends named Tommie Seymour came over. We talked about what we would get into for the day before we went back outside. Tommie and Ernie were the only ones that seemed to understand what I was going through at home, and they did what they could to help me out. When we stepped outside, most of the guys next door were gone so we went and sat on Kurt's porch. We were sitting there talking when we heard the sound of deep bass coming from down the block. We all looked around, waiting to see who would come driving by with their sounds thumping. It was the newest phenomenon erupting in 'hoods all across the city.

Our neighborhood was home to some of the most notorious drug gangs from the crack era. From the Best Friends and the Chambers Brothers to White Boy Rick, who grew up around the corner from us, our streets were flooded with neighborhood superstars. The sounds blaring from their fancy rides drew the envy and attention of all the younger guys and girls in the 'hood, including ours. Whenever one of them would zip past in their Jeep Wrangler or Jeep Cherokee with the music thundering out of the back, we would stand around talking to each other about our dream rides. For the first time in our young lives, we were witnessing guys our age living the American Dream, and we all wanted a share.

Moments after we heard the sound of the music, a small, white Dodge Omni stopped at the corner. The music was pumping loudly from a house speaker situated in the back hatch. "That's Miko," Tommie said as he got off of the porch to greet the tall, light-skinned, muscular man. We watched from the porch as they talked for a few minutes, then Tommie came back up and told us what they had talked about. He said Miko was looking for someone to "roll" for him, which was the name we used for selling drugs. He said Miko was paying up to $350.00 a week plus ten dollars a day food fare for anyone willing to sit in one of his drug spots. The catch was, whoever decided to do it had to be willing to sit in the spot 24 hours a day, seven days a week. I didn't care. All I could think about was having somewhere to lay my head and a way to feed and clothe myself. I didn't give any thought to the potential danger that was ahead of me, including getting robbed, killed or jailed.

Ernie didn't want to do it and Tommie said he couldn't. They both turned to me and told me that rolling for Miko would be a way for me to get off of the streets. I had already given consideration to what they said before they said it, and without further discussion, told Tommie that I would do it. He walked back down to the car and told Miko that I was down to roll. Miko called me over and asked me my name. I told him that my name was Pumpkin, which was the nickname that my aunt had given me. It was also Tommie's nickname and one of the things that cemented our bond. We both knew how hard we had to fight so that others wouldn't think we were soft because of our unflattering nicknames.

"You got to come up with another name, lil' homie," said Miko as he took in my disheveled appearance. "What's your real name?" he asked.

"James," I responded as I thought about a new nickname.

"You should call yourself Jay," he replied.

"Yeah, that sound slick," I said as I thought about my new nickname.

Miko talked to Tommie for a few minutes before he got back in the car. He told me to hop in the passenger seat, then we sped off down the street to the sounds of Cybotron beating from the speakers. It was the perfect soundtrack for our neighborhood. The fast-paced techno-house music coincided with the rhythm of our young lives.

"You had something to eat yet?" Miko asked.

"Some chips and cookies," I replied as I thought about the last time I had a full meal.

"I'mma shoot up to Burger King before we go over to the spot."

"Alright," I responded as I watched the houses and cars zip by.

We pulled up to the Burger King on Gratiot, which was a stone's throw from the Ninth Precinct of the Detroit Police Department. Miko turned down the music as we pulled into the parking lot. When we got out of the car, I felt a nervous energy course through my body at the site of a police car, which was pulling out of the lot. In that moment, I didn't know how much time I would be faced with if I were caught selling drugs, nor did I think about the fact that I could get killed or charged with any number of crimes that were associated with selling drugs. All I knew was that I would be able to house and clothe myself. This ignorance was something that the older guys preyed on.

We headed over to a street named Flanders where the spot was located. We pulled in front of a dilapidated two-family flat that looked like it would fall over if the wind blew too hard. The house sat in the middle of the block between two other houses that looked like they had seen better days. When we got out of the car, I noticed a silhouette in the doorway. The porch steps creaked as we ascended them. I carefully stepped over a gap where a step used to be before I reached the top of the splintered porch.

"Hey, Miko," a dark-skinned, slender woman said as she opened the door for us to come inside.

"What's up, Dee," Miko responded as we stepped into the dark living room.

"Who is lil' man?" she asked as she gave me the once over.

"This my little brother, Jay," he said, introducing me. "He gonna be holding down the spot over here," he continued as he retrieved a plastic bag from his underwear and walked toward the dining room. "Where that mirror at?" he asked as he stepped over to the table.

"I got it," Dee said as she went into the other room.

"These are nickels and go for five dollars a piece. It's a hundred rocks in this bag," he explained, holding it up so I could see.

"Alright," I said, nodding my head.

"How much does that come up to?" he asked.

"Five hundred dollars," I said calmly.

"Okay, lil' nigga. I see you can count. All the sacks I give you will be the same, but it's up to you to count them. That way, you'll know I ain't cheating you," he said as he gave me a valuable rule of the game.

In the world of criminality, no one is to be trusted. It is a predatory and parasitic world, and nearly everyone is out to get over in some way, even on those they employ. This was American greed at its finest.

Dee returned with a mirror. Miko poured the contents of the bag onto the mirror and then counted the rocks out into piles of twenty. I watched his every move and did the math in my head. I was amazed that that small bag held what was a small fortune in my mind.

"When you sell the first two rocks, keep that for your food and cigarettes or whatever you want for the day. When you get down to the last 20 rocks, call me so that I can bring you some more, alright?"

"Yeah," I responded as I took the bag.

"Keep the sack in your drawers and don't let anyone else hold the sack. When someone comes through, Dee will let you know if they are straight. Don't show them shit until they show you the money. Once you have your money, give them a rock. Don't sit there and haggle with them over the size of the rock. This ain't the store, and the customers aren't always right. But at the same time, treat them the way you want to be treated," he explained, schooling me to the game.

"I got you," I responded as the excitement of selling drugs began taking over.

"Let me show you where the heat at, in case somebody get out of line," he said to me as he led me into the back room where he pulled a sawed-off shotgun from beneath a soiled mattress.

I had never held a shotgun before and I was intimidated by the menacing look of it. It looked like it would knock me to the ground if I pulled the trigger, but I took it and held it like I knew what I was doing when he gave it to me.

"That button right there is the safety. If a nigga get out of line, take the safety off, point it at him and shoot. Trust me, this will tear they motherfucking head off," Miko said as he explained the workings of the gun to me.

I didn't know how to respond because I hadn't thought about shooting anyone. I had no idea that crack could turn people into stone-cold killers. I had seen people smoking weed and drinking, but the most that ever happened was a fight.

"I'm going to pick up your partner named Tee. He good people and will have your back, but this is your spot," Miko said. "So run it the way you want it ran," he continued, turning the spot on Flanders over to me.

Ten minutes after Miko left, the first customer came to the door. Dee answered it and told me what he wanted. I came to the door and retrieved his money through the Armor Guard we had on the door for protection. I took the crumpled twenty-dollar bill and gave him four rocks. He looked them over and smiled before leaving the porch. When he left, I took the twenty-dollar bill out of my pocket and looked at it for a minute. It was my first official sale, and in that moment, things became

51

very real for me. I was officially a drug dealer. Within a few hours, customers started flowing through the spot like water. My pockets were quickly filling up with five-dollar bills until I had a fat knot bulging from my pants pocket.

The first week shot by and I was excited when Miko came through to pay me. He deducted about 75 dollars for rocks, which I had spent during the week on clothes that the customers came through trying to sell. He told me to take the rest off of the first sales that I made for the day. When I was finished, he told me to call him and he would take me out to Eastland Mall to shop. All I could think about was what I would buy. At the time, Fila was the hottest shit out and Guess jeans and overalls were the clothing apparel of choice.

When we hit Eastland, I couldn't wait to go to Foot Locker and cop a crispy pair of Fila's. I felt cocky as I pulled my knot of money out of my pocket and paid for my shoes. It was the first time I had been able to go into a store and get exactly what I wanted without having to worry about how much it cost. We continued shopping and Miko bought me a few other items to go with my gear. He was embracing me like a little brother and told me he always wanted me to be fresh.

Things were cool for the first few weeks. I stayed fresh with the latest gear and kept a knot of money in my pocket, but it wasn't long before things started going crazy. The sacks started coming up short and I thought Dee was stealing from me. I couldn't figure out how she was doing it because I kept the sack in my underwear, and if I didn't have it, Tee kept it with him. Whenever we both had to leave, we hid everything in the vacant flat upstairs. It wasn't until a month or so later that I found out Tee was stealing the rocks and putting them in his joints. I had no idea that he was smoking fifty-ones, which was the name we had given crack-laced joints.

In addition to Tee stealing, the Chambers Brothers had a spot a couple of houses down. The guy they had running the spot was crazy and strung out on fifty-ones. He foamed at the mouth and would run up and down the street with no shirt on ranting and raving. He was unpredictable and would sometimes jump on the customers. About every other week, the police had to chase him on top of the roof of the house that they were selling out of. He would eventually tire and come down and the police would take him in on a misdemeanor charge.

The one thing I liked was when he came down to our spot and bought up nearly the whole sack. Our rocks were bigger than theirs, so he would buy ours and chip them down. He would smoke what he wanted and still make the money he owed the Chambers Brothers. Whenever he came through, I made sure to let him see the sawed-off shotgun. Despite how crazy he acted, he turned out to be my best customer. If it weren't for him, things would have been a bit slow.

Within a few weeks, I was into the full swing of hustling. The money came quick and I found ways to spend it quicker. The more I made, the more I spent. I didn't realize it then, but I was overcompensating for the things I felt were missing in my life – love and acceptance. As good as the money was on Flanders, at the end of each night I felt empty and lonely. Tee was a few years older, so there wasn't much we had in common besides making fast money. I couldn't relate to Dee or her husband because they were high all of the time. One of the things I respected about them, however, was that they never smoked crack in front of me. I could tell when they were high because they acted jittery and paranoid, but I never saw them use. It wasn't until a few weeks later that I would learn the inner workings of the drug trade and the power of drug addiction.

One day, a customer named John came through to buy some rocks. He was what we called a "runner." He would make crack house runs for a small gathering of smokers who hung out at his house. He would get all of their money and find the best spot to cop at. In the process, he got the extra rocks from whatever deal he could negotiate, plus they would share their rocks with him. He was a frequent customer and usually bought two or three hundred dollars worth of rocks at a time. This time, after buying one hundred and fifty dollars worth of rocks, he asked if we would be interested in rolling out of his house. He told me he had a spot on Wilshire that he was interested in opening. I told him that I would run it by Miko and we could come through and check it out.

I called Miko and told him that I had a prospective spot to set up shop. He told me he would come by and pick me up so that we could check it out. When he arrived, he told me that he was proud of me for thinking about expanding the business, and if things went right, he would take care of me. That got me excited and I thought about what it would feel like to make more money. We hopped in the car and drove back down toward our part of the neighborhood.

John lived three houses off of the corner of Wilshire and Chalmers. On the corner of the block was a grocery store, and two blocks over was a Seven Eleven. The street was lined with well-kept brick colonials and Tudors, and John lived in a big, pretty brick house that was a stark contrast to the house on Flanders. Miko asked me if I was sure I had the right house and I showed him the address that John had written down.

John opened the door and let us inside. He told us the story of how he lost his job, wife and kids as a result of smoking. Allowing us to sell out of his house would allow him to keep his home and support his habit. It was in this spot that I learned everything I needed to know about being in the streets. I learned how the human psyche responded to addiction and desperation; how money and power breeds arrogance and leads to some of the most sadistic behavior imaginable.

When we stepped inside of John's house, we were surprised to find that it still had the appearance of a home instead of a crack house. There were relics of his former life as a middle class family man. Framed pictures of his wife and children were hung on a wall in the dining room. The living room was well furnished with a floor model television and sectional couch. It felt like the woman of the house would descend from the stairs and ask if we wanted refreshments, but that never happened. Instead, we got down to business.

Before long, the house on Wilshire began to reflect a sinister energy that seemed to haunt our neighborhood. This was the 'hood I grew up in, but little did I know, I was contributing to the death and devastation that led to its ultimate demise.

During the embryonic stages of the crack epidemic, my old neighborhood was still considered one of the better neighborhoods on the east side of Detroit. Most of the houses maintained pristine exteriors, but on the interior, the families were being slowly consumed by the madness of addiction. The promise of the Black middle class was slowly eroding as crack entrenched itself deep into the heart of the 'hood. This was a recurring cycle that manifested in our community. In the sixties and seventies, it was heroin that wreaked havoc, and in the eighties, we were faced with the greatest evil of our generation – crack cocaine.

We set up shop on Wilshire quickly and developed what would become the urban version of a traditional business model. We installed Armor Guard in the doorway between the kitchen and the stairway leading to the basement. We did this so that our customers could walk right in instead of being clustered outside around the door waiting to be served. For customers who wanted to stay and smoke, John charged them a couple of dollars or a piece of their rock. It worked to our benefit because some of the customers would end up spending their whole day and their entire paycheck down in the basement. It also cut down on the excessive traffic, which was a nuisance to our neighbors. Within three days, things began picking up and I got a firsthand education in street life.

John had numerous friends who smoked and most of them worked at one of the factories in the area so their money was always good and consistent. Our spot was one of the first in that part of the neighborhood, which was convenient for our upscale clients. The only competition we had came from some guys who had a spot a couple of blocks over. Their rocks were small by comparison, so they didn't pose any threat to us.

After a few days, I grew bored sitting upstairs all by myself so I ventured down into the basement. That was my first time seeing anyone smoke crack. I sat behind the bar with the shotgun and took in the scene, which reminded me of a scene from a movie. There were mirrors, razor blades, and pipes spread across the bar alongside a bottle of 150 Proof Old Florida Rum, which was used to make torches. I watched men and women smoke their pipes with such intimacy that it looked like they were making love. The look of ecstasy that came over them when they inhaled the thick, white smoke into their lungs was mesmerizing. I had never witnessed anything transform a person so quickly or dramatically as a hit from a crack pipe.

I had seen people smoke weed and drink, but all that did was mellow them out or give them the munchies. I had seen a few people get really drunk and act a fool, but that was a rare experience for me at the time. Watching crack addicts get high literally blew my young mind. What was interesting is that the drug impacted them all differently. There were some who got so paranoid that they hid in the closet beneath the stairs or jumped behind the bar and sat curled up in a ball on the floor.

A week after I ventured down into the basement, a lady who lived around the corner stripped all of her clothes off and ran out of the house naked. She said that someone was chasing her. John gave chase and eventually brought her back into the house where she sat naked at the bar smoking. I tried not to stare at her breasts or the triangle of hair between her legs, but I couldn't help myself. I was intrigued by the female anatomy and my fascination with women was just beginning.

One particular episode had me on the floor laughing. One day when I was down in the basement serving a customer, I noticed another customer crawling on the floor picking up every white speck that he came across. I asked what was going on and another customer told me that he was 'ghosting.' I asked him what that meant, and he told me that the other smoker had smoked all of his crack and was having illusions that the floor was covered with rocks. This became a common occurrence. It was crazy watching grown men and women on their knees searching the basement floor, hoping they would find a crumb of crack. I was so insensitive to their plight and ignorant to the seriousness of addiction that I would laugh at them until my stomach felt like it was going to burst. I didn't realize it then, but I was growing desensitized to the suffering of others. I had begun developing a warped view of adults and the respect I once held was slowly diminishing.

The money on Wilshire began flowing in a steady stream and I met a wide range of people in the first month or so of business. Every personality type imaginable came through the door. Our clientele consisted of White people, Black people, men, women, and upper-middle class on down to ghetto. We also had some of the best boosters come through. For just a few rocks, I bought leather coats and silk shirts that were worth hundreds of dollars. They sold me televisions, VCRs, and handguns for little or nothing. Even though I wasn't old enough to drive, I also rented Cadillac's, Monte Carlo's, and Regal's for a couple of hours in exchange for a few rocks. They ran errands for me, lied for me, and would have killed for me or killed me, all for the love of crack.

Women would come over to clean up the house and wash our clothes for a rock. Things always started off innocent, but it wasn't long before they were cleaning up naked. This was during the early days of crack when it was still considered a glamorous drug, so the women coming through were still attractive and still dressed with pride and dignity. Within a few months, these same women wore the visible signs of addiction – dirty clothes and muddled hair. Sex was also there for the taking. Women who were married with children older than me exchanged sex for rocks. They would offer to give blowjobs or fuck the entire crew.

The first time I saw what crack did to women came about two weeks after I started working on Wilshire. John had a woman come through who worked at one of the local strip clubs. He told us that she would perform for us if we gave her a rock. There were a couple of the guys from the 'hood hanging out with us and they wanted to see what she was about. None of us had any real experience with grown women and we were excited to see what she had to offer that our teenage girlfriends didn't. After taking a couple hits off of her pipe, she took all of her clothes off and began dancing sensuously. She rubbed and caressed her body before lying on the floor and spreading her legs. She masturbated in front of us, and then asked for a lit cigarette. We all stood around speechless as we watched her slide the cigarette into her pussy. Using her stomach muscles, she sucked the smoke into her vagina, then removed the cigarette and allowed the smoke to waft back out. That was the first time I had seen a woman's pussy spread all the way open. She had clearly raised the bar and every woman that came through after that competed to top her feats. I took my cues from the older hustlers I was around, and it wasn't long before I began to objectify women.

A month or so later while working another spot on Bewick between Warren and Shoemaker, a customer, who everyone called the head doctor, came through. She was so proficient with her oral skills that she offered me a money back guarantee. She told me if she couldn't make me cum in a matter of minutes, the blowjob was on her. I was fourteen years old standing on the side of a crack house getting a blowjob, experiencing something that grown men experienced. I was being sucked – figuratively and literally – into a world unfit for a child. Her head game was official and I gave her a rock for her services.

Like many women who came through the spot, she said all the right things, making me feel and think that it was okay to be having sex with a grown woman. I didn't realize that she was a pedophile who preyed on the raging hormones of young drug dealers. Nevertheless, at the age of fourteen, I had sexual command over grown women who were willing to do anything for a quick high. They made me feel like my pleasure was the only thing that mattered. Before long, I began developing a distorted view of women and girls. I couldn't relate to girls my age anymore because they weren't ready to do the things I was accustomed to doing. In fact, I grew very impatient with girls my age, and if they wouldn't have sex with me, I would dismiss them and let them know that I could get pussy and head whenever I wanted to.

I had been raised to respect and honor women; however, in the world that I was living in, those rules no longer applied. It was hard to respect people who didn't respect themselves. Looking back, I believe the crack epidemic led to the misogyny that exists within our community and in hip hop culture specifically. Growing up, it was nearly unheard of for men to refer to women as hoes and bitches; however, in the streets, these terms became the norm.

Day by day, we were all being stripped of our morals. In fact, it seemed that the level of disrespect grew in proportion to the deceit and manipulation that we experienced dealing with our customers. Some women were notorious for stealing sacks and pockets full of money while they performed fellatio. We learned through trial and error that no one was to be trusted, yet we didn't always go by what we knew.

My lessons continued with each day in the basement. The smokers would get into squabbles over things that would seem crazy to the casual observer, but I quickly learned that this subculture had its own rules. One of the biggest causes of conflict was when one smoker cleaned another smoker's pipe. They used alcohol to extract the oil residue left behind after they smoked the rock. They would pour the contents of the pipe on a mirror and set it on fire, leaving behind a powdery residue. They would then scrape this residue off of the mirror, reinsert it into the pipe and smoke it. Between this and the fights over someone smoking more than their fair share of the rock, there was always drama; they were always trying to get over on each other or steal from each other.

I learned a lot from watching their antics, including how to cook up my own batches of crack. I would gather all of the crumbs that shook loose inside the bags of rocks I had. I would place them in a glass vial, add baking soda, and then heat it up with a torch. I would cook it until it congealed into an oily mass. I would then dip the vial in ice water and watch as the cocaine hardened into rock form. It was a valuable lesson that I would later use when I ventured out on my own as a dealer.

The most important lesson I learned was that crack was nothing to be played with; it wreaked havoc in people's lives and destroyed families. There were people I grew up respecting and admiring who I now looked upon with shame and disgust. I witnessed some of the big homies fall prey to the pipe; guys I once looked up to were now groveling at my feet, begging for rocks on credit. I saw women who were at one time beautiful teachers, homemakers, students and store clerks reduced to unkempt crack whores.

My early experiences in the streets caused me to lose my focus, my respect for the community, and ultimately, my own identity. I was raised to be respectful of adults and caring toward people, but in the streets those were signs of weakness. I quickly learned that the streets were unforgiving and would rape you of everything if you were too compassionate or caring. However, after weeks of watching the guys I sold crack with, I soon became a callous, apathetic, cold-hearted predator on our community just like them. I wasn't as quick to anger or resort to violence as some of the guys I ran with, but it wouldn't be long before I recognized that anger and violence were a necessary part of the dope game and I would have to employ them if I wanted to survive.

Over the summer, Miko opened up a few more spots throughout our neighborhood. We operated like any other corporate structure. We were all about expanding into other areas and taking advantage of new clientele. Miko was making a lot of money off of my hustling ability and dedication, sitting in spots twenty-four hours a day. Like many CEO's, he made all of the money while I did the bulk of the work. At the time, I didn't understand how much I was being exploited. All I knew was that I stayed fresh and my pockets were fat. I didn't have any long-term plans or an exit strategy. I allowed my self-worth to be defined by what kind of shoes and clothes I wore and what others thought about me. It was the nature of the game.

As cool as Miko appeared, he was really out for himself and I was just a means to an end. When we started out, Miko was driving a Dodge Omni, which only cost him a few hundred dollars. By the end of the summer, he had purchased a new Jeep Wrangler and Pontiac Grand AM outfitted with a top of the line Kenwood sound system. Although modest by today's standards, these cars were two of the most popular modes of transportation at the time in the 'hood. In contrast, all I had to show for my hard work was a bunch of clothes and shoes. But I was young and didn't care; I thought that was how the game went.

As time went on, I started seeing things a little differently; I realized that I was being used and Miko didn't really give a fuck about me or my life. Once I discovered this, I started doing things my way. I told Miko that I wanted to make more money and be paid by the sack. I was surprised when he agreed to my terms. In exchange, I started recruiting more guys to roll for him. Outside of Tee, our whole crew consisted of guys that I had recruited to come and roll for Miko. These were guys I hung out with on a regular basis but now I was in a position of power.

When I first ran away, a lot of the guys that I grew up with ridiculed and shunned me like I had the plague. I wore borrowed clothes for days at a time and was often hungry and dirty. As soon as I started getting a little money, however, the same people who cracked jokes on me started showing love. Looking back, I know it's the love and acceptance that a guy gets once he starts making money that keeps so many of us chasing the street dream and grand illusions of financial success.

Like most teenagers, I wanted to be accepted and exalted by my peers, and when I came through the 'hood with the fresh Fila's, Bally's and Jordan's, I felt like a superstar. The girls talked about how good I looked in my Guess jeans and Calvin Klein outfit. The attention and illusion of respect that I got was just as addictive as the drugs that I sold. It was this allure that many were willing to die or kill for, including me.

Back then, when I came through the 'hood with a four hundred dollar Fila jogging suit, word spread through the 'hood like wildfire. Today, it's a little different. Instead of jogging suits, it's Cartier glasses and Rolex watches, but the experience is the same. During that era, not everyone could afford the things I was buying or wearing, and at the ages of 13 and 14, my wardrobe cost more than the adults' in my 'hood.

When I pulled up in front of Kurt's house on an Elite 150 Deluxe moped with my pockets bulging, people broke their necks trying to find out who I was down with. The same guys that said I was stupid for selling dope were now trying to get down with us. Instead of treating them badly because they had played me, I told them I would put them on.

At the time, I was making ten dollars off of every hundred dollars worth of rocks that I sold, plus an extra two dollars in tops. Instead of selling five-dollar rocks, we were now selling bigger rocks for twelve dollars. I kept the extra two in addition to the ten that I made off of every hundred. I went from making $350.00 a week to making $300.00 off of every thousand-dollar sack that I sold.

The spot on Wilshire proved to be very lucrative in this regard. On a good day, three to four thousand dollars worth of rocks could be sold. Sometimes it took a few days to get off one sack, but for the most part Wilshire did very well. I would let some of the homies work a sack and make most of the money. I might tell them to kick me down $50 and keep the $250 for themselves because they were the ones responsible for the sack. No matter what I did that day, they had to stay behind and roll, but they got first shot at whatever the boosters brought through. They also bought the beer, food and weed for the day.

Over time, we ended up with a nine-member crew and all but two of them were homeboys that I had brought on board. Everybody had spots of their own to work and we typically worked in groups of two. Wilshire was mine, but since Miko trusted me the most out of our crew, I often spent time riding around with him looking for new areas to open spots. Some days I would work other spots and let some of the other homies work Wilshire since it was doing the best. At the end of the day, I wanted everyone in the crew to shine. I was loyal to a fault and wanted more for my homies than they wanted for me. I saw what we were doing as a means to take care of ourselves. I didn't take into consideration that we were essentially killing our childhood and destroying our community by selling the poisonous rocks.

After a while, Miko started recruiting some of his guys to sell for him. This decision created a lot of animosity amongst the crew. Miko felt like we were spoiled compared to guys who were rolling for other drug crews and he was trying to replace my guys with his own. We knew some of the guys he brought in, but we weren't cool with them, which added to the tension.

A few months later, the spot on Flanders got raided and it revealed a lot to us. Ernie was rolling the spot by himself when the police kicked in the door. They didn't find any dope, but they found a pistol and charged Ernie with carrying a concealed weapon. Miko didn't post his bail because he said Ernie had just started working for him. His failure to bond one of our homies didn't sit right with us. Ernie was risking his life and freedom and we felt the least he could do was bond him out. Adding insult to injury, Miko started telling guys that they could roll out of Wilshire. I felt disrespected because he was cutting my guys out of the picture. In turn, some of my guys started running off with his dope, and things quickly went down hill from there.

One day, I came to check on Wilshire because one of my guys was supposed to be rolling there that day. When I got there, a guy named Henry was sitting in the spot rolling. I was pissed and told him to give me the sack he had. He refused and I punched him in the face. One of my guys then punched him a few times and he took off running out of the house. Henry called Miko and told him that we had jumped on him.

Miko came over and asked me what was up. I told him that I didn't want Henry rolling on Wilshire. He sided with my decision because he had just really met Henry, but the cleft between us was widening.

Some of the crew had started smoking laced joints and fucking up the sacks. One day, Miko knocked one of my homie's teeth out because he had smoked up most of the sack. It was fucked up because we had all grown up in the same 'hood; however, the evil roots of crack were embedding themselves deeper and deeper into our neighborhood, leaving no home, no family and no friendship untouched. As the summer heated up, the madness intensified and I found myself in over my head. I was no longer just addicted to the fast money, I was now addicted to the violence of the lifestyle, and it was only a matter of time before I found myself addicted to crack itself. Yep, I violated the sacred code, "Don't get high off your own supply." At 14, I became a victim of the devil's smoke.

Chapter 6

The butterflies in my stomach stirred as I stood at the front door of our small ranch home on Blackstone. The familiar feeling of running the block in Brightmoor warmed my body as I waited for Brenda to answer the door. My palms were sweating and my heart raced as I waited for her to open the door. My hand was heavy as I reached up to bang on the door. When Brenda opened the door, she had an angelic smile on her face. She rushed out of the door and into my arms.

"I miss you so much," she said as she leapt into my arms and smothered my face with feather soft kisses.

"I told you I was coming home one way or another," I said as I embraced her tightly.

Before I was able to step inside the house, I was awakened from my dream by the sound of someone tapping on my cell door. A smile creased my face as I stirred from my sleep. Normally I would be pissed if someone woke me from my dreams, but this time it was different. I knew we were about to turn this dream into reality and it would only be a matter of time before I was back on the block.

I hopped off of the bunk and looked out of the window to see who was at the door. It took my eyes a minute to adjust to the darkness, but I could see a shadowy figure standing at my cell door. It was after two o'clock in the morning and I knew that the only person likely to be out at that time was Gigolo. We had developed a method for getting out of our cells whenever we felt like it. We would take a sheet and tie a knot to it, then slide the knot beneath the door, pull the sheet up between the door jam and shake it until it popped open. We would come out at night to sneak and use the phones or light up our cigarettes on the wall lighter.

"Wassup?" I whispered through the crack.

"I need to holla at you for a minute," G said as he slid the knotted sheet beneath my door.

I hooked it onto the door and we shook the door until it popped open. I grabbed a couple of squares and slid out of my cell headed for the day room.

"Wassup?" I asked as I fired up the square.

"I think Gigolo and Jabo want to roll with us," he revealed as we sat on the floor beneath the officer's booth.

"You talked to them?" I asked.

"Yeah, but I didn't go into any detail about what we were going to do," he said, assuring me that he hadn't divulged our sophisticated plan.

I was relieved that he hadn't said anything because I wanted to be present at all discussions regarding the escape. Even though G had sparked the idea, I was responsible for the planning and orchestration of the plan. He recognized that his initial plan to bludgeon the officer and take his uniform would have never worked. We may have made it to the elevator on the sixth floor, but there was no way we would have made it out of the building with one uniform at three o'clock in the morning. Instead, I devised what I felt was a fail-proof plan.

"Let's see if they're woke," I suggested as I stubbed out my cigarette.

"Alright," G responded as we crept over to Gigolo's cell. When I peeked into the cell, I could see Gigolo sitting at the desk talking to his bunky. I tapped the window and he came to the door.

"Let me holla at you for a minute," I said.

We popped the door, then went and got Jabo. I asked them what they thought about escaping from the county jail. Jabo hadn't been to court yet, but knew he was facing a lot of time, and Gigolo was still waiting to go to trial. My sentencing date was only weeks away and I felt like I had nothing to lose; however, their situation was different and I wanted to be sure that they would be down to rock with us before I told them what was up. Both of them said that they were down to bust out as soon as we put the plan in motion. I told them we would leave on the Sunday coming up, which meant we had five days to finalize everything.

I wanted to tell L what was up, but I knew he would try to talk me out of it. L was a real religious brother and often quoted from the

Bible. We respected his wisdom, but at the time, I wasn't willing to trust my freedom with a God I couldn't see. For the four years I was on the streets, the only thing I believed in was the power of money and guns, so I wasn't about to allow him to talk me out of it, nor did I want to hear a sermon about trusting the Lord. I wanted to be free so that I could be with Brenda and our unborn child. I had missed out on the birth of my daughter, but I would be damned if I missed the birth of my next child.

Gigolo suggested we get as many sheets as we could from the guys on the rock and the deputy when she passed them out. I hid the pipe in my mattress and we waited patiently for Sunday night to roll around. We did our best to conceal our excitement from the rest of the guys on the rock, but when we were alone in one of the cells kicking it, we couldn't stop talking about what we were going to do when we got out. We talked about the sex we would have, the alcohol we would consume, the money we would make, and the food we would eat. We didn't give any real consideration to what it would be like living on the run for the rest of our lives. All we were focused on was the power of the moment.

During that week, I talked to Brenda nearly every day. She gave me updates on the growth of the baby in her womb, and we talked about the things we missed about being with each other. We continued to plan a life together despite the fact that I was waiting to be sentenced. I kept telling her that I would be home soon, but I never alluded to the fact that I was about to commit an act of desperation in my efforts to get there.

When Sunday rolled around, we spent the day making the final preparations. We gathered the food we had collected from the commissary and made sure everyone had the extra socks and T-shirts that they needed to wear when we made it down to the streets. In the county, we weren't allowed to have gym shoes, so we decided the best thing to do was pull a few pair of socks over our shower shoes to absorb the blow when we hit the ground.

All day it felt like time was moving in slow motion. I thought the night would never arrive, but finally it did. After the deputy completed his 2a.m. count rounds, Gigolo popped his cell door and came down to my cell. He had his county shirt tied around his face like a ninja. I wrapped my face the same way and helped him pop my cell door. My bunky asked what was up and I told him to go back to sleep and mind his business. He was a metro-sexual, feminine-acting cat and we never really spoke so he went with the program. I had slid the pipe out of my mattress when we first locked down for the night and grabbed it as I prepared to exit the cell. It was the first time Gigolo had a chance to hold it and feel the weight of it.

"Damn homie, this a bad motherfucker," he said, feeling the weight of the pipe as I helped G pop his cell door.

Finally, we went to get Jabo out of his cell. We sat around for a minute smoking what we thought would be our last square on lockdown. When the final Newport was put out, it was showtime. Since G was the biggest and strongest among the four of us, he was the first one to take a turn at breaking the thick, Plexiglas window. The first hit to the window sounded like a gun blast. My heart pounded in rhythm with his hits on the window, one ferocious blast after another. My body was on fire with adrenaline and excitement and I couldn't wait for my turn on the window. The noise from G hitting the window was so loud that we couldn't hear the guys on the rock screaming for us to stop. Finally, after he was near exhaustion, G stopped and handed me the pipe, which was warm to the touch.

When I approached the window, I heard someone screaming from one of the cells for us to stop before we got everyone in trouble. Gigolo went to their window and told them to shut the fuck up and get back in the bed. I laughed a little before I went to work beating on the window, increasing the damage that G had started. Finally, the edge of the window gave way and we were able to push the rest of the window open. I tried to squeeze between the two beams that were inside the frame and realized that I could only get part of my shoulder through it, so we went to work bending the beam with the pipe. We wedged the pipe between the wall and the beam and rocked it back and forth, bending the beam a little bit at a time. After a few minutes, I tried to slide my upper torso through the window, but still couldn't fit all the way through.

We had made enough progress to know that we were only minutes away from being able to climb down the sheets we had tied together toward freedom. We went back to bending the beam as the guys on the rock hollered at us to go back to our cells. We didn't give a damn about them being afraid. The only thing that mattered to us was our freedom.

We continued to bend the beam for about ten minutes before we stopped. G tried to squeeze through the window and we got excited when we saw how much progress we had made. We each took a turn seeing if we could fit through the window. When we got around to me, I tried to fit my head out, and just as I was working my way out, a female voice hollered up to the window. She asked what we were doing. I jumped back from the window and told G what was up. We said fuck it, we had come too far to turn back now so we kept on bending the beam. We didn't realize that she was a deputy outside doing a perimeter check. Within two minutes, a squad car was outside flashing a light up to the window.

"Damn, this is fucked up," I said as I turned toward the rest of the crew. My heart sunk down into my shower shoes when I realized we weren't going to be getting out of county jail that night.

"Man, we might as well go back to our cells," someone said somberly.

We looked around at each other, then agreed to go back to our cells. Before I got back to my cell, I realized that we had left the pipe in the day room so I ran back, grabbed the pipe, and threw it out of the window before rushing back to my cell. I knew the deputies would be rushing the rock at any minute so I did everything I could to remove any evidence that I had been out of the cell. I removed the socks from my shower shoes, shook the glass out, took off my extra T-shirt, and then jumped on my bunk. I pulled the scratchy, wool blanket over my head and did my best to play sleep. I was sweating profusely, but I had no immediate plans to come up from under the covers.

It took the deputies at least twenty minutes to finally figure out what rock the escape attempt had occurred on. It felt like the longest wait in my life. I could hear my heart beating and I was sure that the deputies would hear it echoing through the day room when they opened the door. Finally, a bright light washed over the room as they turned on all of the lights.

A sergeant barked out orders as the deputies went cell by cell snatching us all out. They slammed us up against the wall and forced us to strip naked in the middle of the day room. They threatened to beat our asses and bust our heads with flashlights if we didn't come clean. I imagined in my head that when I turned around, there would be several men standing with their fingers pointing at me, G, Gigolo and Jabo. But when I turned around, I realized how well we had concealed our identity because everyone appeared to be confused. They didn't know who or how many of us had tried to escape. The fact that no one said anything seemed to infuriate the deputies and they tore through our cells like human tornadoes. They threw our pictures, letters, and commissary into the middle of the day room floor along with our mattresses. Lucky for us, their emotional reaction resulted in no charges. They had contaminated the scene of the crime, and now every inmate present had glass particles on their property. When one of the captains realized their error, he ordered us back into our cells; however, it was too late, the damage had been done.

They told us that we would be on lockdown until they got to the bottom of what happened. It was this threat that led someone to rat us out. There was one other guy who was supposed to go with us, but he backed out at the last minute. He was the person we suspected had given us up because he was the only other guy who knew of our plot. The reason I won't mention his name is because I can't prove that he ratted on us. My gut and street intuition tells me that he did, but I will never label a person a rat unless I have undeniable proof that he told. To me, that's one of the ugliest labels you can place on a person so I am very careful about using it.

We were allowed to collect our belongings before they finally locked the rock down at about five o'clock in the morning.

I laid back on the bunk and fought back tears of defeat. I had never wanted for anything so bad in my life. I thought about Brenda having to go it alone and my heart crumbled like a graham cracker pie crust as I thought about serving a long prison sentence. It was in that moment that the gravity of my situation hit me. Up to that point, I hadn't made any preparation for being away from my family and friends. I also hadn't stopped for one minute to think about the victim of my crime or his family. I was wrapped up in a delusional state of selfishness and self-denial. I was sick and didn't even realize it until years later.

A few hours later, the deputies returned to our rock and headed straight for Gigolo's cell. They cuffed him and his bunky and escorted them off of the rock. I stood at my window listening in an effort to see what was going on. Initially, I thought they were doing something routine since they had his bunky. Moments later, they came to my cell and told me to step out. They cuffed me and told me that I was being placed in the hole and charged with attempted escape. They boxed up the rest of my belongings and escorted me off of the rock. The deputies took me through a tunnel to the old side of the county jail where the hole was located. When I reached the rock, they took me to a cell and tossed my belongings in before ordering me to step inside. They then removed the cuffs and told me that the hearings officer would be through to see me along with an officer from Internal Affairs.

Gigolo called down the tier and asked who they had just brought in. I told him it was me. We talked for a minute and found out that they had told him the same thing. Moments later, G was brought down to the hole. We acknowledged out loud that we hadn't done anything, just in case they were listening or had a plant in our presence. We agreed that we would demand a lawyer when questioned and stand mute when we went to their internal court. Our strategy proved effective and we were never charged with the attempt to escape. However, we were found guilty in their kangaroo court and sentenced to fifteen days in the hole.

The days in the hole went by slowly. I spent most of the time lying on the floor peering through the cracked window facing Gratiot where cars drove by all day with their sounds bumping loudly. If I wasn't doing that, I watched the roaches crawl down the tier as we talked about different aspects of life. Sometimes we would sit back and recite the verses of rap songs that we loved or kick it about our childhoods. It was through these stories that I learned of the years of childhood abuse and neglect that the other men had suffered. We were all wounded boys with deep psychological and emotional scars. We all came from homes were ass whoopings were the norm and vile words were handed out like candy to trick-or-treaters on Halloween. We weren't bad people, but we had all made some very bad decisions in response to the bad things we experienced in life. We were fathers, brothers, uncles, drug dealers, robbers and killers. We weren't all of one thing, but a mixture of failure, neglect, promise and purpose. Sadly, we would all grow to live our adulthood out in prisons across the state with varied experiences.

One week later, I was returned to court and sentenced to serve 17 to 40 years of my life in prison.

Chapter 7

"The police are outside," John warned, moments before the sound of loud banging reverberated through the house. I rushed down the stairs to see what was going on. John was known for being paranoid and raising false alarms, so I wanted to see what was up before I made any drastic decisions about getting rid of the crack. When I looked out of the front window, I noticed two squad cars and decided to get rid of everything before they kicked in the door.

The police continued beating on the door while I gathered all of the rocks and threw them down the heat vent located in the dining room. I wasn't sure where they would end up, but I knew for certain that the police wouldn't get them. Finally, John opened the door and they rushed into the house with their guns raised. They didn't have a search warrant for the premises and I am unsure if they asked John for his permission to enter. Little did I know, it would not be the last time my Constitutional rights were trampled on. Sadly, for most of the young Black males in our community, there is no expectation of protection by the Constitution. When it comes to our interaction with the police, we are not given the same respect that other citizens receive. It is not uncommon for police to brutalize us and violate our Constitutional rights under the guise of crime prevention.

When the police entered the house, they told John that someone had called and informed them that a homicide had been committed. They told us that one of the neighbors witnessed a shooting in the backyard and they were out to investigate. John assured them that no one had been shot or killed, but that didn't stop them from rummaging through the house.

It was clear from the set up of the house that we were running a drug operation. In addition to the Armor Guard, the house had the usual signs of a drug den. The living room table was strewn with leftover Coney Island and bottles of warm Old English 800 malt liquor with cigarette butts floating around in them. Piles of unwashed clothes sat in the corner next to a row of gym shoes and the basement was full of customers who were clueless to what was going on upstairs.

A few officers went back outside and entered the basement through the side door. I heard a lot of commotion followed by piercing screams as they went to work beating our customers. A middle-aged Black officer and a young White officer ushered me, John and one of the older homies named Lee into the dining room. I was calm at first because I knew I had gotten rid of all the dope; however, when I heard the screams coming from the basement, my hands began shaking like a pair of dice at a crap game. I had no desire to experience whatever they were getting that had them screaming as though they were on the verge of death.

We were ordered to place our hands on the wall in front of us. The young White officer searched the living room and dining room before turning his attention to us. He patted Lee down and took all of the money he had in his pocket. Lee protested and showed him his check stub. The officer returned Lee's money and told him to sit on the floor facing the wall. He then came over to me and asked me where the dope was stashed as he patted me down. He searched my pockets, then stuck his hand in my waistband and pulled them away from my body so that he could see if I had anything stashed in my underwear. Without provocation, he punched me in my nuts. It felt like someone had sucked all of the air out of my body. I grabbed my nuts and slumped to the floor where I lay still while he retrieved money from my pocket.

"Tell me where the dope at!" the Black officer said with a smirk on his face as they counted the money they had taken out of my pockets.

I was in too much pain to respond and what I wanted to say would have cost me another beat down. In that moment, what little respect I had for the police was lost. Whether I was doing right or wrong, they had no right to beat me. They were supposed to be there to uphold the law and lead by example, but instead they proved to be worse than us.

Switching tactics, the officers asked me where I had gotten the money. I told them from my uncle. They told me that I was lying, then snatched me up from the floor and slammed my face into the wall. I braced my fragile body for the barrage of blows that I expected they would deliver, but instead of beating me more, they placed me in handcuffs and told me they were taking me in for loitering in a suspected drug house.

As they escorted me out of the house, they asked where I lived. I gave them my mother's address as they threw me in the back of the squad car. I took in the view of my neighborhood as we rode the short distance to my street. For the first time in my life, I noticed the subtle nuances and beautiful architecture of the buildings in my neighborhood as the people we passed appeared in vivid colors. Something about being held captive heightened my senses, and the reality of what I was doing with my life started hitting me.

When the officers pulled up in front of our house, all of my neighbors came out. Some of them wore disappointed expressions and others had that "here we go again" look on their faces. There were even a few who had smirks on their faces as though they were getting some sick satisfaction from seeing me cause my parents such grief and embarrassment. Looking back, I can only imagine what those times were like for my father.

My mother wasn't home, but my father was there. The officers uncuffed me and walked me into the house where they talked with my father for a few minutes. In his presence, they were polite and professional. They told him that they found me hanging out in a drug house and I had a lot of money in my possession. They never mentioned how they beat my ass, and when I told my father what happened, he looked at me like I deserved it. To this day, it troubles me that we allow these abuses to go unchecked. No matter the circumstances, police abuse is never okay.

Finally, they told my father that they would turn the money they confiscated in to evidence, but I knew that was some bullshit. I didn't know the law at the time, but I knew enough about life to know that we would never see those officers or that money again. It was one of the many lessons that I would learn about the officers who police the 'hood. Most of them were no different from us; they were opportunists, and when they saw a chance to get over, they took it. I'm not saying that all officers are crooked, but my experience in the 'hood has led me to be distrustful of the men and women in blue.

I stayed at my mother's house for a couple of weeks before I fell back into my old patterns. Since I had had a taste of the streets and the feeling of being independent, things were different. I had grown accustomed to coming and going as I pleased. I was used to living by my own rules, eating what I wanted, getting up when I felt like it, and going to sleep when my body and mind were too tired to stay awake. Going back to my mother's house, I knew these were things she would never tolerate. I tried to straddle the fence between the streets and her house, but it was nearly impossible.

The day after the police took me home, I went back around to the spot. I sold rocks during the day and came home late at night. I could sense that my late night antics were rubbing my mother the wrong way. She had a rule about being in her house at a reasonable hour, which meant we had to be home by the time she got in bed. It didn't matter how old you were, she didn't play that running in and out of the house at all hours of the night. She tried to deal with it for the first week or so. I think she kind of understood what I was going through, but was unable to handle it. We never talked about why I had left in the first place, and we never sought counseling as a family, so we did a precarious dance around the big elephant in the room until our feet got tangled up. Two weeks into my return home, things came to a head and I left for the last time.

Meanwhile, the spot on Wilshire was banging. We sold thousands of dollars worth of rocks every day. Everyone in the crew was making money. We would ride up to Royal Skateland in Miko's Jeep Wrangler and Pontiac Grand AM with the music blaring. We would all get out in our Fila suits with our pockets bulging, dancing and talking shit like we owned the 'hood. The girls flocked to us and the guys wanted to be us. The older girls doted on me and told me how good I looked, and I ate it up like Thanksgiving dinner.

We were addicted to the life, and like any other addiction, we were always looking for ways to make it more exciting. Sometimes we would hit Belle Isle and stand around outside of the cars with the music blaring as we sipped on Old English and smoked weed. But that wasn't enough excitement, and in a matter of months, we raised the stakes. Our crew had expanded, and a few of the guys had started getting high on fifty-ones. I resisted the temptation for a while. I had just started drinking and smoking weed on a regular basis, and I wasn't trying to take it any further than that because I had watched a few of my guys fall off. They stopped caring about making money and there primary focus was on getting high. There were a few who were able to manage their addiction, however, and that's how I got sucked into the quicksand of crack addiction.

One day, Lee came over to the spot on Wilshire to hang out with me and Tee. We knew that Tee was smoking so we never allowed him to keep the sack, but I didn't know that Lee was also smoking laced joints until I caught him. I had gone upstairs to use the bathroom when I noticed Lee sitting in the master bedroom on the bed. When I came closer, I saw that he was crushing up a rock and mixing it with a small pile of weed. When he noticed me, he played like it wasn't a big deal. He told me that it wasn't like smoking the pipe because the weed absorbed the effects of the cocaine.

Lee was the epitome of the manipulative older homie. Sadly, many of our young men grow up looking up to the older homies in the 'hood because they make them believe that they have their best interests at heart. When things aren't going good at home, they have all of the answers. When these guys don't have anywhere to live, they show them how to hustle and take care of themselves. In reality, they are the worst predators on our community. Anyone who will encourage a child to sell or use drugs is sick in the head and a danger and threat to the health of the community. Most of the guys I know serving long prison sentences for drugs and violent crimes were introduced to the game by one of the older guys in the 'hood.

What I didn't know is that no matter how you smoke crack, it is highly addictive and deadly. I watched Lee as he lit up the laced joint. The joint crackled, and I could see the oil from the cocaine burning through the paper. The thick plume of white smoke smelled sickly sweet and the effect on Lee was instantaneous. He inhaled again deeply before passing me the joint with a nod. I took it and held it in my hand for a minute before he encouraged me to take a hit. I put it to my lips and sucked the devil's poison into my young lungs. It felt evil going down and I knew something wasn't right. My heart began beating erratically and my lips grew numb. My whole body felt higher than it had ever felt, and I thought my heart was going to burst out of my shirt. My hearing became crystal clear and my conscience began to fuck with me. All of the shit that I had been doing wrong began to play tricks on me. I was paranoid; I thought that my mother would appear at the door any minute with a belt in her hand to whoop my ass.

Lee assured me that what I was feeling was normal. I went to look out of the window about ten times, checking for the police. After a while, the effects began subsiding. Tee joined us and we smoked a few more laced joints. I paid for them out of the money that I was going to make off of the sack that I was selling. By the end of the night, we had smoked up all of the profit from that sack. I called Miko to get another sack, and while I waited for him, I grew more paranoid. I thought he could tell I was high just from our phone conversation. I thought about everything he had told me over the past few months. He had warned me to never smoke crack, and it was like he was sitting on my shoulder whispering in my ear. When he finally showed up, I was really tripping.

Lee and Tee were acting all skittish and paranoid, and it affected me. I picked up on their vibe and began feeling uncomfortable. I thought to myself, "I'm never smoking that shit again in my life," but I knew I was lying to myself. A few days later, we ended up smoking some more, and then it became a regular thing. At first, we would just pay for it out of our own pockets; however, there was no way that what we earned in a day could keep pace with the addictive influence of the laced joints. Between the three of us, we were smoking over a thousand dollars worth of rocks a day.

I didn't even notice how fast I was going downhill. By the end of the day, the money I had hustled for went up in a cloud of bluish-white smoke. Within a few weeks, I was fucking up the sacks. I would cut some of the rocks or claim that the sacks Miko gave me were short. My fourteen-year-old world was spinning out of control.

Around this time, I was also working a spot on a street named Maiden right off of Conners. It was a two-family flat and we rolled out of the downstairs flat. It was a decent looking house, and the couple who lived there was cool. They had a son who was a couple of years younger than me, but they didn't appear to be bothered by the fact that I was selling out of their house. One day, I hooked up with one of their nephews who smoked laced joints. He was in his early twenties and used to sell crack for the Best Friends. We clicked instantly and stayed up all night smoking laced joints. Together we decided that we were going to run off with the next sack that Miko dropped off, which was worth a thousand dollars.

Once we got the sack from Miko, we chilled with some people that the guy knew and smoked all day. I didn't know anyone there, but they had no problem taking advantage of all the crack I had with me. Once all of the rocks were gone and my high had subsided, I realized that I didn't have anywhere to go but back to the 'hood.

I spent the day trying to duck Miko, but there was no getting away from the 'hood. When he caught up with me, he was in the car with two of his goons and he ordered me to get in the car. I thought about taking off running, but decided against it. I was quick on my feet and had a ready response to his question about the dope and my whereabouts. I lied and told him that the spot had been raided and I had been taken to the youth home. I even told him that he could take me around to my mother's house and ask her because she was the one who had gotten me out that morning. I didn't anticipate that he would take me up on my offer, but to my surprise, he put the car in drive and sped off toward my mother's house.

I sat in the back of the car nervous because I knew that my mother had no idea what was going on in my life. When we reached the block, I didn't have the nerve to go through with it. I didn't know what they would do to my mother, and I wasn't about to jeopardize my family because of my bullshit, so I told Miko that I had smoked up the sack. He was really fucked up about it because he had known for a while that the other guys were fucking around, but he never suspected that I would be the one to go out like that. I was still a child and it never occurred to him that I would be gone off of that shit. His goons didn't seem too surprised and were very eager to make an example out of me. They didn't care about my age or my size. They were street-hardened veterans who no longer felt empathy.

There are very few people who know about this part of my life or this side of the game. Like many who fall prey to addiction, I was in denial. I thought that I could handle myself and anything that the streets threw my way; however, no child is equipped to deal with the ugly brutality of the streets.

Miko had no choice but to do something because I had fucked over his money. He was bound by the code of the streets, and he knew that the moment he went against the code and turned soft was the moment he would become the prey in a land of predators.

We drove around in silence for what seemed like hours. Several times I thought of jumping out of the car and taking off, but I didn't have a desire to get shot in the back of the head. Finally, after nearly an hour, we pulled up in front of the house on Maiden. One of Miko's goons grabbed me by the back of my shirt and dragged me into the house. I pleaded with Miko and told him that I would work off the money I had messed up. Very bluntly, he asked me, "How you gonna work off a sack when you a crackhead?" His words hit me harder than any of the punches that they threw. I had in essence become that which I despised and had taken advantage of. I was a customer and consumer of the poison I had once took pride in selling to others. I was the scorn of the dope game and my word meant nothing.

As soon as we got into the living room, Miko turned around and punched me in the face. I staggered backwards, and before I could regain my composure, one of his goons punched me in the back of the head. I swung on one of his goons and did my best to fight back. I never swung at Miko, but I didn't care about scrapping with his goons. Despite my best efforts, my adolescent strength was no match for their adult strength. They quickly overpowered me and administered a thorough beat down. After beating me down until I was lying in a pool of blood, Miko stopped them.

My nose was bleeding profusely and one side of my face was swollen. It was hard for me to breathe, and as I lay there, I thought I was going to die. When they were finished with me, Miko told me to get up from the floor. He told me to clean myself up and wait at the house for them to come back. I was dazed and confused. I looked at his goons and thought about the rifle that was in the back room, but I didn't have the heart at the time to shoot anyone.

Despite the fact that I had smoked up the sack, I felt betrayed by Miko. I looked up to him like a big brother, but when it came down to it, I was nothing more than a laborer. I knew he had held back and didn't allow them to hurt me the way they had done other guys, but it didn't take away from the scars to my psyche. The way I saw it, if Miko could turn on me, then anyone could turn on me, and in that moment, I made a silent vow to kill the next person to put their hands on me.

I stared at myself in the mirror for a few minutes as I thought about what my next move would be. I felt lonely and vulnerable. My lips were swollen and cracked, and my eye had a lump the size of a plum beneath it. As much as I wanted to, I could no longer cry. My feelings grew colder by the minute as I thought about revenge. I didn't know what to do or where to turn, and I was afraid that Miko and his goons would return at any minute and finish beating me until I died. As that thought crossed my mind, I looked around the bathroom for something to defend myself with in the event they came after me again. After a few minutes, I heard them exiting the house and a wave of relief came over me.

I slumped down on the bathroom floor and curled myself up into a tight ball. Thoughts of my mother and father tumbled through my mind. I thought about everything they had told me about God and how none of it made sense in that moment. I cursed their blond-haired, blue-eyed God. How could God allow this to happen to me, I wondered. Where were the caring, protective arms of Jesus when I needed him? Where were my mother and father while I was lying on the pissy bathroom floor of a crack house?

The sound of someone coming from upstairs caused me to pull myself up from the floor. My face was throbbing, and each time I took a breath, it felt like I had been stabbed in my side. I stood in front of the sink and rinsed the blood from my mouth with cold water, then I heard a soft voice asking if I was alright. I looked up and nodded my head indicating that I was okay. Sharon, who lived upstairs with her one-year-old son, looked at me with pity as she grabbed a face cloth and washed my face with cold water. She was the niece of the guy whose house we were selling out of, and from the moment I started selling out of their house, her and I had gotten cool. She was beautiful and I had a little crush on her, but she looked at me like a little brother. She told me that I needed to get out of the game and leave Miko alone. As she talked, I felt a deep sense of shame and embarrassment overtake me. I wasn't sure if she knew that I had smoked up their crack, or if she had seen me get my ass beaten. Whatever the case, I knew that I never wanted to see her again. She told me to come upstairs when I got myself together so that she could talk to me. I told her that I would, but deep inside I knew it would be the last time I saw her.

When I gathered myself, I walked the short distance to my Uncle Keith's house. He lived several streets over on Chelsea. He was street savvy and all of the guys in the 'hood looked up to him. I was set on revenge and thought he would understand. I was thinking irrationally, but back then that didn't matter to me. All I knew was that I wanted to get back at Miko for what he had done to me.

When my uncle saw me and heard what happened, he jumped into his Jeep and drove around the neighborhood looking for Miko. When we couldn't catch up with him, we returned to his house. He asked me what was going on with me, and I gave him a modified version that didn't include me smoking laced joints. He told me that I was heading down the wrong path and needed to go home. I understood where he was coming from, but returning home was no longer an option for me. I stayed the night at my uncle's, and the following day, he dropped me off at my oldest sister Tamica's house on Margaret and John R.

When Tamica saw my face, she started crying. She wanted to go find Miko and beat his ass. We grew up fighting side-by-side with each other. No matter who she got into with, I was right there and vice versa. When she calmed down, we talked about what happened and she told me that I could stay with her. After months of surviving on my own in the streets, I had a chance to start anew. My oldest brother Alan was on his way home from prison and it looked like we would be able to put our family back together.

With Alan's arrival home, my older brother Art started coming back around and the three of us hung out together nearly every day. Before long, we were all deeply entrenched in the drug trade and the pathological behavior of the drug trade became deeply entrenched in us. The real war on drugs had just begun, and it played itself out within our family, leaving behind many casualties.

Chapter 8

The night before I was sentenced, I stayed up pacing the floor. I thought about everything I had gone through that led me to that moment. I pictured the people and the incidents that shaped my worldview. I thought about everything I had missed out on and all that I would miss out on. I never went to my prom or walked across the stage at graduation. I thought about my younger sisters, Nakia and Shamica, who were 16 and 10 when I got arrested. I wouldn't be there to protect them from neighborhood boys, or watch them graduate. I thought about Brenda and the struggles she was about to face trying to raise our child alone. I knew she didn't have the family support that she needed to raise a baby in a healthy household.

I talked to Gigolo, G, White Boy and Jabo until they were ready to go to sleep. They wished me luck and told me that they would pray for the judge to be lenient. Finally, at 3am, the deputy came to get me. He cuffed me and led me to the elevator where a few other guys were waiting to go to court. We were all at different stages of the process so our outlooks were different. Some still held out hope that they would beat their case, and others, like myself, were preparing themselves for life upstate.

When we reached the bullpen, I saw a few familiar faces from the 'hood, but I wasn't in the mood to talk to anyone. Every time a door opened and closed, I thought about my chances of fleeing to freedom, but I knew there was no way I would make it, so I prepared to take my sentence like a man.

I carried a picture of me and Brenda with me to the bullpen outside of the courtroom. While I sat on the bench waiting for my name to be called, I stared at our picture until my thoughts were interrupted by a guy who had just entered the bullpen. He told me he recognized Brenda, and initially I got pissed off. Reading my reaction, he quickly explained that he grew up down the street from her and used to run with her uncle. We talked for a minute until our attention was drawn to a light-skinned guy with a long ponytail who had just come into the bullpen.

"What do y'all think the judge will do to a man serving a life sentence if he raped another inmate," he asked out loud as he looked around the room for an answer.

A few guys replied that there wasn't much the judge could do if the guy was already serving a life sentence. After taking in their answers, he told them that he was the guy he was referring to. Before he could finish his sentence, I knew he was the guy that my bunky had told me about. He didn't look like he was capable of raping another man, or at least that wasn't the vision of Seven that I had in my mind. In my mind, I imagined a brute foaming at the mouth with scars everywhere and a menacing baldhead, but he was just the opposite.

The guy I had been talking to from the neighborhood appeared to be irritated and told him to get the fuck away from him talking that gay shit. Seven laughed, then went and sat next to a White guy who was sitting on the bench. The guy from the 'hood told me that he had done a bit before and couldn't stand the sexual predators that he encountered during his bit. He said that most of them were weak and only preyed on the weak White boys. I took it all in as I watched Seven talking to the White guy. I could tell from his body language that he was up to something, but it wasn't my business. I had my own problems to deal with at the time, so I sat back and waited for them to call my name.

A few minutes passed, and I was called to stand before Judge Robert Evans for sentencing. When I entered the courtroom, I saw my parents, Brenda, and my ex-girlfriend Nycci from Ohio. I smiled at them but my heart was cracked in half. I quickly turned back around to face the judge who reminded me of my grandfather.

I didn't know what to expect at the sentencing. My lawyer assured me and my family that I was looking at no more than ten years. It was his assurance that led me to take a plea. While I wasn't excited about doing the next ten years in prison, I knew it was a good deal. Most of the guys I had talked to on the rock told me that it was in my best interests to take the plea because the charge itself carried a life sentence. We had all seen guys get sentenced to 40, 50 and 60 years for similar charges. While ten years wasn't anything to sneeze at, it sounded better then fifty years or life in prison.

Finally, after a short wait, I was called up for sentencing. My lawyer wasn't present so I agreed to allow his partner, Gerald Evelyn, to represent me at the sentencing. We talked briefly and he told me what to do when the judge questioned me about the plea. I had a GED and did well whenever I went to school, but I wasn't able to fully grasp the subtleties of the law as it applied to my plea agreement. It was my understanding that my lawyer had already gotten me a deal for ten years, so when I approached the bench, I was surprised to learn that there was no pre-existing sentence agreement in place. That meant I was taking a risk and could be sentenced to any number of years, including life. I didn't fully understand at that moment that I could have withdrawn my plea and proceeded with a trial.

There were so many emotions and thoughts running through my head that it was impossible for me to think straight. In many ways, I was still a child, and everything about the system was intimidating, so I went along with the program. Finally, after asking me about the case, the Judge said he was ready to sentence me. He asked me if I had anything to say and I told him I did. I apologized to the victim's family and asked them to forgive me for what I had done to their loved one. I then asked the Judge for leniency. After I was done speaking, he looked down at what I now know were the sentencing guidelines to determine how much time he was going to give me.

When he finished with his calculations, he told me that I would be sentenced to serve a total of seventeen to forty years in prison. When the numbers leapt from his mouth, my knees buckled. I was only two years past the age of seventeen and had hardly begun to live. I couldn't even comprehend the thought of spending nearly two decades of my life behind bars. My shoulders slumped forward as I lowered my head. I could hear my mother and Brenda crying behind me, but I was too afraid to turn around and face them. I knew if I turned back, I would break down. Instead, I turned and walked toward the door leading me back to the bullpen.

When I stepped into the bullpen, everyone grew quiet. I sat back down on the bench where I had left my bag and rested my head against the wall. My eyes felt like they were going to burst at any moment. Slowly, I started shutting my mind down. I had turned my back on everything that I thought would make me happy in life. I no longer wanted to think of the things that used to be; I had a bit to do, and I knew I couldn't afford the distraction of looking back.

Really, there was nothing to look back for. The way I saw it, seventeen years later, none of those things would be the same. Whenever they released me, I would be starting my life over from scratch. All I had shared with the people in my life would be no more. As I sat there deleting the files from my past, my lawyer called me to the visiting booth. He told me about my appeal and my rights. He may as well had been explaining to me how to build the Great Wall of China. His words were empty to me and meant nothing. My sadness was slowly replaced by a deep, dark anger that caused my body to grow tense and hard.

I was thankful that no one in the bullpen asked me any questions, because in that moment, I know I would have been facing another charge. After waiting a few more minutes, I noticed Seven luring a White guy into the small bathroom area inside the bullpen. Evil and perversity dripped from his pores like sweat and it sickened me to think that I would be spending the next seventeen years of my life around such depraved men.

Moments later, the guards came to get me. They returned me to the hole where I had been for the last week or so. When I hit the rock, Gigolo called down and asked me what happened. I told him how much time the judge had given me, and he got quiet. I knew he was thinking about his own chances at sentencing. We had all rolled the street dice and crapped out. A few of the guys asked me how I felt and I told them that I was alright, but that was as far from the truth as Detroit is from Alaska. I was beyond hurt. I couldn't stop thinking about the two children I would be leaving behind. My life wasn't supposed to be spent behind bars, but I had given up on life and now I had to pay the price. That was the hardest part for me. I didn't want to own up to what I had done and it only made matters worse.

Two days after I was sentenced, I was transferred upstate to prison. My first stop was Riverside Correctional Facility where they quarantined all prisoners under the age of twenty-one. We took a battery of psychological, behavioral and physical tests to determine what facility we would be shipped to. They also determined our educational and security needs.

I was herded into the back of a van along with ten other inmates. The ride from Detroit to Ionia was about two and a half hours long and we barely spoke to each other the entire ride. We were all lost in our own thoughts of freedom. We sat in the back with our heads lowered as the van whisked us away from the city. For two and a half hours, I stared at the handcuffs, hoping they would disappear and I would be set free. But no matter how hard I thought or imagined, those handcuffs weren't going anywhere.

When we finally pulled up to the prison, my heart started pounding. The concertina-wired fences were menacing. They looked like they were hungry for tender flesh. The fall sun beamed off of the metal, making them come alive as we circled the parking lot. Finally, we pulled through a checkpoint in front of the prison. The deputies checked their pistols before they got out of the van, then came around to the back. They ordered us out as they held their pistols tightly. We shuffled off of the van and stretched our legs out before we were led inside the building. We watched as the deputies checked their pistols in with the correction officer behind the desk. Once they had met all of the security requirements, we were finally led inside of the prison.

One of the things that I noticed when we pulled up was how neatly manicured the lawns were and how new the buildings looked. The prison stood in stark contrast to the dilapidated schools that sat like scabs across Detroit's decaying landscape. It wasn't until years later that I understood the politics of it all. The state was more willing to invest money in the upkeep of prisons than they were in schools. They had it all backwards. Instead of treating the disease, they spent millions of dollars treating the symptoms. Looking at the buildings was also a reminder of what the bigwig politicians really thought of the Black community; we were disposable. In reality, we were being set up to fail.

The intake process was similar to what we went through when we entered the county jail. We were forced to strip out of our personal clothes and dress-out in state blues. We were given a box to send out whatever pictures, books, and clothes we had brought with us from the county jail. We stood around ass naked in front of more people than I had ever known in my entire nineteen years on earth. Through this slow, gradual process, I started becoming detached from my own body. I no longer felt like I belonged to myself. I didn't realize it at the time, but I was being turned into chattel for the state.

In order to keep from going insane, I learned to detach my emotions from the experience, with the exception of anger. I held on to the anger because that was the only time I felt like I had control over my life, even though I would later discover that I was giving them the little control I had left whenever I lashed out in anger.

We were called up one-by-one to the desk where an officer waited. We went through the whole bend and cough process again, then we were given a number.

"Mr. James Angelo White, please step forward," the officer said.

When I stepped up to the desk, she asked me my name. I gave it to her, then she told me that my new name was prisoner number 219184. She urged me to remember that number like I had remembered my own name. I thought about her words as I stepped to the next window to retrieve my state-issued clothing. I slipped into the blues and went to sit on the bench where a few more guys were waiting.

When the last guy was dressed out, we were taken to building seven where we were given our cell assignments. The officer told us to take our bedrolls down to our cells and report back to the day room in five minutes.

When I went down the hall, I was expecting to see a cell with bars, but instead it was a small room with a single bunk, small desk, and a big steel door. In the back of the cell, there was a window with a few panes of glass missing. It was still early in the evening, but I could feel the cool, fall air blowing through as soon as I entered the cell.

I placed my bedroll on the hard, green, plastic mattress. I then returned to the day room where the rest of the guys waited. The officer led us around to the infirmary where we were given a physical exam. They checked to see if we needed glasses or any other medical equipment to stay alive. They also checked our blood pressure and pulse, and then told us that they were going to test us for HIV and other sexually transmitted diseases. Back then, HIV was relatively new, and most of what we had heard on the streets was distorted and void of truth. We sat around joking about the disease, feeding into the myth that it was only for gay White men. We didn't feel like we had a reason to be concerned.

When I entered the examination room, I told the nurse that I didn't need the HIV test because I had never used IV drugs or had sex with men. She laughed at my ignorance before setting me straight. She asked if I had ever had unprotected sex. I told her yes, with a little swagger in my voice. She told me that if I had ever had unprotected sex, then I could have contracted it. She explained that there were no visible signs that a woman had HIV. She said that a woman could be as pretty as Phylicia Rashad and still be carrying the virus that caused AIDS. The more she explained the disease to me, the more I thought about the women that I had had unprotected sex with. A parade of naked women danced through my head, but not in a good way. I was very promiscuous from the time I turned fourteen. I could count on one hand how many times I had worn a condom and had been burned four times. As she drew my blood, I watched carefully to see if there were any traces of HIV in it. I don't know what I was looking for, but if I had seen anything, I would have freaked out. She finally told me that she wouldn't have results for a couple of weeks. That was the longest wait ever.

Once we were done, we returned to our cells and the officer told us to get our cells together. I went in, made up my bed, and lay down until we were called a half hour later. We were taken down to a large room where we went through orientation. The officer told us how prison worked and what to do and not to do. He gave us a rulebook and told us if we violated the rules, we would be locked down in our cells, or placed in the hole if we did anything serious. He told us to never gamble, borrow money, or engage in homosexual sex. He also cautioned us against playing basketball. He said that all of these things were hotbeds for conflict. He then told us that some of us would do easy time, others would mess up and get in a bunch of trouble, and some wouldn't make it at all. He was vague in what he meant, but over the course of time I would learn exactly what he was talking about. Once we were done, we were returned back to our cells.

This time, the door was locked behind us and we were told that they were about to do count. A few minutes later, an officer came by and looked in my cell before writing something on a long sheet of paper. I learned later that that was how they kept up with us and made sure none of us escaped. When the officer left my door, I went to the window at the back of the cell and stared out into the darkening sky. I felt a deep sadness grab me as I thought about how bad I had messed up my life. I started talking to God and asking him why he had allowed this to happen to me. I couldn't make any sense of the deep pit of darkness I had fallen into. Every bad thing that ever happened to me came floating back as I stared out at the sky. I started feeling sorry for myself, and then started getting angry with God, my parents, my teachers and everyone else I felt had let me down. I felt unlovable and thought that no one cared enough to find out why I had veered so far off the path. Never once did I stop to think about how much I had let myself down.

I cursed God and my parents. I didn't want anything to do with them because I felt like they had given up on me. As my anger grew, I noticed several alley cats sniffing around a garbage can near the back of what I discovered was the main chow hall for general population prisoners. In that moment, I would have given anything to be an alley cat. Reflecting back, I didn't realize the lesson that was playing out right before my eyes. For me, prison was a hellish existence, but for the cats, it was a place of refuge and nourishment. Where I found anger and pain, they found food and shelter. I now realize that there are all kinds of prisons, and the worst of them, is the prison we erect in our mind. Moreover, physical prisons can become whatever we want them to be. A cell can be a graveyard or a sacred space of higher learning; either way, we make a choice.

When count was cleared, we were allowed to come out of our cells and use the bathroom. That was the first chance I had to see some of the guys who were there before I arrived. I didn't know what to expect. I had seen a few movies about prison and had heard enough stories to last me a lifetime, so I was prepared for anything. When I stepped out of the cell, there were a few guys hanging out in the doorway of their cells. We exchanged glances as I walked down the hall. I didn't recognize any familiar faces when I entered the bathroom. A few guys stood around smoking cigarettes and talking to some of the guys who had come in with me. I didn't say much to anyone; I had a bit to do and wasn't in the mood for idle chitchat. In fact, I was a little annoyed with the guys who acted like they were having a family reunion when they ran into guys they were with in the county jail.

When I finished handling my business, I returned to my cell. I was learning to like the solitude that my cell offered. I stayed up most of the night watching the alley cats and dreaming of getting out of prison. When I was tired of standing up, I sat on the edge of my bed chain-smoking. When I finally laid down for the night, I drifted off into a fitful sleep. I was out for a couple of hours before it was time for breakfast. The bathroom was overflowing with guys trying to brush their teeth and wash their faces before they went to the chow hall. There were at least 70 of us trying to share five sinks and three toilets.

From the very beginning, the pecking order was established; the less assertive and weak went last. Small cliques shared a specific sink and made sure the members of their crew got first access to the sink and toilet. This tribal behavior extended to the day rooms, telephones, and basketball courts. If you were perceived as weak or unworthy of respect, you didn't have anything coming unless you aligned yourself with someone stronger. I refused to be taken advantage of or disrespected in any way so I asserted myself from the very beginning. When a sink opened up, I stepped up and used it without asking for permission. I wasn't disrespectful to anyone, but I made it clear that I had just as much right as the next person.

Over the next couple of days, I got a feel for the joint. The social interaction wasn't that much different from the 'hoods I had come up in. In fact, prisons have become an extension of the 'hood in a way. I say this because there aren't many families in the Black community who haven't had at least one member of the their family in prison.

I ran into a few guys that I knew from the streets. They weren't guys I ran with on a daily basis, but we knew each other from school or through mutual friends. My cousin Shawn's baby's father, Ramon, was in the cell across from me. He had just turned eighteen and was sentenced to serve natural life in prison. There was also a guy from the 'hood named Rock who I went to Cooley with; he was also serving a life sentence. He had been in quarantine for a month or so and put me up on the prison hustles. He got me a job as a porter so that I could hang out during the morning and afternoon. I would go with him to pass out linen to everyone in our unit, which nearly led to a full-scale riot.

One morning, we went to pass out linen to the guys who were locked in the gym. When we got in the gym, a couple of the guys started talking shit because they felt we were giving them the worst linen. Rock told them to quit crying, they shouldn't be worried about it because they were doing short time. They insisted that we were treating the other guys in the cells better than them and acted like they wanted to fight. I remained quiet for most of the discussion, but my anger was simmering. Most of the guys in the gym would be back on the streets in a year or less and they were bitching about some fucking linen while we were thinking about how we were going to get through the next fifteen or twenty years in prison. I snapped and told them to quit crying and shut the fuck up before we wrapped their asses up in some sheets. A few more guys who locked in the cells with me and Rock came in the gym to see what was up. When the guys in the gym realized how serious we were, they laid back, but the tension was still there. A few days later, a fight broke out between one of our guys and a guy who had been in the gym.

By the third week, I had met a few guys from other cities and we all got cool. We talked to each other about how we were going to do our time when we got to the Michigan Reformatory (MR), which is where most of us figured we were headed. A few guys started acting out based on what they thought they were supposed to do in prison. There were guys who pressured the White guys to buy them stuff out of the store and others who started carrying shanks made out of sharpened toothbrushes. I continued to do my own time. Every now and then, I would stand around kicking it with the rest of the fellas, but most of the time I would just listen to their stories. I didn't want to talk about life on the streets. It was still too painful for me to think back to those days.

One day, we were all standing outside smoking cigarettes when a guy named Shorty came out and said he had something to tell us. He was excited and acted like he couldn't wait to let us know what was up. He was doing about a year and a half and was one of the guys who wanted to fit in with our crowd. I tolerated him when he came around, but he wasn't the kind of person that I enjoyed being around. I didn't like people who felt that they had to be something other than what they were in order to be accepted. Finally, after a few more guys stepped up closer, Shorty started speaking.

"Y'all want to get y'all dick sucked?" he asked with a smile.

We all looked at each other like, "I know this motherfucker ain't just ask to suck our dicks." I guess he could sense our confusion and rising anger because he started speaking quickly.

"I got this bitch who will suck anybody dick I tell her to," he said with a confidence that didn't coincide with what I knew about him.

When he said he had a bitch, the only thing I could think of was one of the female officers who worked at the prison. I had never observed him speaking to any of them and didn't peg him as having the type of game to pull a female guard, but my interest had been piqued. It had been months since I was sexually active.

"What bitch you talking about?" someone asked.

"Y'all ain't see the new White boy they just rode in? Man, that bitch a real freak and he said he'd suck anybody dick," Shorty replied, boasting like he had just told us the slickest shit in the world.

"Nigga is you crazy? I'm not letting a man suck my dick. I don't get down with that gay shit," I said angrily. "Don't ever call me out here for no bitch ass shit like that," I continued as I prepared to walk back in the building.

Most of the guys in the circle shared the same sentiments. We all went back inside and talked about what Shorty had just said. A few of the guys stayed behind, and we later learned, took Shorty up on his offer.

The lines had been quickly drawn. We made it clear that we weren't about to become gay just because we were locked up. Being in prison wasn't a reason or excuse to change your sexuality. If you indulged in homosexual behavior, it was because that's what you wanted to do. Whatever people might think of homosexual behavior, it isn't as widely accepted in prison as imagined.

My circle remained small and I was learning more and more about the kind of people that I didn't want to be around. It was hard being alone in prison, but I wasn't willing to spend my time around people who didn't share my value system. I would rather do my time alone than to deal with guys who were fake. More importantly, I was trying to figure out how to get home to my family.

I was missing everything about being home and tried to connect with my father and Brenda whenever I could. The first time that I called home and spoke to my father was the hardest. In the middle of our conversation, he broke down crying and I was at a loss for words. In that moment, I knew I had hurt my father deeply. I could only imagine what it was like for him having to explain to his friends that his son was in prison and would be gone for nearly two decades. For years, my father blamed himself for me being in prison and I know this was the source of that deep pain that poured through the phone. He told me that they were going to come up and see me soon, and then we hung up. I called Georgia and she told me that she was going to bring Brenda up to see me also, so for the next couple of days, I focused on my upcoming visits as I paced my cell floor each night. During the day, I read whatever novels I could get my hands on. I had even started reading the Bible. I focused mostly on those stories that I thought fit my situation like Job's; however, I wasn't gaining the sense of peace that I desired so I put the Bible down and focused on the getaway that novels provided.

One day, I was mopping the floor when an officer called me into his office. He told me to get ready because I had a visit. I was bursting with excitement as I walked back down to my cell. I went into the bathroom and freshened up, then headed to the visiting room. I waited nervously until I was ushered inside. When I set eyes on Brenda, a deep longing overcame me. She looked radiant and her smile was beautiful

94

and comforting. The baby was now showing and she had filled out a little. We embraced and kissed each other tenderly as though it was our first time. The familiarity of her taste and the softness of her body pressed against mine made me want to run through the doors with her when she left. Georgia watched us for a moment, then I hugged her and thanked her for bringing Brenda up. We finally sat down, and for the first few minutes, I just stared at Brenda without saying anything. She placed my hand on her stomach when the baby started kicking and I felt a surge of guilt shoot through my body. She looked so vulnerable and there was nothing I could do to be there for her.

Brenda and Georgia told me what was up on the block. Georgia was pissed as she talked about how my so-called friends had been playing me. She told me how they were running around the 'hood wearing my clothes. Brenda told me how they had been playing her when it came to the money and drugs I had left behind. Basically, everyone had flipped. Instead of being there to help her out, they were out to get over on her. The more she told me, the more hurt I was. I had risked my life and sacrificed my freedom for the streets and they were all turning their backs on me. This was something I would learn was far more common than anyone would like to admit. But the reality is, there are very few loyal people in the streets. In fact, most are out for themselves. It was all good while I was out on the street selling drugs and doing everything to hold down the 'hood, but as soon as I got locked up, they acted like they didn't know me. Over the course of my sentence, I realized that none of them were true friends.

We continued to talk about the baby and its due date. Brenda said that she wanted to marry me when I came home and assured me that she would always be there for me. I listened, but emotionally I was shutting down the part of me that would have allowed that to be a possibility. I knew she wouldn't be able to handle the pressure of being there for me over the long haul, and I wasn't about to drive myself insane thinking about it. I couldn't bare to tell her what I was feeling. She was already going through a lot emotionally, so I just sat and listened. When she left, I never thought it would be the last time I'd see her while I was incarcerated.

Georgia told me that they would come back up in a few weeks if I were still there. We hugged and kissed and then they were gone. When I returned to my cell, I stayed up all night looking at the pictures we had taken on the visit. It was as close as I would ever get to her again on an intimate level. In those small moments, it was pictures of family and friends that brought me hope and comfort.

The following week, I got a visit from my family. My father brought my stepmother, stepbrother, two younger sisters and Brenda along with him, but Brenda wasn't allowed to visit because of an issue with her ID. My father told me that she was in the lobby crying, but she would be alright. He said that she told him to tell me she loved me.

We spent the visit talking about my adjustment to prison. As we talked, I stared at my young siblings and was saddened by their innocence. I was failing them as a big brother. I didn't think about the impact that my behavior had on them until later in my life. Honestly, I don't think we'd do some of the things we do in life if we stopped for a minute to think about the impact that our behavior has on the people in our lives.

For the most part, when a person comes to prison, they become fixated on what they're missing out on in life. Seldom do we stop to think about what our loved ones miss out on when they visit us, take our calls or send us money. We don't think about the wisdom that our younger siblings and children need from us, or the comfort our parents feel in knowing we are home with them. In reality, prison isn't just scary for us; it's scary for them, too. In fact, it may even be scarier for them because the only point of reference they have is television. No parent or sibling wants to go to bed every night wondering if their loved one will survive through the night. During the first years of my incarceration, people from home would always ask me if I was alright. That seemingly innocent question held a lot of fear, and I understand why. When someone gets locked up, so does their family. If we realized just how much incarceration impacts our family, we might not put ourselves in situations that could send us to prison.

When my family left, I went back to my cell and stared at their picture as I had done with the picture of me and Brenda. I didn't know it then, but I was developing a pattern when it came to visits. After each visit, I wanted to be alone. I didn't want to talk to anyone because I wanted to hold on to every morsel of that visit for as long as I could. I wanted the smell of my visitors to cling to my nostrils for as long as possible and the feeling of their touch to be a reminder of my humanity. Most often, I fell asleep not long after I returned from a visit.

I had been in quarantine for a few weeks and knew that my time there was winding down. A few of the guys who had arrived before me had already been transferred to MR so I started to shift my thoughts in that direction. While there were some real life prison scenarios playing out at Riverside, I knew they weren't a real reflection of what to expect. I had heard horror stories about the Reformatory, which had been dubbed Gladiator School. It had earned its violent reputation from the daily stabbings that were as much a part of the culture as the horrid slop that they served for chow. There were a few of us slated to be transferred in the coming week, and the tension began taking its toll on us.

The week before I transferred to MR, me and a few guys got into it with some White guys in the bathroom. I don't remember what the conflict was over, but I am sure it was something very petty. We were all on edge and it didn't take much to set things in motion. After a brief argument, we started throwing punches, and then two of the guys ran, leaving the other one behind. We gave the guy a quick working over and left him lying on the bathroom floor. Then, two days later, a guy from Inkster, who I had gotten cool with, got stabbed in the head while he was sitting on the toilet taking a dump. Surprisingly, he didn't panic. He got off of the toilet calmly and started kicking the guy's ass.

Over the next couple of days, the unit buzzed with our volatile exploits. We were all desensitized to violence and accepted it as the way of the world that we came up in. In fact, I don't recall a time when my life wasn't marred by violence. From the first time my mother beat me for some minor infraction to the final time I pulled the trigger, violence was a pervasive part of my existence and what I experienced in quarantine was simply a warm-up for things to come.

Chapter 9

"Oh my God! Alan got shot! Alan got shot!" my sister Tamica screamed at the top of her lungs as she held the cordless phone in her hand. Tears flowed down her cheeks as she listened to the voice on the other end of the phone. When she got off of the phone, we bombarded her with questions about our oldest brother's condition. I watched my sister's emotions morph from sadness and fear into a deep, abiding anger. When she opened her mouth, fire leapt from it as she recounted what she had been told on the phone.

"That no-good ass nigga Art shot Alan in the neck and now he's laying in the hospital with his right side paralyzed."

The news sucked the air out of the room. We were in the middle of one of the bloodiest summers in Detroit's history, but we never thought the violence would come this close to home. Our brother Art had been accused of shooting our oldest brother Alan. They had grown up fighting each other like siblings did, but we never thought it would escalate to gunplay.

Alan's shooting marked a turning point in our family. The bullet that tore through his neck was symbolic of the force of evil known as crack cocaine that was tearing its way through our family. Prior to the emergence of crack in our community, pistols and handguns weren't so readily accessible to us. With the introduction of crack, however, came an influx of guns and gun violence. My brother Art was never known to carry or use a gun until he got deeply entrenched in the dope game.

We all realized that the days of fist fighting were over, and most, if not all, conflicts would be resolved through gun violence. But the way I saw it, if my brother could think nothing of shooting and killing his own flesh and blood, what did that really say about the value of life in the 'hood. The trust and surety that comes with being siblings had been forever altered. From that point forward, we were all aware that when we argued with each other, it could easily turn bloody, if not deadly.

The fallout from the shooting was major. Our family was up in arms both figuratively and literally. They wanted blood – Art's blood. Over the course of a few days, as my brother Alan sat in the hospital wondering if he would ever be able to use his right arm again, my other brother slunk through the neighborhood wondering if he would ever be able to come around the family and feel safe again. I was emotionally confused. On one hand, I was upset and deeply disturbed by my brother's actions. In fact, it was at that point that I started to fear my brother and what he was capable of. On the other hand, I felt sorry for him because no one in the family wanted anything to do with him. Whenever he called and tried to explain away his actions, he was either hung up on or threatened. Eventually, he mustered up the courage to come over to my sister's neighborhood. He parked a few blocks over and called up to the apartment. He spoke briefly with Tamica, but she wasn't ready for him yet, so she gave me the phone. After talking to him for a few seconds, I agreed to meet him on the next street.

As I left my sister's apartment building, I started second-guessing myself. A deep trepidation started to come over me with each step that I took. It seemed like a million sinister questions bounced around in my head as I walked to meet Art. What if he kidnapped me? What if he shot me like he shot Alan? What if he came and killed the whole family in a fit of rage? When I reached the block and saw my brother's blue Camaro, the questions began to subside. When I looked inside the car, I saw a vulnerability in my brother that I hadn't seen in years. The streets were turning us all into cold-hearted predators, but beneath it all, I could see the brother I had grown up looking up to. I got into the car and we drove off in silence.

After driving a few short blocks, my brother asked me what the family was saying. I shared with him what was being said, but told him not to worry. I tried to reassure him that in time they would forgive him and things would return to normal. I was trying to convince him as much as I was trying to convince myself that everything would be alright. We returned to the silence, convinced even more that things would never be the same in our family.

Before Alan got out of the hospital, he took a phone call from Art. Art apologized for shooting him and Alan forgave him. A few days later, Alan was released from the hospital. He wore a sling on his arm and could barely move the right side of his body. He had a bullet lodged in his shoulder near the back of his neck. The doctors said that it would work its way out and he would regain the full use of his arm.

Around this time, Art had made a nice connection with one of the major suppliers on the east side. This connection propelled my brothers to the forefront of the game. Together, they opened several spots on the east side not far from where we grew up. When they opened a spot on Glenfield and Chalmers, Alan stopped staying at my sister's apartment. He told me to stay behind for a while and he would come get me later when he was established. In the meantime, he gave me a sack to sell so that I would have a few dollars in my pocket. It had been a couple of months or so since the last time I smoked a laced joint and I felt like I was ready to get back to the business of hustling.

Tamica's apartment building was the perfect set-up for me. The building had a built-in clientele with addicts occupying nearly every apartment on all three floors. Once I let them know that I had a sack, all I did was sit outside in front of the building serving them as they hustled up on whatever they could afford to cop. Within weeks, the money was rolling in and I felt my swagger coming back. I couldn't wait to go shopping and get fresh again.

I went shopping down in Highland Park and came back with some fly Bally's, a few silk shirts and a couple Guess outfits. I started hanging around the corner on a street named Savannah where all the neighborhood girls hung at. They adored me and I felt like a 'hood celebrity. I was always generous with my illicit capital, which went over well with the young girls and influential guys.

Tamica's neighborhood was right down the street from Palmer Park, which was transvestite central. Because of the high level of prostitution that took place at the park, it was prime drug real estate. The transvestites who lived in the 'hood spent hundreds, and sometimes thousands, of dollars a day. Sometimes a few of the guys from Savannah would come hang out at Ted's, a neighborhood restaurant where we sold rocks and talked shit all day. We would laugh as we watched streams of balding White men roam up and down Woodward picking up transvestites and crack whores to trick with. Most of them drove luxury sedans and lived in the surrounding suburbs. This was one of the many contradictions in the 'hood. Affluent white men were free to come into our community and buy drugs and sex with impunity. Whenever they were pulled over for soliciting, they were given a slap on the wrist and returned to the safety of the suburbs. On the flip side, the parks we once played in as children were no longer safe – drug paraphernalia, empty liquor bottles and used condoms littered the ground – and the streets that were at one time a source of pride were now the scourges of the city.

I continued selling for a few weeks and things started looking promising for me. My brothers were coming up, and sometimes they would come get me to go shopping with them. At other times, they brought me sacks to flip for them. One day, while I was sitting in front of my sister's apartment building, I noticed a fly young lady going into a fourplex located next door. I knew the man and woman who lived there because they were cool with Tamica and her children's father. I asked Tamica what she knew about the young lady and she called next door to ask her friend Cookie what was up. Cookie told her that the young lady was her niece and Tamica suggested that I go over there and talk to her.

Tamica was always trying to hook me up. We were the closest out of my siblings, and at that time, there was a lot going on in our lives that brought us even closer. She had recently had her second son, and I was there during his birth. In addition, I was there when her boyfriend first started abusing her. Like most teenage girls who fall in love with older men, she was in over her head. Her boyfriend started out slapping her over minor disagreements, but before long, his abuse escalated to the point where I had to go get her from the house on several occasions. I was a scrawny teen and knew that I was no match for her boyfriend, who stood 6'2" and had a muscular build, so whenever she called me and told me to come get her, I grabbed the biggest butcher knife I could find and walked to their house. There were times when he smacked her around or jumped on her and I tried to help, but he would either kick me to the ground or throw me off of his back. I vowed that I would beat his ass when I got older, but by the time that happened, he was no longer fighting her because he realized that me and my brothers would kill him. Sadly, it took several years of abuse before my sister finally left that destructive relationship. She was the perfect example of what happens when an emotionally vulnerable young girl gets caught up with older men.

After talking with Tamica about her friend's niece, I got fresh and went next door to meet the object of my desire. When I knocked on the door, Cookie opened the door with a smile on her face. She told me to come in and meet her niece. She introduced us, then went into the back room with her husband Lonnie. Her niece and I hit it off and talked for the next couple of hours. She said that she would start coming over more often and we exchanged numbers. After a while, Lonnie emerged from the back room. His eyes were bloodshot red and it looked like he was enjoying a nice buzz. We kicked it and he asked me if I wanted a beer. I said yeah, so we headed up to the store to get a couple of forties. When we returned, Cookie's niece was gone, but I stayed over and sat in the back room with Lonnie drinking beer. As we sat and drunk our beers, I noticed the telltale signs that someone had been smoking laced joints. I could see where rocks had been crushed on a small mirror and cocktails had been emptied out to make another joint. Plus, the smell of cocaine was undeniable. After awhile, Lonnie asked me if I smoked weed and I told him that I did on occasion. He then pulled out a small sack of weed and poured it on the mirror alongside a few crumbs of crack. He asked me if I knew where he could get some rocks from. I told him I did and proceeded to pull the sack out of my drawers. He bought a rock, crunched it up, and then laced the weed with it. He then handed me the plate and told me that I could roll my own joint if I didn't want to hit the laced joint. I thought about it for a minute. I didn't want to appear soft or timid in front of him, so I told him I was cool with hitting the joint he had just rolled.

I had stopped smoking laced joints on my own before, so I was confident I'd be able to hit it just that one time and be good. In the back of my mind, I knew I was lying to myself. Crack has a magnetic pull that is nearly inescapable once you start smoking. The high seduces you and makes you think you are in control, but nothing could be further from the truth. Despite me knowing this, I inhaled the thick, white smoke deep into my teenage lungs. The rush from the high was instantaneous, and before I knew it, I was crushing up more rocks for us to smoke in laced joints and cigarettes.

When I left that night, I knew that I would return time and time again when I had a new sack. Over the next few weeks, I hung out at Lonnie's smoking laced joints with rocks I had cut down from the sacks that my brothers had given me. I kept their money straight, but I was no longer buying the clothes and shoes that my brothers were accustomed to me buying. They were oblivious to what was going on because I made up all kinds of excuses about why I didn't have any money or new clothes. They had no idea that they were supplying their baby brother with a toxic drug that was killing my youth.

My brother Alan became more stable and invited me to move in with him on Glenfield. We moved into a small, two-bedroom house on the corner of Glenfield and Queen, which was down the street from his spot. I was still smoking laced joints when I first moved over there, and my supply was now a lot steadier because I was living in the house with my supplier. I would steal rocks as I helped my brothers cut up and count sacks of rocks. They were making so much money that they never noticed what I was taking off of the top of each sack.

Whenever my brothers needed someone to work their spots, they called on me and I sold the rocks for them. I sat in spots on Bewick between Warren and Shoemaker, on Pennsylvania and on Lenox and Jefferson. I thought nothing of the fact that my brothers didn't care enough about me to keep me away from danger. Instead, they were blinded by the greed and power that comes with the dope game. I sat in spots, had sex with grown women, and smoked laced joints for about six months. Then, one day I woke up and realized that I was tired of being broke, so I decided to stop smoking laced joints cold turkey. It was very hard at first because I had free access to the sacks.

Around this time, things also began to intensify in the dope game. It seemed like everybody was out for themselves and my brother

Art got into a major beef with his supplier. It had gotten to the point where we were all on edge, and one day, things reached a boiling point at the spot on Bewick. My brother had commandeered the spot and was intent on putting his own dope down. I was at the house when his supplier and a team of his goons came over. The supplier also brought his woman, who happened to live next door to my mother, with them. In addition to the tension over the spot, there was a rumor that my brother and his right-hand man had hit the supplier's woman's house for a key of yayo.

When the supplier came in with his team of goons, I was a bit nervous. They were all strapped with pistols and kept whispering to each other as they waited for my brothers and our childhood friend Jesse Peeples to come over. When my brother Art arrived, he entered the house with the confidence of a lion despite his small stature. He was barely 5'6" and didn't weigh a pound over one-fifty, but what he lacked in size, he made up for in heart and tenacity.

When Jesse came into the house, he quickly assessed the situation and stashed a pistol inside a bag of candy that was on the couch where he was sitting. The room was tense and attitudes were stretched to their breaking point. My brother Art told me to leave and go tell my mother what was up in case anything happened; however, I couldn't get out of the house because the supplier had taken the key to the Armor Guard door. For what seemed like an eternity, they argued back and forth and no one allowed their hand to move far from their pistol. All it would have taken was one person to panic and the entire house would have erupted into a hail of gunfire.

As I sat on the couch watching the whole scene play out, I began questioning why I was there in the first place. The dope game hadn't been kind to me, and I could feel the effects of the violence and drug abuse stripping away the good that my parents had instilled in me as a child. Yet when the air was clear, it was back to business as usual. My brothers continued to hustle and I continued to hustle alongside them, but with each day, the cost of doing business in the streets got higher and higher.

One day, my brother Art came over and asked me to sit in a spot over on Lenox. When we went to check it out, I felt good about it. They had a nice system in place, and there was a nice thick sista named Michel who would be sitting in the spot with me. She was down to hustle and wasn't bad on the eyes, so it was a win-win, or so I thought. Things went smoothly the first night. The people downstairs answered the door, took the money from the customers, and then brought it up so that we could make the sale. We never interacted with the customers, and if the spot were to be raided, the police would be searching downstairs while we got rid of everything upstairs.

One night around two o'clock in the morning, a customer came to the door. The man downstairs came up and bought a couple of rocks from us. Two minutes after he took the rock downstairs, I heard the sound of a shotgun blast coming from the back of the house. I jumped up and ran into the living room to see what was up, and before I knew it, I heard another blast tear through the door downstairs. Michel and the man who lived in the house scrambled from the back room to see what was going on. Another shotgun blast went off followed by the sound of someone trying to kick in the back door. It didn't take long for us to figure out that someone was attempting to rob us.

My heart began beating rapidly as I thought about what would happen if they made it into the house. My brother hadn't dropped the rifle off he had promised and we didn't have any way of defending ourselves. Michel and I ran to the front of the house and hid in the closet. The sound of them trying to kick in the door reverberated through the house, filling the air with the menacing sound of imminent death. If they made it inside, I was sure that they were going to kill us all so I decided to take action. I told Michel that I was going to make a run for it and she had better follow if she wanted to survive. She agreed and we crept down the front stairs toward the door. We listened intently for a minute to see if they were coming around to the front. When we didn't hear anything, we cracked the door open. I told Michel to be ready to go on the count of three. When I reached three, we both took off running out of the house at full speed. I could hear Michel on my heels but I wasn't about to waste time looking back.

When we reached Jefferson, we stopped running and looked to see if anyone was following us. It was late and I knew that the police might roll up on us, so I stashed the dope I had beneath some bushes on the side of a building. Everything was closed except for a Wendy's drive-thru. I ran the short distance to Wendy's and approached the window. I asked them if I could use their phone to call a cab. The girl working the window looked alarmed and closed the window on me. I was a bit out of breath and apparently looked out of place standing at her window at that time of night. The manager came, and after several minutes of going back and forth, he called us a cab.

It seemed like the cab was taking forever. I knew our assailants would figure out that we had fled, and at any minute, would come looking for us. I couldn't have been more relieved when I saw a green and white Checker Cab pull in front of the restaurant. We hopped in and sped off. We dropped Michel off and I headed over to the house on Bewick. I immediately called my brother and he came to pick me up. We went back to the bushes where I had hid the dope. I picked up the sack and we drove over to the house on Lenox to see how much damage had been done. It was dark as hell in the house and we couldn't really see too well so we left and came back the next day with a rifle and it was back to the grind.

After rolling on Lenox for a few weeks, I was tired of the drama and went back to the house on Glenfield. I spent most of my time hanging out on the block with the guys from the neighborhood. Even though Glenfield wasn't far from where I grew up, it was a foreign part of the 'hood to me so I had to make a whole new group of friends. It didn't take long, however, because Glenfield was one of the livest blocks in that part of the 'hood. It also didn't hurt that my brothers kept me fresh and gave me free reign to do whatever I wanted to do. I always had money in my pocket and my brother Alan didn't mind my friends coming over to hang out at the house.

I mostly hung out with the older guys, which meant I was around a lot of older females, many of whom were feeling me. My interactions with these older females accelerated my development when it came to sexual intimacy, and before long, I thought I was grown. I had a few girlfriends who were my age, but most of the women I slept with were grown. My first main girl was a chocolate brown sweetie named Teresa. She was my age, but had already had a baby. I met her through one of the guys that had gone to elementary school with me. She was a friend of his cousin who lived down the street from me. When we first started going out, she wanted to take things slowly because she didn't want to get pregnant again. Things started off slow, but before long, we were together every day. Like most teenagers, we argued, broke up and got back together again. In between our break-ups, I started messing with another girl named Chris who lived across the street from me. She knew that I was with Teresa, but didn't seem to care.

It wasn't long before I moved on to the next girl in the neighborhood. This went on for a while until I met an older female named Kay-Kay. She hung out at her cousin Lynn's house, which is where all the real action was. Before long, my whole crew was hanging out at Lynn's every day with all of the females on the block. Most of them were in their early twenties, and most of us were in our mid-to-late teens, with me being the youngest. Not once did I stop to consider there was something wrong with adult women sleeping with teenage boys. All I knew was that they had what I wanted and didn't have a problem giving it to me.

This distorted introduction to relationships led me to develop a negative view of dating and romance. Most of the women and girls I had been intimate with seemed to only care about who was getting money and who could provide weed and drinks, so even though I was being pleased physically on a regular basis, I went to bed feeling empty and alone every night. The ideas that I had about romance and courtship were shattered by the experiences I had selling drugs and sleeping with adult women before I had developed emotionally. Sadly, there is a double standard in our community when it comes to these unhealthy relationships. When a young boy enters a sexual relationship with a grown woman, he is patted on the back and celebrated. However, when a young girl enters into a relationship with a grown man, he is seen as a lecherous pervert and condemned; and in some cases sent to prison. The reality is that no adult, under no circumstances, should have a sexual relationship with a child.

It took years for me to first recognize that my emotional growth had been stunted due to these unhealthy relationships, and secondly, for me to overcome all that I had experienced in order for me to have the kind of relationship that I desired and deserved.

Things began settling down when my brother's girlfriend moved up from Chicago along with her three children. Our house started feeling more like a home and things were looking promising. It wasn't long, however, before the brutality of the streets reared its ugly head again. One day, we were all standing outside kicking it when a female named Pig came running down the street screaming and crying. She told us that her cousin Shannon Bell had gotten shot and killed.

"Damn, I was just talking to him the other day," was the first thought that came to my mind. I hadn't seen Shannon since our days in elementary school, but we ran into each other on Glenfield and hung out whenever he came to visit Pig and her sister. Then, in a flash, he was gone. Shot dead at the tender age of fifteen. There was no immediate shock when we heard the news as Detroit was experiencing another long, bloody year, but later on while reminiscing with the rest of the crew, we all had that lingering question in the back of our minds, "Who's gonna be next?" and "How soon?"

Though we never said it out loud, our body language spoke for us. The tenseness of our movements, the alertness of our eyes as strangers approached us, and the impulsive way we reacted to any potential threat, spoke volumes. It was very clear that the stakes had been raised. The innocence of our youth was slowly disappearing and life in the 'hood had been cheapened. Over the years, the body count would continue to accumulate, and "here one day, gone the next" became a neighborhood slogan.

Not long after Shannon was killed, a guy named Pops, who lived across the street from us, was shot nineteen times. Fortunately for him, he survived, but the scars were deeply embedded in all of us. We all hung our heads in silence when we went to visit him in the hospital. He had holes all over his body. All we could think about was revenge, but revenge against who was the question. His assailants were faceless, nameless men. They were men who could be anyone, at anytime, and that reality drew us into a sinister silence.

The 'hood was at war with itself, turning on itself like a possessed cannibal, carnivorously destroying life and leaving in its wake torn families, abandoned children and a vicious cycle of gun violence; however, the real tragedy of seeing my homies die and get shot at such an early age was that I became desensitized to life. I no longer believed in the good or joy that life had to offer, and I started growing colder inside; to be anything else was to be considered weak.

I no longer cared if I lived or died. In fact, I started looking forward to the day of my demise. It gave me a sense of control. If I embraced death, then I wouldn't have to live in fear of dying, at least that's what I told myself. The reality was that I was truly afraid of living because living was too painful.

My dreams of growing old with my family were an illusion that shriveled up like a prune sitting in the sun. In essence, I had given in to the monster under the bed. I grew reckless and moved through life uncaring and numb from fear, paranoia and the copious amounts of malt liquor that I consumed. Around each corner, I thought there was a bullet with my name on it and saw fast-approaching vehicles as death machines chauffeured by the grim reaper himself.

With everything I had experienced, I knew it was only a matter of time before I became a dead man walking or a death machine; it was all in fate's hands. If I were quick on the draw, I would be the latter, but if not, then I would be joining the hundreds of young men and women who were lost in the war that rages through our community. How can a child expect to exist like this without going insane? It would only be a matter of time before I found the answer.

Things on Glenfield began deteriorating as fall approached. One night, I was sitting in the living room when I heard a loud commotion on our front porch. When I looked out of the window, I noticed a man with a gun pointed at my brother Alan's head while his girlfriend stood nearby with her hands in the air. I immediately leapt into action. I didn't stop to think about anything other than saving my brother. I grabbed a pistol out of the closet, ran out of the back door, and then circled around the house. I hollered for the gunman to back away from my brother. He pushed Alan and took off running as I squeezed off several shots. My brother and his girl were unharmed and the gunman got away. Not long after that, my brother decided to relocate to the west side to a neighborhood called Brightmoor. I wasn't ready to leave the east side yet, so I stayed behind for a while longer.

Before he moved, my brother told one of his old friends that she and her daughters could share the house with me and she became somewhat of a guardian. I was basically doing the same thing, however, so it was business as usual. During this time, one of my homeboys from the other end of the 'hood came to hang out with me. His name was Boise and I hadn't seen him in awhile. We had gone to Burbank Middle School together. Boise was known for playing drums in school and being one of the best dancers in the neighborhood. We used to skip class and breakdance in the school bathroom along with two other guys named Terrance and Tanzer who lived down the street from Boise. We had forged a little bond in school, so when we ran back into each other, it was all good. We were now a few years older and our interests were the same – drinking, smoking and messing with women. We told everyone that we were cousins, and I introduced him to this woman named KC. For the next few weeks, we hung out at Lynn's house partying it up. Little did I know, Boise was on the run for two counts of murder. It wasn't until I moved to the west side and we lost contact that I found out what happened. Our next meeting would be in prison at the Michigan Reformatory.

Finally, after countless days of drinking and sexing, my brother Art told me that I needed to move off of Glenfield. Every time he came over, the house was full of weed smoke and teenagers who thought they were grown. My teenage body and mind were a bit worn down so I welcomed a change of pace. I thought I was ready to get my life back on track, so I called my father and let him know that I wanted to come home. He had a conversation with my stepmother and they agreed to allow me to move into their home on the west side.

The neighborhood right off of Southfield and Puritan was a far cry from Glenfield. The streets were lined with big brick houses and manicured lawns. There was very little traffic so it was nice and quiet, and I hated every bit of it. It was close to being winter, and I didn't know anyone in the 'hood, so I was miserable. Every chance I got, I returned to the east side, but once I enrolled in school, my view of the neighborhood changed. In addition to the 'hood being full of women, it was a haven for money-getters and 'hood celebrities. Within a few weeks, I felt like that was where I belonged, or so I thought.

Chapter 10

The clanging of steel cage doors slamming shut was the sounding bell for the young gladiators housed at the Michigan Reformatory. On any given day, when the doors banged open for yard or chow, we would count on some drama, and my first day at MR was no exception to the rule. In fact, what I witnessed on the first day was the rule of the 'Big Yard.' It made what I experienced at Riverside seem like mere child's play by comparison.

When we arrived at the prison, I noticed the stark difference between MR and Riverside. The college-like campus, manicured lawn, and well-maintained infrastructure were replaced by an antiquated behemoth of a prison. The large, grey walls surrounded the prison with a finality that stamped out any thoughts of freedom. The block-long tiers seethed with the looming threat of violence and mayhem, and the guards stood ready to break the heads of anyone who dared to go against the grain.

Just on appearance alone, the Michigan Reformatory had earned the moniker Gladiator School. One look at the dusty yard littered with black and brown bodies was enough to transport one back to the coliseum in Rome where blood sports were daily entertainment.

We were hustled out of the van and into the old, cavernous building. We all remained silent out of fear that our voices would betray the poisonous thoughts swimming around in our minds like sea snakes. When I looked at the motley crew of inmates who had transferred in with me, I could see the same fear in them that was gurgling in the pit of my stomach. It wasn't a fear of being harmed or violated; it was the fear of the unknown.

To break the tension, we joked around with each other before we all turned our attention toward the one White guy who had made the trip with us. He was one of the few White guys who had enough swagger to hang around our little circle. He wasn't trying to be anyone but himself, and that was a quality that we appreciated.

All too often in prison, I ran across White guys from the suburbs or one of Michigan's rural towns who tried to emulate the swagger of hip hop artists or guys from the streets in their desire to be accepted. Sadly, this places them in a position where they were either victimized or put to the test to see if they were really gangster. The funny thing about it, the ones who didn't try to be anything other than who they were were accepted, which was the case with Kevin. He was down-to-earth, minded his own business, had a crazy sense of humor, and was just plain cool. He could take a good joke and give out a good joke, so as we waited to be processed in, we joked with him about sticking with us so the booty bandits wouldn't get him. He told us to fuck off and joked that we should be sticking with him because he could whoop all of our asses. We laughed and joked some more as we headed down to the infirmary to get our initial check-up before being sent to the intake rock.

After undergoing another basic physical exam, we were directed to go to I-2, which was the intake rock. There were two main blocks at the Reformatory, with five floors each. On each floor, there were two sides – the inside and the outside. We were led down a murky green hallway until we reached a door leading to I-Block. When we exited the door, we went up a flight of stairs and were met by a Black female officer named Ms. Ingram who gave us our assigned cell numbers. I was assigned to I-80, which was close to the middle of the rock. When I looked down the tier, it felt like it would never end.

Once Ms. Ingram had given us our cell numbers, she began clanging the bars open. We walked down the tier searching out our cell numbers, and once we were inside, the bars slammed shut. On the way down, I noticed a few guys sticking mirrors out into the hallway. They called the mirrors 'hawks,' because like birds of prey, they were used to zero in on any potential prey.

When I stepped into the cell, my head started spinning and I became nauseous at the sight and smell of my new residence. It smelled like raw sewage had been dumped on the floor. The hard, green, plastic-covered mattress was peeling and cracked and the pillow was as flat as a flapjack. The sink dripped with rusty brown water and the toilet was full of shitty water, which was the source of the horrible smell. I held my nose closed and prayed the toilet didn't overflow when I flushed it. The toilet was stained with the remnants of week-old feces and flushing it did nothing to rid the room of its stench.

Within a few days, we all realized that the one-hundred-year-old Reformatory had one of the worst plumbing systems in the state. Whenever someone a few cells over flushed their toilet, the waste showed up in another toilet. Nearly every morning, I was awakened by the smell of someone else's bowel movement floating in my toilet like an unwelcomed guest.

I scrubbed the cell from floor to ceiling and washed down my mattress and pillow. When I was finished, I made up my bed and laid down. I listened to the various conversations going on around me. Most of them were war stories full of 'hood exploits, or grumblings about the state of the prison. I drifted off into a dream about my old neighborhood, and just as it started getting good, I was awakened by the sound of our doors being opened for yard.

We filed out of our cells and walked slowly to the big yard. The group of us that had come over from quarantine together hit the yard. We had been given ten dollars by the state to purchase store items and couldn't wait to get some cigarettes and a few food items to supplement the meager scraps we were served at chow.

The sun was out but the fall air was crisp. When we exited the building, the sounds and the sights were overwhelming. It looked like there were over a thousand men moving back and forth through the prison. I had never been in a place with that many people. We followed the flow of the crowd until we reached the yard. When we entered, there were between fifty and a hundred guys standing around the store line staring at us. We stood out from the rest because of the small blue jackets we had been given in quarantine. We had just arrived so all we had were new state blues. Most inmates who were able bought regular clothes from one of the MDOC-approved catalogues, or had them sent from home as soon as possible. We did all in our power to reclaim whatever sense of normalcy we could. Sometimes just getting dressed in regular clothing was enough to make us feel free, if only for a moment. It was also a small way of expressing uniqueness and independence in an environment where you're seen as just a number.

The veteran inmates were in full predator mode, searching our faces to find who amongst us was weak enough to be considered prey. It was as though they were able to smell weakness a mile away. Immediately, we saw a couple of guys walking off with Kevin in tow. They had their arms draped around his shoulders. All we could do was watch helplessly. We were on enemy terrain, and at the end of the day, it was every man for himself. No matter how cool we all were, we knew we had to stand up for ourselves before we could expect someone else to ride for us.

Once we got our store items, we headed over to the basketball court to observe the games. It was easy to see that the basketball court was one of the proving grounds on the yard. Once you stepped onto the basketball court, you had to stand ready to defend yourself on every level. No blood, no foul was the rule of the blacktop. It was common for inmates to play basketball with a shank in the sole of their shoes. A hard foul could easily lead to a stabbing, or worse, a riot.

The games we checked out were tense and very competitive. There were a few guys who stood out immediately on the court. There was a tall, slinky guy who I would later learn was named Bone. He played above the rim and dunked damn near everything that came off of the rim. He was one of the many basketball legends that I would meet over the years.

When yard closed, we headed back to the rock and waited for chow time. Our movement was restricted because we were in close custody, which meant we were only allowed out for yard for an hour a day. I didn't have any books so I spent the first few days looking out of the window when the other rocks were out on the yard. When I wasn't looking out of the window, I slept. In fact, I think I slept more during the first year of my bit than I have at any other point in my life. It was a clear sign that I was suffering from the depression that came with losing my freedom. Sleep allowed me to dream, and dreaming was my way of connecting with life on the street.

After a few minutes listening to my neighbors talk about what they had witnessed on the yard, I dozed off. Before I could get into a deep sleep, I was awakened by the sound of keys jingling loudly as several officers ran down the rock. I strained to see as far down the rock as I could before they were out of my sight. The rest of the guys on the rock grew quiet as we listened to find out what was going on. After nearly an hour, the officers and nurses rolled a gurney down the tier with a body on it. They had a white sheet draped across the inmate's face, and we later learned that it was Kevin they had wheeled out of the building. By the time we came out for chow, the word spread through the prison that Kevin attempted suicide after being pressured for sex. It was a sobering reminder to all of us that we were living in a jungle of desperation and hopelessness.

The next morning on the way to breakfast, I witnessed my first stabbing. We took the back steps down, and as we were walking, a slim, dark-skinned brother slid past us and stabbed a guy in front of us several times in the neck, then calmly discarded the shank in the mailbox at the bottom of the steps. We jumped back when the guy started stabbing the other man, then walked around the scene. The guy clutched his neck and took off running back up the stairs. By the time we reached the walkway headed toward the chow hall, a group of officers were running into the building. On our way out of chow, they stopped us and shook us all down. No one said anything and we were allowed to go back to the block.

I stayed up late that night thinking about all of the violence around me. I looked around the cell to see what I could make a shank out of. Making shanks became a skill that I perfected over the years; the more time I did, the more capable I became at manufacturing a weapon on the fly. A plastic bottle that would normally be discarded became a tool to be melted down and sharpened to a point that was sharp enough to puncture a lung or take an eye out. The carts we used to cool off fresh baked bread became a smorgasbord of high quality steel shanks, which we called "horses" or "bone crushers." Working in the bakery and using a whisk also gave me instant access to a hundred icepicks. Whatever crude piece of metal I could lay my hands on became a tool of violence.

After nearly two weeks at the Reformatory, I was moved to J-Block. My first day over there, I witnessed another brutal act of violence. On the way to chow, a thick-necked, light-skinned brother hit another brother in the head with a lock attached to a belt. The bulky Master lock knocked a chunk of meat from the victim's head. Instead of panicking, he turned around and began punching the guy in the face. His attacker continued to swing the lock wildly, hitting him in the head several more times until he began losing consciousness. Their scuffle caused traffic on the steps to back up, which alerted the officers to the scene.

The Gladiator School was proving to be everything we were told it was. Over the next couple of months, I witnessed one act of violence after another. The whole time, I knew it wouldn't be long before I was sucked into the drama of the big yard.

Within a few weeks, most of the guys who had transferred in with me were sent to other prisons. We weren't seasoned convicts yet and the administration saw fit to send us to the newer correctional facilities. Several of my associates went to Brooks, which was located in Muskegon, and a few of us were sent to a prison in Carson City. I was excited because I knew that my brother had been there before. I was unsure whether he was still there, but I figured there would be someone there who knew him, so when I arrived at the facility, my spirit lifted a little at the thought of seeing my brother Art.

The prison sat on a sprawling piece of land that contained two prisons and a farm on the other side of the gate. The lawns had been manicured by inmate landscapers and the buildings were modern. There were microwaves, a pool table, and a universal weight machine in each unit. The food was of higher quality and we got at least four hours of yard time a day in addition to access to the gym. The inmates appeared to be less hostile and more optimistic compared to the Reformatory. I didn't realize it then, but the facility had been designed to decrease violence and increase the control that the officers had over inmates.

In many ways, the prison gave us a false sense of hope that things would get better. By creating a more livable environment, the state was creating more docile inmates. This worked well for those who were easily made complacent by the token treatment we received, but I hadn't been locked up long enough to be pacified; I was still in the rebellious mode. Whenever I got into something, the officers would ask the older inmates to talk to me. The older inmates would come see me and ask me to be cool so that I wouldn't get myself in trouble, or even worse, get them in trouble. They told me that one inmate could mess it up for the rest of them. I wasn't sympathetic to their pleas and felt insulted that they thought they could tell me what to do. When I became conscious, I found the perfect name for the inmates who felt compelled to do the officers' bidding – House Niggas. Just like the passive slaves who identified with Massa, these bootlicking Negroes worked harder for the administration than they did for themselves. They were content to have a microwave and more yard. While it was a convenience, I knew damn well that it wasn't home and I wasn't trying to get comfortable.

I started off in 5-Block, which had single man cells. It was a unit for predators and inmates with behavioral problems; however, they would put anyone in 5 if they didn't have the bed space in the other unit. For the first two weeks, I kept to myself for the most part. The only person that I talked to on a regular basis was a brother named O'Neal-El.

One day we were talking, and he told me that he needed to finish a book he was writing. I asked him what he was writing about and he told me he was writing about his neighborhood. He was a member of the infamous drug crew Young Boys Incorporated and wrote stories loosely based on his experience in the streets. He wrote his stories in neat block letters on folded prison stationary. He asked if I wanted to read one of his stories and I started laughing at the idea of an inmate writing a book. He told me that he was serious, and since I wasn't doing anything, I said I would read it.

I didn't really know what to expect, but when I started reading O'Neal-El's stories, I couldn't put them down. They were only about 80 or 90 pages, but they were detailed. When I finished, I felt like I had grown up alongside them wearing Top Tens, Max Julian coats and campaign hats. After I read a few of his books, he asked me if I had ever heard of Donald Goines. I told him I hadn't and he suggested I go to the library and check him out. He told me I would love Donald's work if I liked what he had written.

I sent a kite over to the library and requested to be placed on a callout. The next week I was given a callout to go to the library. I asked the clerk if she had any Donald Goines' books. She pointed me to a separate room, which contained a lot of books by Black authors. Upon entering the room, I checked the shelf for Donald Goines and found one of his books entitled, Eldorado Red. It was the last of his books left on the shelf, so I checked it out. The clerk gave me a form to fill out that said I would be charged five dollars if I lost the book or it got stolen. The only books we were required to fill out these forms for were books by Black authors. I was offended by what I felt was overt racism. The idea that I couldn't just go into the library and check out a book by a Black author without being under a cloud of suspicion was offensive to me. I understood that these books were very popular among the Black prison population, but they were no more popular to us than Jackie Collins and Sidney Sheldon were to White readers yet they didn't have to fill out a form ensuring that they returned their books. I mumbled to myself about how racist this practice was as I looked around the room for other books that may have been of interest to me.

The room was full of books with unfamiliar faces and names. I had never heard of Marcus Garvey, Ivan Van Sertima or Cheik Anta Diop. However, in that moment, I knew there had to be something to them because they were in the same room as Donald Goines. I picked up a couple of books and perused the back covers to see if they were of any interest. I may as well have been reading Sanskrit because I was unfamiliar with words like revolution, colonialism, or repatriate. I quickly slid the books back on the shelf and returned to the main area of the library. I gathered up a few more novels and went to the desk to check them out. I was told that they would hold a few Donald Goines' novels for me to check out later.

Once I got my books stamped, I left and returned to the unit. It was nearing time for count so when I got to my cell, I opened up the dog-eared pages of Eldorado Red and became instantly hooked by Donald's vivid tale of inner city life and the underground lottery. His storyline had me on the edge of my seat and I yearned for more with each page I turned. I tried to savor the last few chapters of the book, but I just couldn't put it down. Before the end of the night, I was done and thirsting for more. I read the other novels I had selected, but none were memorable and none left me with the feeling I got when I read Donald's work.

It felt like my next callout was taking forever, but when that day came, I nearly ran to the library. I didn't want anyone to beat me to the room and get Donald's books before I could get them. When I reached the library, it was as though the clerks knew I was coming. They had witnessed the intoxicating effect that Donald's work had on inmates and knew I would be back. They smiled as they handed me the books that had been reserved for me. I held Dopefiend and Whoreson in my hand as though they were the Holy Grail. I checked out a few more books and quickly headed back to my cell where I read throughout the day and late into the night. By the time I laid down at three o'clock in the morning, my eyes were on fire. I couldn't wait for sunlight so that I could indulge what was fast becoming my deepest passion.

The following week, I transferred to the unit next door where the cells were double-bunked. My bunky went by the name Murder, which seemed quite funny to me at the time considering he was about 140 pounds soaking wet. We hit it off immediately. He was originally from Chicago, but had family on the east side of Detroit where I had grown up. After a few weeks of kicking it, we realized that our sisters lived on the same street. He watched television most of the time while I read. He wasn't into sports as much as I was and only seemed to like watching movies and old westerns, none of which appealed to me at the time. I didn't have my own television, so I stuck to reading whenever I was in the cell.

In addition to reading, I started taking an Office Occupation class, which was really a fancy name for typing, or at least that's how it seemed considering that's all we did. After a couple of weeks, they opened a Food Tech class and I switched over to that. Murder and I found different ways to ensure that the other person had some alone time in the cell. This is something that is negotiated between bunkies to ensure they don't get on each other's nerves. Sometimes it's something as simple as stepping out of the cell and allowing your bunky to put on deodorant and lotion after a shower. We made sure to respect each other when we were asleep and be considerate enough to take a bowel movement when the other one was out of the cell. Bunking with anyone can be a challenge, especially when you have a toilet in the cell that must be shared.

I continued reading Donald's collection until I had read every one of them. Once I was done, a few guys turned me on to Iceberg Slim, Chester Himes and other authors like Harrold Robbins, Sydney Sheldon and Robert Ludlum. Some of their work I could get into, but none of them inspired me the way Donald did. Outside of reading, listening to rap was my other passion.

Growing up, music was my first love. I grew up in a household where you could hear music as diverse as Anita Baker, Prince and Luther Vandross to Parliament Funkadelic, Jimi Hendrix and Pink Floyd. My parents, aunts and uncles loved music so I inherited my love of music from them as naturally as the bloodline we shared. When rap entered my small world, I was hooked like a fish on the line. As a teenager, I rushed to the record store to get the newest release when my funds would allow, and when I couldn't afford to, I would swap music with my friends and dub their cassettes, building up a nice collection in the process.

When I entered prison, music became my getaway as much as it had been on the streets. It wasn't uncommon for me to sit in the day room and listen to other inmates freestyling in the ciphers or reciting the lyrics from their favorite rapper. It was in this arena that I met a tall, gangly brother who went by the name DJ X. He had a deep, raspy voice and would rap non-stop while beating on his chest. One day, he was in a cipher rapping and began using a bunch of names that I wasn't familiar with. I had heard a few of the names while listening to X-Clan and Public Enemy, but I didn't have a working knowledge of who they were. Listening to Boogie Down Productions and Rakim, one would think I was conscious, but back then, I was more concerned with the beats and the rhyme structure. When Chuck D said he was a supporter of Chesimard, I assumed he was talking about someone in his crew. I had no idea he was using the government name for the woman who would become one of my favorite sheroes – Assata Shakur.

When KRS One took the picture for the cover of his acclaimed album, "By All Means Necessary," I didn't know he was updating Malcolm X's famous photo and saying; however, I soon found out that I knew more than I thought I knew. I identified with the rebelliousness of their music as well as the African aesthetic; however, I was ignorant to our history and culture, and it was time for my awakening. When DJ X rapped, he spit with such authority that I assumed these people were gangsters. I mean, you have to admit, there's a menacing gangster quality about the name Malcolm X.

When DJ X was done rapping, I asked him about some of the names he had mentioned. He stared at me with an incredulous look on his face. He couldn't believe that I didn't know about Nat Turner and the other brave men and women he had mentioned in his song. I assured him that I was ignorant, and he suggested that I check out the Autobiography of Malcolm X when I went to the library. So on my next trip, that's exactly what I did.

When I picked up the Autobiography of Malcolm X, the picture on the cover was familiar. I had noticed a few brothers wearing T-shirts with Malcolm's image on the front. I had also seen a few clips on the news regarding Spike Lee's making of the movie, but I didn't stop long enough to pay attention to what all the hoopla was about. All I knew was that White people appeared to be very upset. The more I thought about it, the more familiar the name started to sound. Not long before I came to the joint, a school named Malcolm X Academy had opened up in Detroit, and there was White uproar about that as well.

As the pieces of the puzzle started coming together, I knew that Malcolm X had to be a serious gangster. However, when I read the back cover of the book, I was a bit let down. I saw that Alex Haley had co-written the book and that immediately started to change my image of Malcolm. I just knew I was about to read another in a long list of stories about Black people who just wanted to get along. I had grown tired of the Martin Luther King "I Have a Dream" and Rosa Parks back-of-the-bus stories. To me, they only served two purposes. One was to make White people feel guilt-free, and the other was to appease Black people and ensure that we remained docile in our approach to independence.

Though I wasn't born during the Civil Rights Era, I had witnessed enough police brutality in the 'hood to know that I would never endorse a non-violent movement. Despite my initial apprehension and obvious ignorance about the true meaning of human and civil rights, I decided to go ahead and read the book, and without question, it was the best and most important decision I could have made at that point in my bit.

While Donald Goines' collection of novels was the beginning of my growth as a man, it was Malcolm's autobiography that ultimately snatched my eyes open. The rawness of Donald's writing and his ability to articulate the pain of inner city life created a burning desire in me to read, but Malcolm's classic tome imbedded in me a burning desire to do something meaningful with my life. Once I finished reading Malcolm, I began reading with a purpose. I wanted to know as much as I could about the world we lived in. I read everything from political science to erotica to contemporary fiction and philosophy; however, it was my reading of Black history as told by people of African descent that allowed me to put things in perspective. It helped me understand why the majority of the prison population looked like me and why there were so many deep-rooted racial antagonisms inside of prison. It was evident that the Prison Industrial Complex had replaced the slave plantations.

My reading of Black history gave me a sense of pride and dignity that I didn't have prior to coming to prison. In school, the things we learned about Black history were designed to keep us dreaming of a better tomorrow, one that would only come when White America felt sorry enough to treat us as equals. This never set well with me, and for the most part, left me feeling angry, inferior and confused. I couldn't understand why White people hated us so much and why they didn't want us to have the same opportunities in life that they had.

I soon realized that the little bit of Black history that they taught in public schools really served a White elitist agenda. I didn't learn about freedoom fighters like Nat Turner, Toussaint L'Overture, Ann Nzingah, Assata Shakur, Malcolm X, and Huey P. Newton until I came to prison. I didn't know there were African kingdoms like Mali, Ashanti, and Timbuktu until I read classic works by scholars Chancellor Williams, Cheik Anta Diop, Dr. Ben Jochannan, and J.A. Rogers. It was then that I discovered our great contributions to the world and realized my self-worth. I had descended from greatness, therefore nothing was impossible for me. I learned that my ancestors were more than passive observers of history; they were in fact an integral part of the development of civilization as we know it today.

The more I read Malcolm X's autobiography, the more things started to make sense to me. Coming into prison, I was confused about religion. I had long ago given up the blonde-haired, blue-eyed Jesus that my mother worshipped. I had been raised to believe in Jesus, but my mother never tried to force religion on us, at least not intentionally. There were never any critical questions raised regarding religion and its origin in our household. When we went to church or Sunday school, we were expected to accept whatever the preacher and the Bible said was true.

I never had any point of reference outside of Christianity when I came to prison, and like many who find themselves in serious trouble, I always turned to Jesus with the hopes that he would pull me out of the fine mess I had found myself in. My motivation was clearly to get my ass out of hot water; I wasn't seeking any real relationship with God. So when things didn't turn out the way I had prayed for, I said to hell with God, Jesus, the Bible and anything associated with it. However, there was a small part of me that desired a sincere spiritual connection to the source of all life, and I was now on a quest to feed that desire.

Malcolm's autobiography was the first book to make me question Christianity. His insights into how Christianity had been used to make African people passive in the face of such horrendous treatment by slave masters made me look at things differently. I started to question why all of the characters in the Bible were depicted as White. I didn't, and still don't, have any personal biases toward White people, but I wanted to know where all the Black people were in the Bible. I knew we hadn't just fallen from the sky. When I asked others who were Christian, I was either met with a blank stare or told it didn't matter, that God wasn't a color. It was the politically correct thing for them to say, however their unease and nervousness suggested that they knew differently. The fact of the matter is that color does matter, and proof of this is revealed in how churches continue to portray Jesus as White despite the lack of historical data that says he looked anything like how he's depicted. In fact, it is well known that the Jesus we know today is a figment of Michael Angelo's imagination as painted on the ceiling of the Sistine Chapel.

The more disenchanted I became with Christianity, the more intrigued I became with Islam. Malcolm's experience in Mecca and his description of Islam as a religious brotherhood that didn't discriminate made me feel good. From the time I was a child, I envisioned a world that was all-inclusive and a God that was all-loving, regardless of color. So once I read about Islam, I began researching the Islamic organizations in prison. At the time, there were four dominant Islamic groups in Michigan prisons. There is the Sunni Muslim sect, which holds traditional Islamic beliefs. There is the Nation of Islam, which has strong Black nationalist views and its members follow the teachings of the Honorable Elijah Muhammad and Minister Farrakhan. There is also the Moorish Science Temple of America, which follows the teachings of Prophet Noble Drew Ali. This group is one of the first Asiatic Islamic groups in North America and has the largest followings in prison. Finally, there was the Melanic Islamic Palace of the Rising Sun, which was officially disbanded in 2000 and officially designated a gang. Similar to tactics employed by J. Edgar Hoover and COINTELPRO, the MDOC lodged trumped-up charges against the organization's head officials and labeled the organization a Security Threat Group. It was this organization that drew my interest the most due to their militant Afrocentric ideology. I was impressed by the discipline and cultural perspective of the few members I had encountered, and admired the red, black and green badge that they wore because it reminded me of X-Clan and other rappers I identified with.

The Melanic Islamic Palace of the Rising Sun was comprised of Black nationalists who combined the teachings of other organizations that had preceded it like the Black Panther Party and the Organization of African American Unity. Even though the Bible and Quran were the spiritual books of choice, they weren't exclusive. The members were encouraged to read other spiritual texts and drink from the many spiritual streams that our ancestors used to quench their thirst for spiritual rejuvenation. It wasn't uncommon for a spiritual advisor to quote David

Walker's Appeal or George Jackson's Blood in My Eye during a sermon, then open to a passage in the Bible or a surah in the Quran. Instead of trying to razzle dazzle us with an imaginary paradise in the sky or a terrifying threat of eternal damnation, the spiritual advisors set out to help us understand our daily realities, and this approach resonated with me. It made me think about Malcolm and his approach to reaching the downtrodden amongst us. Instead of standing at the podium as though he was on the mountaintop, Malcolm came down and walked amongst the people. He was the people; he related to their struggle, their pain and their frustration because he had lived it. This is what I witnessed when I finally relented and decided to attend one of the Melanic's Saturday morning services.

I had ducked the brothers who asked me to attend various services for several weeks. It was still early in my bit and I didn't like getting up early in the morning. Plus, I didn't want to get labeled as soft for attending an Islamic service. In prison, there is a negative stigma attached to some of the guys who attend service. Muslims have a reputation of sticking together and taking care of their members' problems, not unlike any other family or social group where the individual's problem become the group's problem. Unfortunately, however, there are inmates who take advantage of this reality. Some need protection, some are opportunists who seize the opportunity to have their basic needs met, and others are in search of the acceptance they didn't get from their own family, so I was very careful about my decision to attend Melanic services. Eventually, after reading several more books and holding a few conversations, I decided to check out a service.

The services were unlike anything I had ever experienced in a church. The podium was decorated with a large red, black and green flag and a picture of Nat Turner, who I would later learn was the organization's prophet. The brothers wore neatly pressed blues and polished shoes. Most of them wore black fezzes and stood until they were given instruction to be seated. The brothers at the door wore stoic expressions as they directed guests to the front of the room where we stood as the members proceeded to do the call to prayer. I was impressed by the preciseness of their movements as they formed a ten-man prayer pyramid. When the final row of the pyramid was filled, the brothers moved in a counter-clockwise motion as they called out to our ancestors. It was an awesome display of power, respect and spirituality. In an uncompromising display of solidarity, the brothers paid homage to those who came before us while praising the Creator for a chance to do something meaningful for our people.

Once the prayers had been said and the laws of the organization read, a brother was called up to speak. He talked about the importance of unity and shared the history of Nat Turner. I was even more intrigued as I listened to the story of Prophet Nat Turner who organized the largest uprising of enslaved people on the shores of North America. While attending school, I had never heard of a Black person fighting for their freedom through armed resistance. Later on, I found the prison administration hypocritical because they portrayed our organization as advocating violence because we embraced Nat Turner as our prophet. How can a country that celebrates George Washington, who led the fight for independence against Britain's tyranny, condemn us for honoring a man who fought against one of the vilest systems known to man? In their eyes, it is heroic for White men and women to fight for liberation but criminal for people of African descent to take a stand against those who oppressed them. In the coming weeks, I would learn just how much the administration despised those who wanted to change from predators on our community to freedom fighters and agents of change.

After that first service, the brothers asked me if I would come back and visit again. I told them that I wouldn't make any promises, but I'd consider it. Over the next couple of months, I visited service sporadically. It didn't have anything to do with their teachings or other people's perceptions; it was simply a matter of timing. I am nocturnal by nature and spent most nights reading until two or three o'clock in the morning, so the last thing I wanted to do was get up at seven o'clock in the morning to get ready for service. Despite this, I kept reading and building with the brothers.

As important as my spiritual and intellectual growth was, there was something more important manifesting in my life. The months had been moving swiftly and the winter was fast upon us. With each frosty day that came and went, I knew I was one day closer to getting the news I had been waiting to hear for the last eight months. It was late December and I called home to get an update on Brenda. It had been a few months since I saw her last and we were only talking occasionally. The cost of phone calls had long ago taken their toll and Georgia couldn't afford to take calls on a daily basis. Brenda did what she could to help with the phone bill, and I did my best not to call too much. When Georgia answered, she told me that Brenda was due to have the baby any day. She said Brenda wasn't available to speak, but told me to call back in a few days. Instead, I waited about a week and a half before I called Georgia again.

On January 7, 1992, I stepped outside of the unit into the frosty winter air. My hands nearly froze the moment I took them out of my pocket to dial the number. The cold winter air sliced through the thin fabric of my state coat like a bayonet. When Georgia answered the phone, I knew that my son had been born into the world. Her voice cascaded through the phone like the music from a symphony. I listened intently as my eyes watered with tears that froze as soon as they hit the air. I had mixed emotions as I thought about what the birth of my son meant for Brenda and I. I was happy to hear that he had been born healthy and Brenda decided to name him after me, but my chest felt heavy, as though I had swallowed a cinder block. A deep sadness engulfed my entire being. It hurt like hell knowing that I wouldn't be there to guide my son through life. In addition to letting my daughter down, I had let Brenda and my newborn son down.

In the few weeks preceding my son's birth, I had been learning a lot about the conditions of young Black males. I was concerned about my son getting caught up in the same cycle of violence, drugs and crime that had claimed so many from my generation, including me. I didn't want my son to become another in a long line of young Black males who became statistics, and I didn't want my daughter to end up like Brenda and the countless single mothers who fall hard for males like me who wouldn't be around to raise the children we helped create. The more I thought about it, the angrier I became. I didn't know how to process what I was feeling at the time and it began eating away at me. I felt guilty about being an absentee father, yet I didn't want to take responsibility for the actions that led me to be taken out of my children's lives. I was learning a lot about White supremacy and the role it played in filling America's prisons with young Black males. This new knowledge provided the perfect target for the toxic anger that was consuming me.

When I returned to my cell, I lay on my bunk and thought about my son. I imagined what he looked like. I wondered what characteristics he had inherited from me and which ones he had inherited from his mother. Brenda was a pretty young lady, and I thought I was a decent looking brother, so I was sure that our son would be a cute baby. As I thought about him, my heart began filling with an unbelievable joy and I knew I had to find a way to be a part of my son's life. In that moment, I made a vow to find a way to be a father even though I was in prison. I knew one of the first things I had to do was change my thinking. I could no longer think destructively about other Black males. I could no longer justify shooting, beating or selling drugs to those who looked like me. I had to reclaim my humanity and soften my heart so that I could be the voice of reason and spirit of wisdom that my children could always rely on. I knew I was in for the fight of my life, but I was prepared for the battle.

I knew that "nigga" in me had to be choked and subdued by the African warrior I was destined to become. There could be no more settling for less in my life. I had given up on myself and my family, but I would be damned if I gave up on my children. I knew it wouldn't be an easy victory, but I was determined to fight against the side of me that had me believing that I couldn't be anything more than a thuggish criminal and predator on my community. No matter how many times I was knocked to the ground, I was determined to get up over and over until I was able to stand on the firm, proud, strong legs of an African man and father. Without compromise or apologies, I had begun my journey of transformation.

The first year or so was the hardest because I was deeply entrenched in the anger phase of my transformation. The more I read about White people's treatment of people of African descent, the angrier

I became. I felt justified in my rage toward White staff and inmates. I empathized with my ancestors and felt tears pour from my heart with each story of lynching and rape that I read. I was growing dangerously intelligent. What I didn't realize at the time was how distorted my thinking had become. Instead of going beneath the surface and delving into the root causes of my negative thinking and violent behavior, I covered up my pain by directing it toward White people. This allowed me to justify my outbursts and remain unaccountable for my role in how things in my life were turning out.

It wasn't until nearly eight years later that I had a real awakening and grew into the fullness of my potential. In the meantime, I waged a daily battle with my old way of thinking, and sadly, the New African warrior that I had become wasn't always the victor. One day, after learning that Brenda hadn't sent the money off that she promised, the "nigga" in me assumed control of the ship. True to form, chaos ensued, and I found myself heading down a dark, murky path. For the first time during my bit, I would learn the true meaning of hell on earth.

Chapter 11

The thought of killing myself smashed into my consciousness like a drunk driver. Images of my tattered life boiled and raged inside my mind, and a deep, piercing pain shot through my heart. It felt as if someone had plunged a fiery sword through my most vital organ. I looked down at my shirt expecting to see thick, crimson blood gurgling from my chest where I knew the hole was. Instead, all I could see was the red, white and blue Fila logo perched on my T-shirt. I clutched my chest as I struggled to cross back over to the space in my mind that was capable of making a rational decision, but it was too late; I had already welcomed into my most sacred space the idea of ending it all – the pain, the loneliness, and the sense of abandonment that I felt.

I looked around Ralph's basement, hoping that someone would take notice of what was going on inside of me, but they were lost in the merriment of the alcohol we had consumed that night. Instead of alerting them that something was seriously wrong, I made a joke about what I was feeling. With a sinister grin, I asked Ralph, Jamal and Mike what they would do if I blew my brains all over the walls of the basement.

"Nigga, you trippin," Mike responded before taking a swig from the 40 ounce bottle of Old English 800 he had been holding.

"Don't be playing like that," Ralph replied with a laugh.

Jamal just looked over at me for a moment before he fired up a cigarette. Suicide was something we never talked about, and in their case, I guess had never thought about. Back then, I didn't understand the power of depression and how it could lead me to think about ending my life, bringing an end to the pain I had been holding inside. My vocalizing the thought of painting the walls with my brain matter was a cry for help that none of them took seriously. What had happened inside of us that allowed us to laugh away a question so serious?

We continued to drink for another half an hour or so before Ralph decided it was time for us all to leave. We exited his side door and headed for our respective homes. Mike lived one block over on Murray

Hill, Jamal lived two blocks over on St. Mary's, and I lived a block in the opposite direction on Ferguson. When we reached the corner of Midland, we exchanged pounds, then I turned and walked toward my block. With each step I took, my feet grew heavier. It felt like the weight of the universe was on my shoulders and I would surely buckle under the pressure. At that moment, as I neared our house, I decided I would end it all. I had a sawed-off shotgun beneath my mattress in the basement with plenty of shells. A smile crossed my face as I thought about the guilt that my parents would carry around in their hearts when they found my bloody, headless body in the basement. Maybe then they would stop and think about what they had done when they tore our family apart, and maybe for once, my mother would feel the pain that I felt as a result of her absence in my life.

The pain from my mother's absence had crawled around inside of me like a cockroach trapped inside of a television screen. I thought to myself, if I were no longer here, maybe she would finally think about her decision to push me out of her life and ignore me. Maybe she would cry as she thought about all of the times she told me she wished she had never had me. The fact that she hadn't played a significant role in my life since their split made me believe her, and if I was unworthy of my mother's love, I figured didn't need to be here.

I fumbled with my keys as I struggled to let myself in the side door. The house was quiet when I entered, but I knew that my stepsister Vanessa would be up talking on the phone. The moment I thought about her and my nephew Megale, a tinge of guilt shot through me. I knew she would be hurt and my nephew would be confused. I inhaled deeply and descended the basement stairs as I stuffed my emotions back down where they couldn't impede my progress toward death. I didn't bother to turn on the basement lights; I knew the layout of the basement, which doubled as my bedroom, like the back of my hand.

When I first moved in with my father, stepmother, stepsister and nephew, they showed me the area where my bedroom would be with such pride. Instead of feeling safe and warm, I felt cold and cutoff from the rest of the house. In my mind, the basement symbolized my standing in the family – I was at the bottom of it all. I didn't feel welcomed or wanted. Instead of looking at it as though they were trying to give me a private space to call my own, I felt like a burden and that was their way of dealing with me. My mother didn't want me, so why would they?

I plopped down in one of the big Lazy Boy chairs that made up the décor of the basement and lit up a Newport. I allowed the calming influence of the nicotine to circulate through my body before exhaling, then closed my eyes and thought about how things had been since I moved in with my father. On the surface, everything looked good. The house sat in the middle of a pleasant street. My stepmother's cooking was spectacular and my relationship with my stepsister had evolved into an ideal sibling connection. My father and stepmother both worked for Lafayette Clinic at the time and provided us with money when they got paid. I had enrolled in Cooley High School, made a few friends in the neighborhood and had a couple of girlfriends who skipped school with me whenever the mood struck us; however, I didn't feel at home, and I wasn't happy. The longing to be loved and accepted by my mother ate at me, and I felt like an unwelcomed burden to my father and stepmother.

I knew my father and stepmother had some concerns about my behavior. Prior to moving in with them, I had been arrested a few times for various crimes. I was no longer the honor roll student I had been. I rarely attended class and had lost interest in learning. Whenever I was kicked out of school and my father had to sign me back in, I never stayed. He would take me through the front door, and as soon as he left, I went right out the back door. The most troubling thing about this part of my life is that no one ever stopped to ask me what was wrong. They never questioned how or why I had changed so dramatically in such a short span of time. Years later, during conversations with my father, I would learn the struggles he faced trying to be a father and a recent divorcee all the while trying to make a new relationship work.

As I sat there puffing on my cigarette, I began having the most negative dialogue with myself. I thought about every beating I had endured at the hands of my mother. I thought about the day she hurled a cast iron pot at my head after I asked her a question. I thought about how my brothers treated me, and how they never stood up for me. I thought of everything I could think of to make myself more miserable until I had worked up the courage to reach beneath the mattress and grab the sawed-off shotgun. I held the heavy steel in my hands before sitting back down in the chair. I caressed the barrel as tears began streaming from my eyes. I remembered telling my mother that I wanted to be a doctor, and more tears fell. I would always tell her things like that because I wanted her to love me and be proud of me more than anything in the world. I started getting angry because I couldn't form the words to say that she was so wrong. In my eyes, she was blameless, so I knew there had to be something wrong with me.

I then started to think about my father and his role in the drama. I started getting pissed at him for not being stronger in his position as head of the household. I felt like he went along to get along. I wanted him to come in and put his foot down when she beat my ass for nothing, but he never did. I tried to make myself dislike him, but I couldn't. Despite his shortcomings, I knew that my father loved me and he was a good man. I thought about how things were when it was just me and him, and more tears came. I knew my death would break his heart, but I had to end the pain.

I checked the shotgun to ensure there was a slug in the chamber before taking off the safety. I inhaled deeply and prepared to place the barrel in my mouth. I thought about the flash of pain I would feel. I wondered if the heat from the barrel would melt my lips when I pulled the trigger. I had heard that the pain would be minimal, but I wasn't quite convinced that blowing my brains out would be a painless ordeal. I wondered how much of my head would be spread over the basement and how loud the gunshot would be. This final thought stopped me cold. If I blew my brains out, the sound would startle my nephew from his sleep. I imagined my stepsister trying to calm him down, and the image of her consoling him made me put the gun back beneath the mattress. There had to be another way.

I lit another cigarette before climbing the stairs up to the top floor. As I walked through the house, I absorbed all of the details for what I felt would be my last time. When I reached the upstairs bathroom, I tiptoed inside and closed the door. I didn't bother to cut on the bathroom light; I used the sliver of light that crept through the window from the street lamp outside. I opened the medicine cabinet and began going through the different bottles of prescription medicine inside.

I read a few of the labels with hopes that they had a warning sign on them, letting me know just how potent they were; however, I didn't find any that said, WARNING! MAY CAUSE DROWSINESS. Once I had read each label, I started searching all over again until I came across a bottle that had a lot of pills in it. It didn't have a warning sign, but I figured if I took enough, they would do the trick. I removed the bottle from the cabinet and opened the top. I poured a handful of pills in my hand and looked at myself in the mirror. The sliver of light coming through the window gave my face a ghostly appearance; I looked as if I were already dead. In reality, a large part of me had been dead for a couple of years. My eyes were heavy with the sadness and loneliness of an orphan.

I took one last look at the pills in my hand, inhaled deeply, and then swallowed them greedily. When the last pill snaked its way down my throat, I hurriedly left the bathroom and headed back downstairs to the kitchen. I turned on the faucet and gulped down some water, trying to ensure that the pills would stay down. When I was done, I slunk back down into the basement and waited for death to claim me. I sat in the Lazy Boy chair and lit up another cigarette. I puffed incessantly, hoping that I could hurry death along. After awhile, I was struck by the thought of how unfair it would be for me to allow my two-year-old nephew to find me dead in the basement. He was usually the first one to come downstairs in the morning. It was one of my most pleasant experiences. Each morning, I would lie in the bed and listen to the pitter-patter of his little feet as he navigated his way through the living room, dining room, and finally the kitchen where the stairs to the basement were located. I could sense when something caught his attention because he would stop for a moment before continuing his journey. When he reached the stairs, he would crawl down backwards, stopping periodically until his eyes had fully adjusted to the light. When he reached the bottom step, he would stand up, then come over to my bed and stare at me. Sometimes I would watch him through squinted eyes as he tried to figure out if I was awake. Finally, he would tap me on my face and call my name.

"Uncle Jay! Uncle Jay!" he would say as he tapped my face. "I want some cereal," he would continue until I got up and fed him.

The thought of him not being able to awaken me caused me to jump up from the chair. I was a bit dizzy, but I was able to make it back up the stairs. I went straight to Vanessa's bedroom and tapped on her door lightly. She told me to come in, and I sat on the floor beside her bed for a minute before I said anything. She asked me what was up. I explained to her that I was trying to kill myself and had taken a lot of pills. I told her that I was letting her know because I didn't want Megale to find me dead in the morning. She was silent for what felt like an eternity. When she spoke, I could sense the uncertainty in her voice. I assumed that she smelled the alcohol on my breath and may have thought that I was drunk. She then asked me what I had done. I told her about the pills I had taken, and that's when she took me serious. I told her that I was about to go back to the basement and die, and she told me that she was going to get my father. I begged her not to, but deep inside, I was happy that she was taking action. For the first time in a long time, I felt like someone cared about me.

I left Vanessa's room and walked back down to the basement where I laid across my bed. A few minutes later, I heard the heavy footsteps of my father coming down the stairs. He hit the light switch, and the bright glare of the light caused me to scrunch my eyes into a tight ball.

"What's wrong?" my father asked as he sat on the bed beside me. He placed his hand on my head and checked my pulse.

I told him that I didn't want to live any longer. He told me that I shouldn't say that or feel that, then started telling me about all of the things I had to live for. He then stopped and asked me what I had taken, and I told him. He got up and walked upstairs, and to this day, I don't know what he went to do, but when he returned he had a cup of coffee. He held my head and urged me to drink the coffee. I sipped the bitter liquid as I listened to him breath deeply. He continued to talk to me for an hour or so as we drunk coffee and smoked cigarettes. When we realized that the pills I had taken were harmless and I wasn't going to die, we decided to call it a night. My father sat in the Lazy Boy chair and watched me until I fell into a fitful sleep.

The next morning, none of us mentioned anything about what had happened the night before. There were no discussions of me getting counseling, no one asked me what I had been thinking for me to consider ending my life, and there was no call from my mother. Vanessa never said anything about that night and neither did I. Though I knew I wouldn't attempt to kill myself again, I had no idea how I was going to cope with the pain that I carried around like a malignant tumor. All I knew was that I had to find a way to get rid of what I was feeling inside.

Although I was enrolled at Cooley High School, I rarely went to class. Whenever I decided to go up to the school, I hung out across the street behind the fruit market drinking and smoking cigarettes. If I wasn't hanging out at school, I was hanging with the one guy in my 'hood that I connected with the most. Ralph was from Long Beach, California, and had moved to the 'hood around the same time I did. We made friends with other guys in the neighborhood like Daniel "Big D" Lyton, who was the center for the famed Cooley High School basketball team that would go on to win three state championships while we were there. There was also our Puritan Avenue crew who hung out on St. Mary's every day. On my block, there was Toke, Quinny and a few other guys I was cool with. However, the bond that I had with Ralph was different because we were the two new guys in the 'hood.

I had lived in a few different neighborhoods across the city so I had to learn the fine art of making friends quickly. One of the things that I realized from past experiences, however, was that no matter how cool I was with the guys in the new 'hood, I would never have the history that they had with each other. As we got older, this became evident as beefs and rifts occurred between me, Ralph and the rest of the guys on my block.

With Big D, it was different because he was more mature than the rest of the guys on the block. Our bond was solid and we would always kick it whenever I showed up at school or hang out when he got his father's van. The thing that really cemented our bond was our love for hip hop and street culture. We would walk up to the record shop anytime one of us had some extra money and cop whatever new rap album came out. After that, we would sit in my basement and dub tapes for each other as we ate my stepmother's cooking. Our bond remained solid over the years, but I was growing apart from the rest of the 'hood.

Ralph and I began dabbling in the dope game again. I sold weed at school and we hung out with my older brothers in a neighborhood called Brightmoor. My sister Tamica was the first of my siblings to move to this gritty neighborhood at the far west end of the city. She lived on a street named Blackstone, which became one of my favorite places to hang out. It reminded me of my old neighborhood on the east side, and every chance I got, I called my brother Alan to come get me so that I could hang out in Brightmoor. He had a house a couple of streets over from my sister on Patton near Lyndon, so if I wasn't hanging on Blackstone with Tamica, I was at Alan's house. He was selling weight and the house was cranking. I loved sitting at the dining room table with my brothers counting money, but I loved spending the money they gave me even more. When I went up to Cooley, I would wear the newest Troop apparel they had bought for me, or whatever else was out at the time, and I always had money to drink and eat at the Coney Island. Around that same time, things had started to heat up in Brightmoor.

One day, I noticed a car sitting a couple of houses down with four guys in it. They looked suspicious so I told my brother Alan about the car. I didn't know if they were police or not, but I wanted to give my brother a heads up. He checked it out and said he didn't know what was up but I shouldn't worry about it. We went back to doing what we were doing, then decided to order a pizza. When the pizza arrived, his girlfriend Teresa got a few plates out for her children and us, and we started eating. Before I could get the second slice down, the sound of a loud crash burst through the air.

"Police! Police!" the voices screamed out as several men barged into the house. We froze in our tracks and placed our hands on top of our heads. The first guy to reach me pushed me into the wall before snatching the gold rope that I wore from around my neck.

"Hit the safe in the bedroom," I heard a muffled voice say as two men started ransacking the back bedroom. Once they grabbed the safe and started to flee, it dawned on me that we were being robbed. On their way out, one of the guys carrying the safe hit me in the head before he exited. That's when Alan sprung into action. He grabbed a pistol out of the closet and ran out of the door, but it was too late. They were gone.

Immediately, we started thinking about who could have put together the robbery. We called my brother Art and sat at the dining room table thinking about who had put the play down. My brother was relieved that no one had gotten hurt and they hadn't gotten away with anything other than the necklace they had snatched from my neck. A couple of hours before the robbery, my brother Art had come over and picked up the money, so their plan came up short. When we finished talking, we concluded that the only person it could be was a guy named Mike who lived a few doors down. He had sold Art a few guns and was one of the only people outside of family who had seen the location of the safe.

We sat outside waiting for Mike to return home. When he did, we went down to his house. I carried a rifle and both of my brothers had pistols with them. We accused him of setting up the robbery and threatened to kill him if we didn't get the necklace back. We were beyond reckless and allowed the emotions of the moment to dictate our actions. Mike stuck to his guns and assured us that he hadn't had anything to do with the robbery. After a few minutes and a few more threats, we left and went back to the house. Moments later, while we were sitting in the living room talking about the incident, Mike came back down to the house. Before he could get two words out, Art began shooting at him with a .357 Magnum. The sound of the gunshots caused the house to shake. Teresa grabbed her children and ran for cover as me and Alan looked on.

For Alan, that was the beginning of the ending. There was no way he could leave his girl and her children at the house with a full-fledged beef going on. For the rest of the night, we remained vigilant, but things on Patton were never the same. We continued to make money over there until Alan was picked up for a parole violation. He was extradited back to Illinois where he had served time on two other occasions and was sentenced to serve more time.

We were saddened to see our brother go back to prison, but we continued to live the lifestyle. With Alan locked up, me and Art began spending more time together. Everyday, he would come and get me from my father's house and we would ride around all day picking up money and dropping off drugs. When we weren't handling business, we went skating at Northland Roller Rink during the weekdays and Rolladium out in Pontiac every Sunday, which is where we hung out with our homeboys Billy Davis, Jesse Peeples and Terrance Majors from our old neighborhood on the east side. For the first time ever, me and Art started hanging out everyday. I was getting older and able to hold my own so he liked having me around. But as they say, good things always come to an end.

The more I hung with Art, the more I became a victim of he-say, she-say in the 'hood. Some guys that lived down the block from me on Ferguson had an issue with me hanging with my crew from Puritan, even though I was barely in the 'hood. Then one day, things got heated and we got into a shootout over some trifling neighborhood gossip. When Vanessa caught wind of the shootout, she called Art and told him what happened. When he came over to the house, I was a couple of blocks over on St. Mary's with the rest of the crew talking about the shootout.

Art pulled up and told me to get in the car. He asked me what was going on as we pulled off. I gave him the rundown and he started going off on me about hanging out with my crew. He never liked crowds, and back then, I didn't understand his line of reasoning. When we neared the corner, the guys from down the street were coming up the side street. Their older brother was leading the way. When Art saw them, he pulled over and started talking to their older brother. The conversation started off cool. Their brother said he was coming around the corner to squash the beef, but as he talked, one of their cousins began running off at the mouth. Art got tired of listening to the shit talking and pulled off. When we neared the corner of the next block, he hit a U-turn and pressed down hard on the accelerator. Before they could get out of the way, he had run a few of them over.

Just as we were driving through the crowd, one of the guys started shooting. The car window exploded as Art yelled for me to get down. When we got to my street, Art told me he had been hit. We had a female named Peaches with us, and her and I rushed him to the hospital. We checked him in under an alias so that he could get treated for a gunshot wound to the arm. They told him that he had to stay overnight so I went back to the 'hood, got Ralph and we drove back to the hospital. We asked Art if he wanted us to go back and shoot one of them, but he told us to leave it alone until he got released from the hospital.

The following day, me and Peaches picked Art up from the hospital, then picked up some money before heading over to Art's ex-girlfriend's house. He had gotten the car in her name and wanted her to call the insurance company to get the window fixed. They got into an argument and he ended up slapping her around. Shortly thereafter, we left her house and headed to his apartment to chill. While we were kicking it, Art said that he had a feeling his ex-girlfriend was going to call the police because she knew he had a warrant out for his arrest. Despite this, we remained at the apartment. I ran a few errands for him while Peaches took care of him. When I returned, me and Peaches sat on the couch kicking it. Art was just coming out of the bedroom when he heard a loud knock at the door.

"Police! Come out with your hands up!" they ordered through the door as they beat on it frantically.

"Fuck y'all, I ain't going to jail," Art said as he scrambled back into his bedroom.

Peaches started crying and my heart began pounding as I thought about us all dying in a hail of bullets. Art reemerged from the bedroom and looked out of the kitchen window into the parking lot, which was surrounded by police cars.

"Damn, why you have to be here little bro," he said as he held a carbine in his hand.

After a few tense moments, Art realized that he was out of options unless he was ready to die. He told them that he was about to open the door. He hugged me and told me to call our father to let him know what was up. He then opened the door for the police to enter. They rushed him like a rugby player, and in a matter of moments, all I could see was a pile of blue uniforms and the soles of my brother's shoes beneath the pile. A couple of officers came over and told me to get up against the wall as they began searching the apartment. They found a pistol beneath the couch that I was sitting on and a few automatic rifles in the front closet. In the bedroom, they found more guns and a scale. One of the officers said that he could charge me with the gun that was beneath the sofa, but my brother told them that everything in the house belonged to him. When they were finished searching the apartment, they took him out in handcuffs and told me and Peaches that we had to leave the premises.

Peaches and I caught a cab to my father's house. When I told him the news about Art getting locked up, he was livid. He started fussing at me for hanging out with Art and warned me that I was going to follow him to prison if I continued down the path I was on. I allowed his words to flow in one ear and out the other.

In less than a one-year span, both of my brothers had gone to prison, and as prophesied, it wouldn't be long before I followed suit. It had become clear that me moving back home was not working out. My father and I began clashing over everything. Then, him and my stepmother separated, and he and I moved into an apartment on Greenfield and Plymouth; however, I was still hanging in the 'hood or down in Brightmoor.

Things cooled down for a moment until I caught a felonious assault case for which they had a warrant out for my arrest. It started over a petty beef between my neighbor Desmond and one of my homeboys named Boo Boo who lived a few blocks over. One day, Boo Boo came over to my house drunk and decided to kick my neighbor's door in. They thought I had something to do with Boo Boo's actions and decided to retaliate by beating on our door at three or four o'clock in the morning. I came running out with a pistol and confronted my neighbors. Desmond's mother denied knowing anything about them coming to our house, but I could hear him and his friend from down the street talking in the background and I vowed to beat their ass when I caught them. My father had rushed out the house behind me and forced me to go back inside. A few weeks later, I caught Desmond and his friend slipping and beat his friend in the head with a bat. He was rushed to the hospital and a warrant was issued for my arrest.

I wasn't prepared to go to jail so I stopped coming home and started hanging down in Brightmoor exclusively. I had tired of all the drama at home and asked my sister Tamica if I could stay with her for awhile. It was 1989, and I was one month shy of my seventeenth birthday. I had no idea that my birthday surprise would be the beginning of the end of my life on the streets.

Chapter 12

The thought of robbing another inmate had never occurred to me until I was discussing my financial predicament with my bunky Murder. I told him how things had gone with the money Brenda was supposed to send me, and he told me that he was in the same position. Neither of us had been assigned a job yet and our only source of income was our family and loved ones. Unfortunately, neither of us had received a money order in time to make it to the store, which we were only allowed to do every two weeks. We were running low on cigarettes and neither of us was in a position to borrow money from other inmates because we didn't know when our next money order would arrive.

This was one of the many sad realities of being locked up. It didn't take a whole lot to survive financially in prison, but we couldn't even count on our so-called friends to drop a hot twenty dollars on our books. The more I thought about how much money I used to spend at the corner store on a daily basis, the angrier I became at the thought of my friends not sending me money. We used to drink fifths of liquor, forty ounces of beer, smoke cigarettes and weed every day, but the way I saw it, I wasn't worth sacrificing one trip to the store in their eyes.

I sat up kicking it with Murder about being betrayed by our homies and our families. We used that conversation to fuel our anger and reinforce our fuck-the-world mentality. By the time we finished talking, it was late into the night and we had devised a plan to rob our neighbor after he picked up his store items. He was a middle-aged White man running his own black market store so we felt doubly justified in robbing him. We talked about how he would give the other brothers one store item for two items in return and then talk down to them when they didn't have what they owed him. He was no different than the other brothers on the cellblock who thought nothing of busting another brother's head or stabbing him to death over a pack of cigarettes; however, in our mind, his White skin put him in the same class as the White officers who policed the prison.

We agreed that I would run into the cell and subdue our neighbor while Murder relieved him of all of his store goods. We hung around our cell watching his every move while also watching the movement of the officer responsible for our tier. When we noticed our neighbor headed for the shower, we knew the timing was right.

We eased back into our cell and cracked the door. I told Murder to look out for the officer once our neighbor returned from the shower and give me a minute to walk past his cell so I could check out the scene. Once our neighbor was in his cell, I stepped out and walked past to see where he was in the cell. I had to walk a little ways down the hall to play it off, and when I turned around, I was shocked to see Murder halfway inside the cell telling the guy to run all of his store goods. While Murder was talking, he was also trying to watch out for the police, and that's when our neighbor took advantage and tried to land a punch. I pulled Murder out of the way and delivered a punch to the guy that knocked him into the cell door. He staggered and covered his face, then Murder jumped on his back and tried choking him as he pulled him back into the cell. We were making a lot of noise, so I tried to silence the guy with a few more punches. What started off as a robbery attempt had quickly escalated into a full on assault; we got caught up in the adrenaline rush and forgot what we had come for.

Just as I started measuring the guy up for a good punch, someone jumped on my back. All I could do was think about his bunky sneaking up on me from behind as I felt someone pulling at my arms. I quickly leaned forward, causing the person on my back to stumble forward. I then reached behind me and flipped who I thought was the guy's bunky over on his back. It was then that I realized it wasn't his bunky after all; it was one of the officers working the unit. Before the reality of what I had just done could kick in, I was rushed to the wall by several other officers and handcuffed.

More officers rushed to the unit, grabbed Murder and threw him in handcuffs. As we were being led away from the unit, we could hear the cackling over the radio. The officers had to send out an emergency call to the infirmary because our neighbor had begun having a seizure. The officer who had me by the cuffs told me that I was going to be charged with murder if the guy died enroute to the hospital.

"I don't give a fuck. I ain't never going home anyway," I snapped, in an effort to take back some control of the situation.

The officer ignored my bravado, as he had seen and heard it all before and knew better than us that we really did care, or at least wanted to. When I got to the segregation unit, I was placed in a shower cage where I stayed in handcuffs for fifteen minutes. Finally, after what felt like an eternity, a hound dog-faced officer came to the shower cage and ordered me to back up so that he could take the handcuffs off of my wrists. I backed up to the slot and put my hands up so that he could take the cuffs off. He put the key in and freed my right hand while tightly holding the cuff.

"So you like to assault White men, huh? You lil' asshole," the officer said as he snatched the cuff through the slot, bringing with it my arm, which he pulled downward in a jerking motion.

"Bitch, when they let me out of the hole, I'm going to kill your hoe ass," I promised through clenched teeth as I felt the skin tearing from my arm and my bone threatening to snap.

"Next time, you'll think twice about who you put your hands on dickhead," he snapped back with a smirk as he released my hand from the cuff.

As I wrapped my shirt around my arm to stymie the flow of blood, I continued to curse and tell the officer what I was going to do to him when I got out of the hole. When the other officers came to take me to a cell, my body became very tense. I didn't know what they would try to do to me. They were White like the first officer, and I didn't know if they held the same sentiments, so when they told me to turn around and place my hands behind my back, I hesitated. It was then that one of the officers noticed me bleeding and asked if I wanted to see a nurse. Something about him showing concern caused me to relax. I told him that I was okay and allowed him to cuff me up.

Even though I knew that the other officer was wrong, I wasn't about to rat him out. It wouldn't have brought me any pleasure, even if he were suspended. The only thing that would have given me pleasure was beating his ass, and I knew his co-workers weren't going to allow that to happen, so I chalked it up to the game.

As I was being escorted to a cell, one of the officers asked me why I was wasting my young life. This was a question I had been asked quite often when I was young, and I never had an answer. All I knew was that I was hurt inside and didn't give a fuck about living or dying. I felt like my life was over, so there was nothing more to waste. The officer went on to mention that they had escorted our neighbor to the hospital and it wasn't looking good for us.

When I entered the cell, I sat down on the bunk and thought briefly about what my father would think when he learned that I had been charged with another count of murder. Though I didn't think at that time that I was ever getting out of prison, I didn't want to kill anyone, especially not over a bag of commissary.

I stood looking out of the window for what felt like hours before a sergeant came to my cell and read off the charges. I was given a major misconduct for assault on staff, assault on an inmate and dangerous contraband for a weapon they discovered in my cell. Within two days, I was transferred along with Murder.

One evening after chow, I was told to pack up all of my property; I was getting transferred in the morning back to the Michigan Reformatory in Ionia where I would be placed on long-term segregation status. In prison vernacular, we called it "lay down." When I first came to the hole, I asked one of the inmates who had been in prison for a while why they had given it that name. He responded with a laugh before saying, "Because down here, all you can do is lay your ass down and read, lay your ass down and write, or lay your ass down and talk shit all day. So it's up to you young blood how you do it, but all I can tell you is, don't take this shit laying down." The administration, on the other hand, chose to use the much more lofty euphemism "administrative segregation." It sounded politically correct and oh so professional, but when they weren't on record, they called it the "hole" just like the rest of us.

During the forty-minute ride back to Ionia, thoughts of what the "hole" would be like tumbled through my head like a gymnast. Horror stories of how inmates in the hole had been found hung in their cells, or mysteriously suffocated with their own socks, or how the officers would come in your cell with the goon squad and beat you two breaths short of death, all ran tirelessly through my mind. What about all of the resistance I had put up? What if the officers at the other prison had called their buddies to give me a nice work over?

After being processed, I was escorted to the hole into a cellblock known as the "Graves." It had earned the moniker from the inmates there because once you were thrown in the "Graves," it was like being entombed in a place where you lost sight of time. It was as though you were dead to everyone in general population, and the cells were so small that you felt like you had been squeezed into a coffin. Essentially, being sentenced to "lay down" was to be sentenced to an indeterminate amount of time in hell.

Before the reality of what I was about to experience kicked in, an officer told me that the sheriffs were there to pick me up and take me on a writ to the county jail. The first thought that ran through my mind was the inmate who I had assaulted had died. It took a minute for me to realize that it was the Wayne County Sheriffs, which meant I was going back to Detroit. I breathed a sigh of relief as I prepared for what turned out to be several months of me going back and forth to the Wayne County Jail. After my first trip to the county, I was returned about a week later and tossed back into the Graves.

The first thing I noticed when I entered the cellblock was the gloomy ambiance. The windows were painted a somber grey and the only natural light present was the few streams that snuck through when the officers were nice enough to leave one of the windows cracked, which was very rare. Being stripped of all personal belongings, with the exception of the bare necessities, made it impossible to tell if it was morning or night unless you asked the officers or the windows were open. Other than that, I had to guess the time based on when my meals were passed out.

As I was escorted down to my cell, I had to navigate my way around spoiled food, empty milk cartons, fecal-stained towels, and piles of shredded and soiled paper. I kept my head straightforward as I walked toward my cell, but out of the corner of my eye, I could see several inmates standing at their bars looking out curiously. I had learned from day one inside of the Reformatory not to look into another inmate's cell. It was an old code of respect. Since we were already being deprived of so much by the system, we didn't want to deny each other the last semblance of privacy, so we didn't look into each other's cell. Not everyone stayed true to this code, and it was often the cause of conflict, leading the Peeping Tom to be stabbed on the yard, or flashed with genitalia. I had no desire to see another man shaking his private parts in anger, nor did I have a desire to stab anyone or get stabbed for looking in someone's cell, so I always kept my head forward.

When I reached my cell, the bars squeaked open and the officer ordered me to step inside. Once the bars closed shut, he removed the handcuffs and left. I looked around at the dingy cell in disgust. The bed was six inches off of the floor and the toilet was stuffed behind a small footlocker. In order to sit down and take a dump, I had to remove my whole jumpsuit so that I could fold my legs behind the locker.

After my initial observations, I stood at my cell bars for the next hour waiting on the officer to make his rounds so that I could get some cleaning supplies to sanitize my cell. To my surprise, it was relatively quiet, but as I would soon learn, this was the calm before the storm. Most of the inmates in the hole slept the bulk of their days away, only waking up to get their food trays. Once the final meal of the day was passed out, the cellblock would come alive with activity.

When the officer returned, I asked him for some cleaning supplies and was informed that the porters would pass them out after lunch, so I continued to stand at the bars until lunch. There was no way I was going to sit or lay down on a mattress that someone else had sweated and farted on without it being sanitized. When the porters arrived with our food trays, I took mine and stood at the bars eating the hastily thrown together meal. The portions were nearly a half-size smaller than what I was used to receiving in general population, but I devoured the small meal in all of five minutes like a ravenous wolf, then placed my tray on the bars. I didn't really like drinking milk all that much, so I left the carton sitting on the locker. When they came around to pick up trays, one of the porters whispered that I had better hide the milk in my locker unless I wanted to be placed on food loaf. I placed the milk back on the tray as I looked at him curiously. I had never heard of food loaf, but from the way he conveyed the message, I could tell it was something very bad. His "man, you crazy" look was also letting me know that it in the hole, no food was to be wasted. That milk I threw back on the tray could have bought me a bag of cereal, a juice, or an extra piece of toast. In the hole, everything pertaining to eating and smoking was to be bartered and nothing was to be wasted. Once they banned smoking, a cigarette smuggled in could net you three dollars in store items.

It was in the hole that I learned to start eating Brussel sprouts and dressing and a few other things I would have never eaten had I been in general population. Every time I ate green beans or Brussel sprouts, I thought about all of the times that my parents tried to get me to eat them when I was a child, and I hung my head in shame.

After the trays were picked up, a porter came back and handed me some cleaning supplies. I swept beneath the small bunk and was surprised at how much dirt and dust came from under the bed. I washed the mattress, toilet and sink down, then made up my bed. After I cleaned up and laid back on the bunk, I drifted off into a fitful sleep.

My mind was full of thoughts that I had stuffed deep down inside where they were safe. All of the issues that I had run from while I was in general population – either by watching television or playing basketball to exhaustion – now came rushing back to the forefront of my mind. I dreamt of how soft Brenda's lips used to feel against mine. I dreamt of how good it used to feel to guzzle down an ice cold 40 ounce on a hot summer day. I dreamt of the late night laughter that echoed through the 'hood as we sat on the porch at two o'clock in the morning playing the dozens. My dreams were a kaleidoscope of all that my life had been, and all that it could have been.

I was awakened by the sound of the chow cart squeaking down the tier. I retrieved my tray and sucked down the bland slop that they called dinner, and this time, I drank the milk. Despite my aversion to plain milk, it sure beat the brownish water that drizzled out of the old porcelain sink in my cell. I sat the tray on the bars, laid back on my bunk, and forced myself back to sleep in an attempt to retrieve those lost and stolen dreams, but to no avail. After the officers picked up the food trays, they passed out mail and the cellblock was pretty quiet for the next few hours. The hum of a few conversations could be heard as inmates discussed religion, politics, and stories of their lives on the streets. Stories shared between inmates were our way of staying connected to the neighborhoods we came from. It was one of the few means we had to touch, taste and smell our former lives, if only for a few minutes. It didn't matter if you were a part of the conversation or not, you could relate, because when it was all said and done, most Black communities were pretty much the same. So when I sat back on my bunk listening to a guy from Flint, Saginaw or Lansing talking about their neighborhoods and what they had been through, it was like reliving my own memories of life before prison.

One of the things about prison is that you have some very amusing storytellers with expansive imaginations who are capable of creating the kind of vivid imagery that would put Hollywood screenwriters to shame. I have always marveled at how a person could remember the exact color of their socks, how much money they had in their pocket to the nearest dime, and all of the ingredients used to make the meal they had on the day they got shot, had sex for the first time, or made their first thousand. When retelling a story, everyone has a tendency to embellish things a little, but in the hole there were a few inmates who were infamous for their ability to tell a lie-filled story that was so entertaining, each night everyone would grow quiet as they recounted their neighborhood exploits.

As the voices hummed about from cell to cell, I found myself thinking about how I had arrived at this point in my life. Growing up, I never imagined that I would be living my life out caged in a cell like a wild animal. "I am too smart for this shit," I thought angrily as I stared up at the paint-chipped ceiling. No matter how many times I closed and opened my eyes, however, my nightmarish existence was still there.

After speaking with several inmates at length, I realized that most of us go through this extreme feeling of disbelief. At some point, we all think this is a nightmare, and at any moment, we will awaken and be back home in the warm comfort of our own bed; however, after years of incarceration, we all learn that prison is all too real. And for me, things were about to get more real than I could have ever imagined.

After getting bored listening to the monotonous conversations going on around me, I decided to get up and write a few letters. The first, I wrote to Brenda, and then to my ex-girlfriend Nycci. Before I knew it, I was writing everyone I knew. The hours spun past quickly as I scratched out letter after letter with a dull two-inch pencil.

When the third shift came on at ten o'clock, I was still immersed in writing letters. It was through writing letters home that I realized writing was my escape. With a pen and piece of paper, I could get away whenever I wanted to. I could stand on the corner in my neighborhood and no one could stop me. I could drive down the freeway to go see my ex-girlfriend in Ohio if that's what I wanted to do, and the bars and wired fences couldn't hold me back. Writing was freedom. So I wrote until midnight when they cut off the power and my fingers became sore to the bone.

When the lights went out, the cellblock had an eerie feel to it. I was on the bottom tier toward the end and there were no lights in the hall near my cell, so I couldn't stand at the bars and read or write like guys who had lights in front of their cell. I climbed into my bunk and prayed that I could drift off into a deep sleep before the dreams of my life before prison came back to haunt me. I had to get away from them; otherwise I knew that I would go insane. There was nothing I could do to change my reality, and I didn't need to be constantly reminded by my dreams.

As I lay there trying to capture sleep, the world around me exploded into chaos. "Get y'all bitch ass up. Ain't no sleep around here," a loud voice called, followed by a sound as loud and startling as a shotgun blast in a small church. Boom! Boom! Boom! The sound came relentlessly as the voice banged the lid down on his footlocker over and over, which set into motion a chain of events unlike anything I had ever imagined.

For the next four hours, the hole became an anarchist stronghold as inmates banged lockers and hurled racial epithets and disparaging homosexual remarks through the air like hand grenades. Some stuffed their toilets with sheets and flushed until water cascaded over the tier like Victoria Falls. I stared out of my cell in disbelief as the floor quickly became a small wading pool. Trash and sheets that had been set on fire flew out of countless cells. After their initial attempts to restore order by turning off the water supply to all of the cells, the officers threw in the towel. As dawn slowly crept upon us, everyone settled down and the cellblock grew quiet again.

The only thing that seemed to be stirring was a giant rat the size of a possum, which the inmates had named "Food Loaf," after the loaf of bread-sized brick of mashed up food that was fed to recalcitrant inmates. I watched as Food Loaf sludged through the murky water to retrieve the soggy bread and rotted apple cores that had been thrown out onto the cellblock floors. He moved with a quiet confidence about him that came as a result of being around hundreds of people every day. The rest of the vermin that darted in and out of the cells were more cautious.

I often wondered why no one had killed Food Loaf, but then it dawned on me. In a lot of ways, he was a lot like us. He was an outcast, and for the most part, everyone despised him, and we could all identify with that. Though the term "rat" had been used over the years to describe someone who told on others to protect their own ass, Food Loaf had won over our respect and was therefore allowed to coexist with us. His mousy cousins weren't as fortunate, however. Every opportunity we had, we killed them because they were invasive of our territory. It's hard to get along with vermin when they get in your bed at night or nibble on the food you had stored away to get through another day.

My days in the Graves were pretty much the same, night in and night out. After a few days, I too learned how to sleep through the mornings and afternoons. After nearly six of months of transferring back and forth between Wayne County Jail and the Graves, I was transferred to Standish Maximum Security Facility where a whole new level of hell awaited me.

Chapter 13

From the moment my sister Tamica moved on Blackstone in the heart of Brightmoor, I fell in love with the neighborhood that sat at the farthest end of Detroit's west side. Initially, I had gone over there to hang out with Tamica and her husband, but it wasn't long before I started connecting with guys in the neighborhood. I knew most of her neighbors from when I used to visit, but one day I noticed that a new family had moved across the street. I established an immediate bond with Mack, who was one of three Cooper brothers. We were both into music, fighting pit bulls, and drinking everyday. He introduced me to his older brother Coop, his mother Ms. Cooper, his twin sisters Karen and Sharon, and younger brother Boe.

Once I started hanging out down there on a regular basis, I also reconnected with what turned out to be my best friend in Brightmoor, Mark Bosley. He introduced me to the rest of his family, including his brothers Jimmy, Sean, Andre, and Michael, his sister Kenyatta, and their mother Mrs. Bosley. They all started hanging out at Tamica's house and we developed a strong bond between all of our families.

Everybody was hustling rocks on the corner of Blackstone, and the street stayed abuzz with drug activity. Even though Boe was the younger brother, he was the major supplier for his brothers. Initially, I just hung out and watched them make money, but after awhile, I started getting dope from my old neighborhood and selling my own rocks on the block with everyone else.

The summer was heating up and I could sense that Boe wasn't feeling me selling dope on the block where he had established things, but I continued to sell rocks on my own for a while. The way I saw it, there was enough money for all of us because we had some of the most loyal customers and one of the hottest blocks in the D when it came to selling crack. On any given day, you would see dozens of customers lined up on our block, and we didn't hesitate to serve them up. Within a year and a half, we had built a solid family-like vibe with everyone on our block. No matter what someone needed, we knew someone in the crew would take care of it.

Our neighbors who weren't involved in the trade embraced us like family because we were always there to bail them out financially. If they had more bills than money, they knew that they could borrow from us until their payday. We also took care of the children on the block, buying them ice cream daily and saving their family a few dollars a week, which meant a lot to families who were barely getting by.

We had a very distorted approach to life. On one hand, we were being neighborly and taking care of the people who lived on our street, but on the other hand, we were destroying our community. When we got into shootouts, we didn't think about the possibility of a stray bullet hitting someone that we loved or the reality that we were making the children hostages in their homes when a beef was on.

We also didn't think about the bandits and thugs that we brought around our loved ones, or the fact that we were taking food out of the mouths of the kids who looked up to us. This sickness was so deeply entrenched in our young hearts and minds that we never gave thought to the fact that someone, at any given moment, could run up in either of the houses we hung out at and start shooting. For a while, none of these things mattered to us; we were all about making money, having fun, and chasing the street dream. It wouldn't be long before our dreams turned into nightmares for all of us. Within a few months, we were hit with tragedy after tragedy, and our families were forced to deal with the fallout.

Not long after we met, Boe was shot and his sister's boyfriend murdered his best friend over an argument about money that Boe was owed. It was a sobering moment for the Cooper family and it was only through the Creator's grace that Boe didn't die that day. During that time, Boe and I weren't close, so I just played the background and offered my support to his brothers. I let them know that if he needed me to retaliate, I was available. My loyalty to the Cooper brothers was extended to Boe even though we weren't cool at the time.

After the shooting, Boe started hanging over on the block more often and we began developing a lukewarm relationship. In the meantime, my bond with Mark had grown to the point where we were like brothers and nearly inseparable. If I was walking down the street, you could trust that Mark wasn't far behind, and it was the same with Mark. Wherever you saw one of us, you knew the other wasn't far behind. In reality, that was the first time I felt like I had a brother who I could relate to like family. My biological brothers were older, and they weren't into the things I was into, so Mark filled that void.

One night, we were at Tamica's house kicking it about how we would get rich selling dope or rapping. The conversation was going good and the drinks were flowing. It was a nice spring night and everyone was enjoying themselves. Unfortunately, it wasn't long before an argument broke out between Mark and his younger brother Jimmy, who was also my close friend. Tamica told them to take it outside, so everyone started going outside. I grabbed a jacket and rushed out of the door in an effort to break up the fight. I didn't realize it at the time, but I had stashed some crack in the jacket over the winter.

While we were standing outside trying to convince Mark and Jimmy not to fight, the police had crept around the corner with their lights off. By the time we realized that they were on the block, it was too late. They whipped up on us and hit the spotlight. Jimmy was still going haywire. The police jumped out and told all of us to get up against the car. Another one of our homeboys named Orlando tried to toss a sack of rocks beneath the car, but it ricocheted off of the tire and bounced right in front of a female officer. Her partner then began searching all of us aggressively.

When the officer reached me, I was as cool as a cucumber because I knew I had sold out of the rocks I had earlier that day. He turned my pants pockets inside out like rabbit ears, searched my boxers, and then patted my jacket down. When he hit my left side, I felt something brush up against my side. The blood nearly drained from my face when he reached inside of my pocket and pulled out a bag of crumbled rocks. Before I could even begin to explain, he had the cuffs on me and was stuffing me in the back of the squad car.

Orlando and I were taken to the 8th Precinct where we stayed overnight. The following morning we were taken to the Wayne County

Youth Home on 1333 E. Forest. When we arrived, Orlando's family was there to post bond and take him home. I knew that my parents weren't coming to get me, however. My father had told me from day one that he would come see me, but he would never bail me out if I got locked up, so I had no expectation of getting out. When we approached the desk, we went through the preliminaries and the woman doing intake asked if I had any injuries. I told her that my hand was swollen from a fight that I had had a few days before. When she looked at my hand, she told the officers that she couldn't admit me without me getting medical treatment. So the officers transferred me to Receiving Hospital where they put me in a holding cell until the doctor was ready to see me.

When the doctor finally arrived, the officers brought me out of the holding cell, handcuffed me, and then shackled me to a gurney. I remained like that until my mother came and got me. They released me into her custody after they determined I needed surgery on my hand. As soon as she got me out, I was right back on the block; being chained to a bed wasn't enough to deter me from the path of destruction I was on.

A couple weeks later, I went to court on the drug charge and the judge sent you to the youth home while I awaited my trial. I was crushed when I realized I would be locked up for the entire summer.

When I first entered the youth home, I was shocked when they told me to strip so that they could spray me down with disinfectant. I felt like a dog getting hosed down in the backyard. I was then sent to 4C, which was a unit for violent offenders. I was one of the older guys on the unit, not only in age, but also in maturity. Everyday there was either a fight on our unit or between our unit and the other units.

After a few weeks in the youth home, I was sent back to court. I had just turned seventeen so the judge gave me two options – go to a juvenile detention center or enter Job Corps. I had had enough of lock up, so I told her that I would go to Job Corps. She told me that I had to report to Job Corps within two weeks or she would issue a warrant and have me rearrested and charged. She was willing to give me a second chance, even when I wasn't willing to give myself a second chance.

Two weeks later, I enrolled in Job Corps. I just knew that I would still be able to hang out in the 'hood because there was a Job Corps on

Jefferson on the city's east side. When I got ready to enroll, the staff told me that the judge's instructions indicated that I could go to any Job Corps in the country, except for the one in Detroit. I nearly broke down in tears when they told me that the only one with an immediate opening was located in Prestonburg, Kentucky, and it was one of the only all-male programs. I wanted to run out of the door and head back to the 'hood right then, but when I looked up at my father, I knew that I had to do the responsible thing and go.

My father was always by my side no matter what trouble I got myself into and came to see me at the youth home every chance he got. I had promised him that I would get my life together, and this was my first chance to show and prove. I filled out the necessary paperwork and was told that I would be leaving in two days. I went back to the 'hood and got drunk with my crew for the last time, then went and chilled with my girlfriend Shelly. My father, stepmother and Shelly took me to the Greyhound bus station where we cried and hugged until it was time for me to board the bus. I looked down at my paperwork like where the fuck is Prestonburg. As I sat in my seat looking out at my family, I reasoned with myself that I was taking a step toward a brighter future. What I didn't realize was that I was about to take a trip back into the past – the deep, dark, racist past of America.

Chapter 14

It was a relatively warm and sunny fall day when I was transferred to Standish Maximum Security Prison. I was a year into my prison sentence and a few months past my twentieth birthday. Instead of entering my sophomore year in college, I was shipped to a prison designed to house the worst of the worst. Upon my arrival at the newly designed facility, I was brought into the control center where several officers stood around glaring at me. I maintained a stoic expression as they talked their tough correctional officer talk. I was no longer new to the psychological warfare that the officers waged against the inmates. This was a protracted war of attrition that had been going on since the first prison was built over a century ago. As I glanced around at all of the technology, an officer began removing the black box that was wrapped around my handcuffs to prevent an escape.

Once he removed the black box, another officer approached with a pair of handcuffs that were attached to what looked like a dog leash. This was the first time I had seen anything like it, and my immediate thought was that it had to be in violation of the Universal Declaration of Human Rights. But I guess in the prisoncrat's mind, being leashed like a dog didn't violate Article 5 of the Universal Declaration of Human Rights, which states, "No one shall be subjected to torture or to cruel, inhuman or degrading treatment or punishment."

Despite what prison officials thought, I definitely felt degraded. I mean, how could I not feel degraded when I was being treated like a common house pet? One officer placed the handcuffs on me as the other officer removed the first pair. They did this in a synchronized way to minimize the time in which either of my hands was free from the other. After removing one pair of shackles and replacing them with another, the officers chatted with each other before the transfer officers left. I was then taken to the hole in cellblock one. I shuffled along in the shackles as two officers held on tightly to the leash that was attached to my handcuffs until I reached the unit. All was relatively quiet when I first stepped into the cellblock. The design of the prison was totally different from the Reformatory, which was over one hundred years old. Inside the unit, there were four wings – two upper wings and two lower wings. I was taken to the lower wing on one side of the unit.

The first thing I noticed was that the hallways were free of debris, and instead of bars, there were large steel doors with window covers on them. Once I reached what would be my cell, the officer in the control bubble hit a button, the cell door slid open, and I was ordered to step inside. Once inside, the door slid shut behind me with a finality that still resonates inside of me to this day. As the officer removed the handcuffs and shackles and prepared to leave, I asked him if my window shutter could remain open and he said no, then banged it shut.

For the first time in my short incarceration, I felt alone as I looked around the Spartan-like cell. A flat green mattress lay folded on top of a thick slab of concrete that protruded from the side wall. Another shorter slab of concrete protruded from the back wall over the concrete bed, and I soon discovered this was the writing surface, or television stand for those who had a TV. A steel toilet/sink combination sat in the corner up by the door and a large steel locker was bolted to the floor adjacent to the concrete bed. I rolled the mattress out, placed the sheets and blankets on it, and then sat back. A few minutes later, a piece of thick paper attached to a string came sliding beneath my door. I didn't know what it was so I just sat on my bunk staring down at it until someone called out my cell number and told me to pull on the line. I didn't know what was going on, so I came to the door and asked who it was. I was informed that it was my neighbor across the hall.

I climbed down on the floor, peeked under the door, and saw that the string was coming from his cell. As I began pulling, I noticed a few magazines slide from beneath his door. I pulled them in and took them off of the line. Inside was a short note introducing himself. He let me know that if I needed something else to read, I could just holler over at him. His name was Lowrider, and he turned out to be a cool older guy. He was quiet and laid back, but wasn't to be played with. After a couple of days, I learned that he was in the hole for slicing another inmate's face up with a razor blade. The other inmate owed him some money and refused to pay up when it was time, so Lowrider responded according to the laws of the environment. This was proof that even the most mild-mannered human can be pushed into graphic violence in order to survive the rigors of prison life. Despite this heinous act of violence, Lowrider was a cool dude. He understood the old convict code that said when someone first arrives, you do what you can to make their time a little bit easier, and that was something I could relate to.

Within a couple of days, I found out that some of the guys I had been at the Reformatory with were there, and they, along with Lowrider, filled me in on the runnings of the prison. It didn't take long for me to get into a nice routine. I had always loved to read, and Standish had a very nice library, so I started sending over there for books whenever I could. I discovered how creative Stephen King really was when I read his novels. It was also at Standish that I got hipped to Terry McMillan and read Roots for the first time along with a few other classics. Reading was my refuge, and I devoured everything I could get my hands on.

I was disappointed that I couldn't get as many books authored by Black writers as I would have liked, but it didn't deter me from sending requests to the library every week. Whenever it was time for them to drop off our library books, I got excited like a kid waiting on Santa Claus to come sliding down the chimney.

In addition to books from the library, I also read every magazine that someone was willing to slide under my door. I quickly learned to make a fish line like the one that Lowrider had slid beneath my door, and I used it to drive up and down the wing to retrieve whatever reading materials people had for me.

My stay on that wing was short as I was going back and forth to the county jail on a writ regarding the case for which I was serving time in the hole. When I returned a few months later, they moved me to a different wing, and it was then that I was introduced to a form of madness that would characterize the rest of my stay in the hole at Standish Maximum.

When I first got arrested in 1991, my father and stepmother were working at Lafayette Clinic, which was a psychiatric hospital close to downtown Detroit. While I was in the county jail, my father was on the local news speaking out against the budget cuts, which caused the State to close a lot of its mental institutions. This trend continued throughout the nineties, and it wasn't until a few years into my incarceration that I was able to make the connection between what I witnessed in prison, generally speaking, and what I witnessed in the hole. Instead of keeping the psychiatric hospitals open throughout the state, they closed them down and herded all of the patients into various state prisons, with most landing in maximum security. Because most of the patients with psychiatric needs are hard to manage in general population, they end up being housed in the hole, where the hostile environment exacerbates their psychiatric problems. In addition to the hostile treatment that they receive from the officers, those with mental health issues also have to face hostility from other inmates who don't understand psychiatric disorders like schizophrenia, bi-polar disorder and the like.

When I returned to Standish from the county jail, I didn't understand what was going on, like many of the inmates. My first day back on the cellblock, they moved an inmate named Reed across the hall from me. As they were putting him in the cell, he and the officers had a heated exchange. I jumped down on my floor and peeked beneath the door to see what was going on as they forced him into his cell. Once inside, I heard them giving him an order to turn around so that they could remove the mask from his face. I stood back up, listening and peeking out of the crack of my door, trying to hear what the officers were talking about as they left. I noticed them carrying a black mesh mask that looked like something out of a fetish magazine. I would later learn that they placed these masks on inmates who were considered spitters or biters.

When lunchtime came, the officers returned to Reed's cell and asked him if he wanted his food loaf. He swiftly told them to get the hell away from his door because he'd rather starve to death than eat food loaf. As I sat there listening, I looked down at the small rations on my tray, and despite how hungry I was, I knew that I couldn't eat my rations without offering to share them with the brother. I liked the fact that he wasn't willing to bow down and accept inferior treatment.

I slid my "car" over to Reed with a small note attached asking him if he wanted half of my food. He wrote back, indicating that yes, he wanted some of my food. I took half of my food and placed it in a few envelopes, attached it to the line, and slid it across to him. He pulled it in quickly to avoid being detected by the officers. For the next two weeks, I shared every meal with Reed until he finally got off of food loaf. I was happy to see him get off of meal restriction because that meant I could go back to my full rations, and he could go back to his.

When they passed out trays, and Reed got his, he called me to the door. Sometimes on first shift, when one of the cool officers was working, they would leave our window shutters open until they picked up trays, or until they got ready to change shifts, so I stepped up to the window. This was the first time they had left Reed's window open, so I had a chance to see him face-to-face for the first time. He was a tall, corpulent brother with a full beard that made him look like a brown-skinned version of the Ayatollah Khomeini.

"What's going on, Reed?" I asked as I approached the door.

"You know what?" he began.

"Naw, what?" I asked.

"Man, you a bitch ass dick sucker. Now get your hoe ass on your bunk and lay down," he said as he broke up into a maniacal laughter.

I stood there with my mouth agape for a few minutes as my temper burnt red-hot. That was the first time I had been blatantly disrespected since I entering prison, and I was completely thrown off. Add to this the fact that I had shared half of my meal with this man for two weeks, not only starving myself, but also risking being placed on food loaf along with him. Of course, I was pissed, and I knew the first chance I got once I was released from the hole, I was going to stab Reed in his neck. I had to, otherwise the rest of the inmates would feel like they could get away with disrespecting me, and I would rather die than live without my dignity and respect. Reed continued to hurl insult after insult at me as I sat on my bunk steaming.

I even had to go back and ask myself if I had done something unintentionally to make him feel slighted in any way, but I decided that wasn't the case. Maybe he was just taking my kindness for something other than what it was; whatever the case, I had made up my mind that I was going to take care of Reed on the first chance I got.

The hardest part was not knowing when I would get my shot at him. I was serving an indeterminate stint in the hole and knew that I would have to be approved by the Director of Prisons due to the assault on the staff charge. I was well into my routine of reading and exercising when the counselor finally came to tell me that she was recommending me for release. I knew it was going to take awhile before she had an answer, but I started preparing myself for my return to general population. I was also mentally preparing for a return trip to the hole because I was ready to go to war with Reed.

A few weeks later, I was released from the hole, and I patiently waited for the day that Reed would be released, but it never came. As I would learn over the years, there were some inmates who did their entire sentence in the hole to prevent anyone from getting to them. Any time they were scheduled for release, they would catch another misconduct so that the Security Classification Committee would have to keep them in administrative segregation longer. Once I realized that Reed would never get out of the hole, I refocused my attention on doing my time in general population.

When I finally hit the yard again, it had been nearly a year since I had been in general population. It felt weird walking from the segregation unit to the regular housing unit. My steps felt unsure and it took a minute for me to adjust to walking without having shackles and handcuffs on. Before I reached housing unit 3, one of the other units was released for chow. I walked slowly, trying to find a familiar face in the crowd, but there were none to be found. Most of the inmates were in their thirties and forties, which made me feel out of place. Their faces were creased with the bitter, jagged lines of stress that came as a result of doing life in prison.

The closer I got to the unit, the deeper the impact their faces had on my psyche. Their faces carried the look of broken dreams, life disappointments, anger, and hopelessness. It was like looking in the mirror of my future. When I reached the unit, I shook off the thoughts of my broken future and focused on the moment.

I was assigned a cell and informed that our unit had already been to chow and yard, so I wouldn't be able to leave my cell again until the following morning for breakfast. I went into the cell, cleaned it, and made up the bed before sitting down. I didn't own a radio, tape player or television like the other inmates around me, so I pulled out the Bible and began reading it. When I tired of the Bible, I picked up the Quran and read a few surahs. I then said a prayer and sat back on my bunk listening to the chatter around me. A few inmates stood at their doors talking to each other about what was on television, and I started feeling sad. I felt left out and alone because I didn't have my own television to help me escape the boredom. Up to that point in my bit, I hadn't received much financial support from my family or friends, and it hurt. Televisions were about $89.00, and the thought that I didn't have a quarter in my account nearly caused me to break down.

I began cursing everyone who said they loved me. In my fragile mind, I felt like it was me against the world. My anger began to boil and rage, which inspired me to start doing push-ups as a way to release some of the pain and frustration. I don't know how many push-ups I did for the first set; all I know is that I refused to get up until my muscles were burning and so tight that I thought they would pop. It was as though I was forcing the mental and emotional pain out of my body through each set. When I had exhausted my muscles and cleared my mind, I washed up and then laid back down to read until I fell into a restless sleep.

I was awakened the next morning by the sound of an officer calling out, "Five minutes before chow lines," on the PA. I hopped up, brushed my teeth, and washed my face, then waited for the doors to break for chow. I wasn't a big breakfast eater, but I needed to get out and see who was around me, and more importantly, if there was anybody there that I knew.

I waited until the last minute to exit my cell. I wanted to be at the end of the line so that I could observe everything around me. I finally walked out of the cell, trailing a few paces behind the crowd of men. There were a few guys getting dressed hastily in the hallway so that they could make it to chow on time. It was funny seeing them wipe the crust out of their eyes. It was clear that they hadn't brushed their teeth or washed their face. We called that pulling a John Wayne, who often hopped on his horse, like a lot of cowboys did back in the day, without washing his face or brushing his teeth.

When I reached the chow hall, I saw someone I knew back when I lived in Highland Park. His name was Day Day, and he was legendary in HP. He was seated a few tables away, so I didn't speak until later in the day when we were on the yard. When he realized that I had just been released from the hole, he sent some commissary over to me and told me if I needed anything to let him know. I couldn't wait to sink my teeth into the candy bars and chips he had sent over.

Day Day also gave me the lay of the land. He told me that there were a few Melanic brothers in the unit, and when we hit the big yard the following day, he would introduce me to them. They were cool brothers, but they were older, and we really didn't have much in common outside of us being in the same organization.

For the most part, the unit we were in was laid back, and for the first couple of weeks, I kept to myself most of the time. I developed a routine quickly, which included working out and reading to pass the time. I did push-ups in my cell every morning before I took my shower, and then sometimes throughout the day to burn off the anger. The rest of the day I spent reading until the wee hours of the morning. When they turned the lights out, I stood by my door reading, using the little bit of light that crept through the window.

After a couple of weeks, I started hooping with Day Day and a few other guys in the unit. Then, one day, Day Day asked me to join the unit basketball team. The games were always competitive and tempers ran red-hot. Players argued with the refs, the coaches, and even other players. There was a lot of bad sportsmanship displayed because winning meant everything to us. We had been told we were losers our entire lives, and none of us wanted to have that confirmed in anything that we did. What we didn't realize is that our poor sportsmanship, which led to constant conflicts, stabbings, and even murder, was a reflection of the poor attitudes about life we had adopted. We took losing personal, as if losing defined who we were. In reality, these were meaningless basketball games designed to keep us distracted from our reality. The basketball courts always remained full while the law library and regular library were always empty. This was one of the many contradictions that existed in prison.

Like the rest of the brothers, I found myself on the basketball court constantly and in the middle of several conflicts. The first conflict came when KO, one of my Melanic brothers, cursed out a brother name Rimmer-Bey, who was officiating the game. He was a well-respected member of the Moorish Science Temple of America, also known as the Moabites. KO refused to back down and the gym became very tense. One of Rimmer-Bey's cronies came over and acted like he was going to ride out, so I stepped up, ready to jump in the fray. We were firm believers that you came to the aid and assistance of a worthy brother, so I wasn't about to back down. Later, I learned that guy who came to Rimmer-Bey's defense was a known hit man back in Jackson. A few of the guys marveled at how I stood up to him, adding to my credibility on the yard.

The next time we broke for yard, the tension was very thick between the Moabites and the Melanics, and I was ready to go to battle. We came out with shanks and were sure they had done the same. Fortunately, cooler heads prevailed and our respective security personnel brought the potential war to a head before anyone was stabbed or seriously hurt.

When the basketball season concluded, I vowed not to participate in the next season because I realized that KO was a hothead serving a life sentence, so conflicts were inevitable. Like many of the brothers in the joint, the court was the place where he took out all of his frustration. I had just gotten out of solitary confinement and wasn't trying to go back over a basketball game.

After a month or so, I was transferred to another unit. I was pissed because it was nice being around someone I knew from the streets. However, one of the realities of the joint was that we couldn't always dictate where we ended up.

When I got to the new unit, I went straight to the counselor to get classified for a job since I had my GED already. When she called me into the office, I just knew I was about to get a job in the kitchen. I wanted to work in the kitchen so that I could eat extra meals and start saving up money to get my own TV and radio. I was tired of being one of the only guys on the tier without my own appliances. I didn't want to bug my father about sending me money because I knew he had to take care of my younger sisters and son. I also felt like I had made my bed, and I had to lie in it. Some days, I dreamed about someone thinking enough about me to send me something out of the clear blue sky, even if it was just ten dollars and a few lines to say "I'm thinking about you." But it never happened.

The counselor told me that she couldn't classify me for a job yet because they considered me a security threat. According to their policy, I had to be in the unit for at least 90 days. I asked her how I could be considered any more of a threat than any of the other men at the prison, and she told me that I had gotten a lot of misconducts in a relatively short amount of time.

I slunk back to my cell heartbroken. I wanted to work more than anything so that I could make a few dollars and get out of my cell regularly. As much as I loved to read, being locked in my cell for twenty-three hours was taking its toll on me. I did everything I could to get out as much as I could, but I was very limited. I went to the library twice a week, Melanic service once a week, and attended yard when it was our hour to be out.

I was fortunate to be around a few cool guys, some who were close to my age. They knew that I didn't have a television so they would sneak me their radios and tape players whenever they could. I also had a few solid brothers in the unit who liked to read, and they sent me as many books as my mind could handle. They fed me books by J.A Rogers, Ivan Van Sertima, Marcus Garvey, and Dr. Chancellor Williams. With each book that they fed me, I felt a part of my soul growing and opening up to commune with my ancestors. I immersed myself in African history and imagined what it was like in ancient Kemet (KMT), which had been renamed Egypt by the Greeks. I thought about the powerful pyramids, which have stood the test of time, and wondered how they had been engineered. I thought about Timbuktu and the vast knowledge they created that was the envy of the world. In the short time I was at

Standish, I learned more about African history than I had ever learned during all of my years in school. As each day passed, I felt myself growing wiser and stronger.

One day I hit the yard, and there was a lot of buzz amongst the brothers. They were excited because a brother named Baruti was being moved into our unit. Baruti was a brother who was held in high-esteem by the other brothers because of his personal self-discipline and integrity. I didn't know much about the brother other than what I had heard about him catching a case in Jackson. They said he had been convicted of open murder for the death of another inmate. From what the brothers told me, Baruti had been charged based on some flimsy evidence and the weak testimony of another inmate. I took this information with a grain of salt because I had learned enough over the years to know that information passed around the cellblock wasn't reliable.

When I finally met Baruti, I was impressed with his calm, quiet demeanor. He wasn't boastful about his jail exploits as were some of the other guys from Jackson who felt like they always had something to prove. Instead, he was a wise teacher who taught mostly through his actions. Every morning when we hit the yard, he exercised, and then ran vigorously, outpacing and outdistancing everyone on the yard. On the days we held study group, he always gave me encouraging words. He told me never to take anything at face value and be diligent in my research. When I made valid points when building with the brothers, he would give me a nod of encouragement to continue.

After a few weeks, he took a liking to me like an uncle or older brother. We worked out together at the pull-up bars along with a brother named Tim Greer-Bey. When I first started doing pull-ups, they laughed because I could only do one or two despite the fact that I had an athletic build and could do push-ups all day. Even though they laughed, they told me to never give up, and within a couple of weeks, I went from doing one and two reps a set to doing ten to fifteen. By the time I was paroled, I was one of the best who ever touched the pull-up bars.

I continued to build with my elders and absorb as much wisdom as I could. It is because of their wise counsel that I was able to leave prison with a sense of purpose. I didn't always listen to them in the

169

moment, but over the years, I found all that they shared with me to be of great value.

I recall one day coming out to the yard and a few of the brothers informed me that we were having a security meeting. It turned out that an inmate in another cellblock had gotten into an altercation with one of our Melanic brothers and had kicked his store goods all over the yard. We were incensed because none of the other brothers had stepped up to do anything. The way prison worked, an attack against one of us, was an attack against all of us. The incident wasn't something that we could overlook as an isolated occurrence because it would reflect poorly on us as an organization, but moreso as men who claimed to be brothers.

During our security meeting, we were briefed on what occurred and who was responsible. It just so happened that the inmate who was responsible for the attack on our brother was working on the yard crew during our yard time. The tension in the air was so thick because everyone knew that we would retaliate. The hard part was trying to figure out when and how we would respond so that we went undetected by the officers and the security camera.

When it was time to decide who would go on the mission, it came down to me and another brother who was a few years older than me. The rest of the brothers backed out and came up with all kinds of excuses. When our head of security asked me if I wanted to help set the play up, I agreed without hesitation. I was tired of hearing the excuses and was tired of the other organizations looking at us, waiting to see if we would do anything about the incident. When I agreed to help retaliate, the other brother said he would ride with me on the play. We strategized with the rest of our security staff to set the play in motion the following day during yard. We had to figure out a way to lure him to an area where we wouldn't be visible to the cameras, and then we had to get rid of the shank after we put our strategy in motion.

When we settled on how we would handle things, I went back to my regular routine of working out and talking to Tim and Baruti. I didn't discuss what was shared at our security meeting, but I suspected they knew what was going on. As a member of security, we were not allowed to discuss information that we shared in our meetings with anyone. We continued working out, and Baruti gave me some information that would take a few years for me to appreciate. He told me to never allow anyone to use me, including my comrades. At the time, I didn't fully understand why he shared such wisdom with me, but over the years, it all made sense. In me, he could see my loyalty to the cause and the brothers, but he also saw the naiveté that was common amongst young, impressionable brothers. We held a quixotic view of the movement and our loyalty was often misguided. We were always eager to prove our loyalty to our organization, and the older, wiser members often took advantage of this.

The following day, it was time to set the play in motion. I had nervous energy coursing through my body from the moment I woke up until it was time to put in work. It hadn't been that long since my release from the hole, and I had no desire to go back, but my sense of loyalty and desire to see our name defended overshadowed whatever thoughts I had of a return trip to the hole. When the yard opened up, I felt like all eyes were on us, even though most of the population didn't have a clue about what we were up to. In reality, I felt a combination of guilt and desire because I wanted everyone on the yard to know what were about to do so that our respect could be restored.

I could feel my hands sweating as I walked across the yard to meet at our regular meeting spot. When I approached, I greeted the brothers and they returned our unique greeting, which was one of the many things we shared that connected us and increased our bond. After a quick briefing, the brother who was responsible for bringing the shank out produced the crude, prison-made knife. The rusty piece of steel with a handle made of torn bedsheets looked menacing as he passed it to me. The other brother who agreed to ride with me produced a shank as well. We went over the plan again before leaving the meeting post.

We walked a few laps around the track, patiently waiting for our prey to reach the location where we knew the cameras wouldn't be able to see us. As many cameras and gun towers that the prisons had, there were always blind spots at every prison. These spots were known by every inmate and considered death traps. It didn't take long before our target began moving in the direction we desired. He was a yard crew worker and we knew it wouldn't be long before he'd be right where we wanted him. As he approached the camera's blind spot, we quickened our pace. Before he realized what was happening, it was too late. When the shank first pierced his skin, he hollered out, "What I do?" He was stabbed a few more times before he took off running across the yard. We slowly walked toward the far end of the track as the other security members came and retrieved the shanks. Once they had secured the weapons, we took off jogging on the track, blending in with the rest of the joggers. When we reached the pull-up bars, we watched as the officer's administered first aid until a few nurses came out and escorted him to health services. Within minutes, the siren sounded and they ordered everyone to go back to their units.

I just knew at any moment the officers would be coming to cuff me and take me to the hole, but they never came. The following day, the yard was abuzz over the stabbing, and our reputation was restored. This was the law of the jungle. Not responding would have left our members vulnerable to attacks by other inmates and put our stores, and other means by which we made money, at stake. This part of prison life was something that always brought me internal conflict. On one hand, I was learning about our history and culture and reading about how much we needed to love and care for our brothers; but on the other hand, whenever a brother did something that we felt violated our code of honor, we dealt with it by stabbing him or busting him in the head. It wouldn't be long before those contradictions challenged me to make some tough decisions about the Melanics and my role in the organization.

The rest of my stay at Standish was uneventful, and it wasn't long before it I was being transferred back to MR. It was especially hard saying goodbye to some of the older brothers because we never knew if we would see each other again. They had given me so much wisdom and encouraged me every step of the way to fill my mind with as much knowledge as I could. I will never forget how the older brothers in the library embraced me when they saw that I came consistently to check out books. It had gotten to the point where they had books already picked out for me when I showed up. Whenever a new title arrived by a Black author, they would hold it for me. When I read it, they wanted a review to see if it was worth them reading, but more importantly, to make sure that I was reading the books. I was going to miss my older comrades, but I was ready to get back around guys my age and decrease my security level.

When I went inside to speak with the counselor, he told me that it would be about two weeks before I'd be transferred. I wanted to get transferred to Ryan Correctional Facility, which was in Detroit, but the waiting list was long. He explained to me that it would be at least a year or so before I got transferred if I chose to go to Ryan. I didn't want to run the risk of getting caught up if I stayed any longer, so I told the counselor to send me somewhere that didn't have a waiting list. He told me that I could go back to the Reformatory if I wanted to, so I chose to return to Gladiator School. When I told the brothers about my choice, they thought I was crazy; however, looking back, I know it was divine order. There were things I needed to learn about life that I wouldn't have gotten anywhere else.

I told Baruti that I was getting transferred back to MR and his eyes lit up with excitement. He told me that his son was there and asked that I connect with him when I got there. Over the next couple of weeks, he reminded me of a few things he had shared with me, and then it was time for me to depart. Little did I know, Baruti and I would be forever connected even though it would be nearly 16 years before we saw each other again.

Chapter 15

"Man, it's a hundred niggas outside our door right now," one of our roommates cried out in a panicked voice. I looked over at Maceo and AD, who I had met earlier that day on the Greyhound bus headed to Job Corps. Out of the ten brothers who caught the bus down to Kentucky with us, Maceo and AD were the two that I related to the most. We connected immediately and made a pact to stick together and support each other while we were at Job Corps. It didn't take long for our pact to be put to the test.

Upon our arrival, we were orientated and assigned to a temporary room along with the rest of the guys that we traveled with. Once we got done with our orientation, we went to check out the surroundings. That's when we met a guy named June from Chicago. He told us that he did store runs for the guys in the unit and was available to do a beer run if we wanted him to. It had been a long day and we all wanted to catch a buzz before we went to bed, so we got our money together and gave June enough to get two cases of beer. When he returned, he told us that he had to drop one of the cases because the campus police was chasing him. When he gave us the other case of beer, we looked at each other to be sure we were all picking up on the nickel-slick bullshit that was seeping out of his pores. I hadn't long left the block dealing with desperate drug addicts who tried every trick in the game to get over. The fact that we had paid him and offered to drink with him increased my anger.

"Dig nigga, you have a few options, and I'm only going to tell you this once. You can either produce the other case of beer you trying to play on, produce the money, or get your ass beat," I said calmly as I approached him.

"Man, I'm telling you they knocked me," June said nervously.

In addition to trying to be slick, June was a coward, and that really pissed me off. I couldn't stand for someone to think they were about to get over on me, and I wasn't good at holding my feelings in.

Before he could continue explaining, I punched June in the face, causing him to stagger backwards as he grabbed his eye. He started hollering like a little girl and then took off running. Maceo and AD burst out laughing as we went back into our room. We didn't know the dynamics of local gang culture, city cliques or other affiliations that existed at the center, so we never anticipated him getting nearly half of the unit to help him retaliate.

When our roommate walked out and discovered a sea of guys standing outside of our door ready to go to war, we knew it was about to get real. Maceo and AD looked at me like let's go out and see what's up. When we opened the door, June was standing in the middle of a group of guys holding his face and talking all animated about what happened. A stocky guy from Chicago stepped up holding a lock in his hand and asked who hit June in the face. I stepped up and told him that I had hit him and was going to beat his ass until he paid my money. My reaction caused a few of the other guys to start talking shit like they wanted to do something. I stepped further into the hallway and told them to come on with it as Maceo and AD followed closely behind.

Though we were outnumbered, we stood our ground, which threw them off of their game. They hadn't anticipated we would be ready to fight although the odds were in their favor.

I had a philosophy about fighting. Once a person got in arm's reach of me, I was swinging first. As we inched out into the hallway, they backed up, and it was then that I knew most of them were bluffing. They had a lot to lose for fighting on campus, and we felt like we had nothing to lose because we didn't want to be there in the first place. Before the tension exploded into an all-out brawl, a guy named Tracey from New York stepped up and suggested we go one-on-one. He was older than most of us, and I later found out that he was the oldest brother on the campus. I could tell that they respected Tracey because they grew silent when he spoke.

"Y'all know June be trying to be slick every time somebody new arrive, and dude and them ain't buying it, so let that nigga go one-on-one if he ain't going to give up the money," Tracey said.

They turned and looked at June, and his facial expression made it clear that he didn't want to fight. His fellas looked at him like, "What are you going to do?" Before he could decide, I decided for him. I ran up on him and started swinging. He slipped the first punch, but wasn't swift enough to slip the next two. He fell, and as he tried to scramble to his feet, I kicked him in his ass and he took off running. Tracey started laughing, which caused the rest of the guys standing out in the hallway to laugh as well. It turned out that they didn't really care for June, but felt like they had to step up and confront us because we were new. When it was all said and done, they invited us outside to drink with them. What they didn't realize was that we had just initiated the first move of a hostile takeover, Detroit-style.

When we were done drinking, me, Maceo and AD went back to the room and clowned our scary ass roommate who was also from Detroit. We joked with him about how scared he sounded when he realized how many guys were out in the hallway waiting on us. He took it in stride and told us that he wasn't the fighting type. We had to respect him for being honest.

Once we were done joking, I laid on my bunk and replayed the day in my head. When the bus departed from Detroit, we had no idea what to expect in Kentucky. There were five of us leaving from Detroit, and at our first stopover in Cleveland, we picked up about twelve guys from Chicago and Milwaukee. Most of the trip, we sat in the back listening to rap by Detroit's Most Wanted, Esham, and Awesome Dre. We were missing home already and music by our local rappers offered us the kind of comfort we needed. Before we reached Kentucky, we connected with a couple of the guys from Milwaukee who were interested in our music. We kicked it and smoked weed together when we got off at the last rest stop.

When we finally reached Kentucky, it was early in the evening and a van from the Job Corps Center awaited us. The driver, who was also a counselor at the center, was a cool chubby brother who spoke with a country twang. He told us that he was going to take us to get something to eat before we got to the campus because the kitchen would be closed by the time we arrived. When we were all aboard, he took off speeding. It was cool until he started flying through the mountain range. I had a window seat, and every time he hit a curve, I wanted to close my eyes, but my mind wouldn't let me. It was by far the scariest fifteen-minute ride of my life, and from the looks on the other brothers' faces, it was theirs as well.

Our counselor pulled into the parking lot of a Wendy's and hopped out of the driver's seat. He came around and opened the door and before we could hop out, he started giving us a lecture about the race dynamics down there. He told us not to stare or gawk at the White women because their men would get mad. We all started laughing, but the serious expression on his face told us it was not a laughing matter. He continued to explain to us how we would be treated by White people while there. He said that they wouldn't speak to us or interact with us, and it was best for us to always travel in groups. As he talked, images of "Whites Only" signs danced through my head. I thought about the things I had learned in school about racial harmony and Martin Luther King Jr.'s dream. I also thought about how my parents had raised me to view all people as people. The neighborhood we grew up in was primarily White, so I believed my parents with all my heart. Unfortunately, they didn't warn me or inform me that bigotry still existed in some parts of the country.

When our counselor was done talking, we got out of the van and headed inside Wendy's. We all joked about his mini-lecture in our effort to lighten the mood. None of us really took it that serious, and most of us thought he was trying to scare us to keep us from running wild. But we were all in for a major shock once we entered the restaurant. The moment we stepped inside, the restaurant grew eerily quiet. Every White person inside, including the staff, stopped doing what they were doing and looked at us like we were crazy. We looked around at each other in confusion. The emotional weight of America's racial history came crashing through the building. I could see the look of dismay on the brothers' faces as we all struggled to figure out what that moment meant to us. I felt violated by their stares of disgust, and started to feel deep-seeded anger slowly bubble to the surface. I was pissed off by the sheer arrogance and audacity of people who looked like backwoods hillbillies to think of themselves as superior.

"Man, fuck these White motherfuckers," I said to the brother standing next to me.

"Yeah man, fuck them. We ain't got to eat in this bitch. You can take my Black ass home," another brother chimed in.

Our voices punched a hole in the silence as the White customers started grabbing their food and storming out of the restaurant. Our counselor urged us to quiet down, but it was too late, we became more boisterous. Before long, we were making a mockery of their ignorance and his fear. Like other Blacks from his generation, our counselor had grown up in an environment where Black people were forced to be silent on race matters. We were from the 'hood, however, and if you violated someone, you were getting your ass kicked no matter what color you were. Instead of storming out like we started to, we decided to stay and eat. In our small way, we were saying, "Our ancestors were forced to go through the back door, but we're barging our way through the front."

A few of the staff offered up fake smiles and weak apologies, but we weren't having it. We began mocking them, ordering our food with exaggerated, buffoonish language. "Issa like to order me sa burga sir," someone said as we laughed and enjoyed our food. It wasn't long before our counselor was laughing along with us, though it was a nervous laughter. Although he seemed cool, we had lost whatever respect we had for him. When we were done eating, he drove us through the mountains to the Job Corps Center.

The campus sat on spacious land surrounded by mountains and forests. When we pulled up, there were small groups of guys sprinkled across the parking lot and basketball court talking amongst themselves. I took in the scenery as I smoked a cigarette and waited on the rest of the guys to get their bags. When we all had our bags, we went inside the building and headed to a large room where they gave us the rundown on what rooms we would be sharing and what trades they offered. They told us the center's rules when it came to gambling, hanging out, and going AWOL, and then explained the misconduct system that they had in place, which restricted our privileges when we violated the rules. After explaining the rules, the staff went through our luggage to make sure we hadn't smuggled any weapons or drugs. A few of us had brought weed, but it appeared everyone had either smoked all of theirs or had it concealed in their underwear.

When we were done with orientation, we headed to our rooms. Once we resolved the issue with June running off with our case of beer, we settled into day-to-day life on the campus. Over the first few days, we checked out every trade they had available. I decided to try out carpentry because it was the only trade that piqued my interest. I felt like I could be creative as a carpenter moreso than a plumber or electrician.

Within a week, we were assigned to our permanent room. Maceo, AD, myself and a brother from Milwaukee named Mark moved down to dorm three into the same room, which was already occupied by a brother named Peanut from Detroit and a brother named Spook from Flint. We each had our own bunk and a wall locker to keep our belongings. Peanut and Spook gave us the rundown and told us that dorm three was considered the troublemakers' dorm. When we stepped into the hallway, we could tell the difference between dorm 3 and the one we had just left. Music was playing loud and guys were hanging out in the halls shooting dice and talking shit. It was right up our alley, and we made ourselves at home.

Within a few weeks, Maceo and I were running a black market store, selling everything from single cigarettes to liquor that we had smuggled in. It was our way of supplementing the nominal income that we earned from Job Corps and whatever we received from home. We took our illegally earned profits and bought clothing, alcohol for our own enjoyment, and whatever else we felt we needed to make ourselves feel comfortable.

Despite our illegal activity, we were both optimistic that we would be able to make it through Job Corps. I enrolled in the carpentry program and started off going to GED class every other day. I hated GED class because the work made me feel like I was in middle school. It wasn't challenging, and felt like I was repeating things I had learned at the age of twelve. When the teacher noticed that I wasn't doing my work, he asked me what was going on. I told him that the work was too easy, and he laughed in my face. He said he had heard that line from a few others who lacked ambition and drive to get their GED. I laughed back in his face and told him I was serious, so he decided to challenge me. He told me if I could pass one of his tests, he would let me take the half-test to prepare for the GED. However, if I failed, I would have to do all of the work he gave me. I took him up on his offer.

The teacher gave me the test, and ten minutes later, I returned to his desk with my test completed. He looked at me suspiciously and asked if I had just randomly written down the answers. I told him that I had learned how to speed-read when I was 8 years old and was done with the test. He had a cynical look on his face until he started grading the test, which I had aced. True to his word, he gave me the half-test, and when I aced that, he put me on the list to take my GED. He later explained that no other student in his class had been able to do that.

A few weeks later, I was on a bus headed to Kentucky State to take the GED test. A few of the guys who were testing for the second or third time bet me that I wouldn't pass the first time. I told them that I would gladly take their money, and I did. I breezed through the test, and had time to spare after each segment, so I hung out on the campus of Kentucky State in between test segments. Sadly, I didn't realize at the time that I was on the campus of a Historically Black University; all I knew was that I wanted to get my GED knocked out so that I could enroll at the university and chase girls.

While we waited on our test results, I was allowed to go to my carpentry class everyday. Things were moving along smoothly until the cumulative effects of overt racism overwhelmed my young, rebellious spirit. After the Wendy's incident, we had a stretch where we didn't have any problems, and then there was like an explosion. It started when one of the staff members discovered that I had a Public Enemy tape in my possession. I was called into the director's office and told that I was not allowed to play or possess their tape because their music was found to be inciteful and antagonistic toward the White staff members. I found his explanation laughable and told him that I would play whatever music I chose, which led him to write me an insubordination report. I loss the privilege to leave the campus, but I didn't care. Before long, I had another tape smuggled in.

A few weeks later, some racist White guy shot our roommate Peanut in the arm while he was out on pass in Charleston, West Virginia. Charleston was the town we hung out in when we had weekend passes. Peanut and a young lady were waiting on a cab when a car load of White guys drove by and told them to get their "nigger asses" out of town. Moments later, they returned and started shooting, hitting Peanut in the arm.

When the report of what happened reached us, we were livid. The campus was ready to explode. One of the Black supervisors called an emergency meeting with us at one o'clock in the morning. He urged us to be calm and told us that he hoped the incident wouldn't make us angry with the majority White staff or other White people we encountered in Prestonburg. He was an apologist, and whenever we brought racial incidents to his attention, he made every excuse in the book for White people, and we had had enough. He was the typical charismatic Negro that White people send into the community to "calm the natives."

Despite our anger, we allowed his words to soothe us and lull us to sleep. A week or so later, we were evacuated from the building when a bomb threat was called in. Someone had threatened to blow up the building if our "city nigger asses" didn't leave town. It was nearly three o'clock in the morning when we were evacuated from our dorm, and we had to stand outside in the cold for what seemed like an eternity while we waited on the bomb squad to clear the building. As we stood waiting, we watched a cross burning in the woods across from the center.

My blood was boiling, and I was ready to fight back. I refused to live in fear, but honestly, I was concerned that the nameless, faceless cowards who made the threat would one day make true on their threat to blow the building up. When the building was cleared, the staff held another meeting. We listened, but we all looked at each and silently agreed that it was time for us to hold our own meetings.

We talked amongst each other and agreed that we would retaliate the next time one of us was hurt or threatened. We knew that we would not lie down and accept such racist mistreatment if we were back in Detroit, Chicago, New York or LA, so we damn sure weren't going to accept it there.

It wasn't long before we were put to the test. The staff always took us on outings, and one night we were given an opportunity to go to a basketball game at one of the local high schools in Plainseville, Kentucky. We boarded the bus intending to enjoy a night out and what we hoped would be a good game. When we entered the gym, a silence came over the crowd as we walked to our seats. We could hear the whispers blazing through the crowd like a wildfire. They didn't want our kind there.

We felt judged and deemed unworthy of sharing a human experience based on our skin color, and that cut us deeply. Our coach, who was also my carpentry teacher, calmed us down and told us to just sit back and enjoy the game. For nearly two hours, we sat there in the midst of our simmering anger and their vile, racist attitudes.

When the game ended, we filed out of the gym and were about to board the bus when Derrick, who was from Chicago, asked if anyone had seen his homeboy named Inches. Inches had earned the nickname due to his small stature; however, what he lacked in height, he made up for in heart. We all looked around and before anyone could search the bus, Inches came running around the corner holding his eye. Hot on his heels were three red-faced White men hollering and cursing about "niggers" looking at their women.

The blood drained from our coach's face when he realized we had reached our limit with the violent, racist attacks. Derrick asked Inches what happened, and before Inches could say anything, a White man came forward and shouted, "That little nigger blew a kiss at my wife." The boldness of his words sliced through our hearts with a coldness that made Chicago winters appear mild, but instead of shrinking from his words, we responded swiftly, audaciously and fearlessly. We were outnumbered 2 to 1, but we were infused with an anger that increased our strength tenfold. Derrick delivered the first blow, knocking the White man down with one punch. Before he could recover, several guys from Chicago leapt on the guy, kicking and punching him ruthlessly.

The two men who were with the White guy had a look of terror in their eyes when they realized we weren't the meek, humble Negroes they had anticipated. We sensed the fear in there eyes, and like lions, we pounced on our prey. The crowd screamed as we beat and kicked them beneath the bus. When my foot met the soft underbelly of the racist idiot who had shot Peanut, I felt like I was delivering a blow for Peanut and all the other brothers who had been victimized while they were in Kentucky trying to improve their chances at life. We continued to beat the three men, and a few other people in the crowd, until we heard the sound of police sirens.

We all ran to the bus when we heard the sirens. Our coach jumped onto the bus, pulled off immediately, and raced us back to Job Corps. Plump beads of sweat slithered down his forehead and his lips trembled as he gripped the steering wheel so tight that the veins in his hands looked like they were going to pop. Once he drove out of the parking lot, we began cheering wildly as we recounted the blows that we delivered and the impact of each blow on our intended targets. None of us knew what to expect when we returned to the center; all we knew was that we were going to celebrate our victory.

When we got back to the center, an emergency staff meeting was called. The coach told the rest of the staff that he didn't see who did what. He explained that Inches had been attacked first, and someone from the school corroborated his story. The only thing they could do at that point was ban us from the high school.

Though we were victorious that night, the racial tensions continued. A few weeks later, I was in the chow hall talking to one of my friends when the security guard came and told me to sit down. I told him that I would sit down as soon as I finished conducting my business. He looked me dead in my face and said, "Boy, when I say sit, you sit." His words scraped my spirit like fingernails on a chalkboard.

"What the fuck you just say to me?" I replied angrily.

"I said, boy, you sit down when I say," he responded with a smirk.

Those were the last words he spoke before I slung my tray at his head. He stumbled back and radioed for help as everyone in the chow hall started cheering and laughing.

Following that incident, I was called into the director's office and told that I was being terminated from the program. He informed me that I had passed my GED, but my termination meant that I wouldn't be able to attend Kentucky State. I stood up and called him a racist-loving asshole as another officer escorted me out of his office.

I returned to my room and packed my belongings. When word reached Maceo, he rushed back to the room to find out what happened. Before I could tell him what went down, he shot out of the room. Moments later, he came back and started packing. He had gone to talk to the director and told him that he was leaving because he didn't want to be around that level of racism.

When we were packed, they put us on the first bus smoking out of Kentucky headed back to Detroit. As we rode the bus home, I thought about the mentality of the brothers that I was leaving behind. I wondered what it was about them that allowed them to be complacent in the face of such blatant racism. I thought about how I could have handled things differently, but none of the options felt good. It wasn't in me to go along to get along.

When we touched down in Detroit, I prepared myself for the lecture I knew I would receive from my father. I knew he was going to be disappointed, but I had to follow my heart.

Once I returned from Job Corps, I lived with my father for a little while, but it just wasn't working out. He had tried his best to get me on the right path, but there was another path that held me captivated. Unfortunately, it was a cracked and distorted path that led to self-destruction.

Chapter 16

They say the third time's the charm, and in my case, it proved to be true when I returned to the Michigan Reformatory in the fall of 1992. Reflecting back, I realize that my third stint at the Reformatory was the most important leg of my journey through the belly of the beast. In the midst of daily stabbings, human despair, and overt racism, the man Shaka was born and the boy Jay was laid to rest. It was at this point that I started understanding things about myself that my father had been telling me from the time I was a child. I finally acknowledged my own intelligence and accepted the fact that I possessed leadership qualities, which I could use for good or bad. But more importantly, I laid the foundation for my transformation and began understanding the power of empathy and human compassion

My transformation didn't happen overnight, however. As with anything worthwhile in life, I found myself working hard to overcome the violent legacy of my past. I waged a war with myself, dug my heels in, and fought until the end to heal my broken soul.

My first two weeks back at the Reformatory was an adjustment period for me. I knew I would be there for awhile and had to figure out how to make the best of my time. I had encountered several of my homeboys from my old neighborhood on the yard and in the chow hall. Tommie Seymore, who had lived around the corner from my old house on Camden, was working in the chow hall. He told me to get classified for the kitchen so that I could be assigned to J-Block where he locked. I also ran into my homeboy Boise who told me to try and get in the factory, but I couldn't because I had a dangerous contraband misconduct in my file. After deep consideration, I decided to get classified for the kitchen.

Two weeks after I got classified, I was told to pack up and move my belongings over to J-Block. I was assigned a cell in the middle of the tier and given a job working on the chow line in the kitchen. The culture of the kitchen was unlike anything I had experienced in prison. It was a world unto itself, where you never knew what each day would bring.

Stabbings over unpaid debts was the norm, and the kitchen was always tense on the days that we received our tokens. Tokens were the currency given to us when we withdrew money from our account. The little brass coins came in denominations of 1, 5 and 10 dollars, and was the heart and soul of business transactions on the yard. We were all security conscious and had shanks stashed throughout the kitchen. This was the reality of life in a prison filled with young, violent offenders. In the midst of the chaos, we were able to carve out a sacred space to study and discuss Black history, religion and revolutionary theory.

When I returned to the Reformatory, a few brothers told me that there was a Melanic brother that I had to meet. They said that he was as avid a reader as I was and was very serious about transforming himself and others. I was excited to meet another young lion who had the same kind of fire that I had. They told me his name was Yusef and he locked in J-Block, so when I moved over there, I sought the brother out. After a couple of short conversations, we discovered that I knew his father Baruti, who I had just left at Standish Max.

As usual, there was a tense feeling out process for both of us. We were veterans of the streets and trust was something that didn't come easy; it was earned in the trenches. Although I knew his father briefly, I had to get to know Yusef on my own. As I had learned from past experiences, family lineage didn't guarantee a solid pedigree.

Over the next few weeks, we began building a bond based on our love of reading and our desire to make a difference in the world. At that time, neither of us knew whether we would ever get out of prison alive, but we prepared as if we would be released the next day. Each time we exchanged a book, we would gather at one of the tables in the chow hall or on the yard and dissect what we had read. This was an important part of our re-building process. We wanted to ensure that we both came away with a comprehensive understanding of what we read. This was also our way of challenging each other to grow and separating the sincere brothers from those who lacked sincerity.

Yusef and I had a lot in common; we were both young fathers and had come from some of the most depressed neighborhoods in Detroit. However, our stories weren't unique. We were surrounded by nearly fifteen hundred young men who had similar stories filled with poverty, desperation, and hopelessness. Indeed, this was a common thread that ran through prison, tying us all together. Most of us came from backgrounds where high-levels of gun violence were the norm in addition to child and sexual abuse. We were the broken souls that dwelled inner-city streets, hopeless and desperate for an escape from our hellish existence.

I continued to build with several solid Melanic brothers like Simba and my dude Smiley Senghor, who I had met while in quarantine a few years earlier. I also had deep discussions with brothers from other organizations because I felt that it was important to understand all of our people. We all held different philosophical and theological views, yet we were all being oppressed by the same beast. With this realization at the forefront of my mind, I sought to find common ground for us to build on. This was one of the most important discoveries that I made during that time. Because of my willingness to learn and understand the teachings of others, I was able to build solid allegiances and bring an end to some of the violence that was standard between groups. However, there was no way to stop all of the bloodshed.

I tried to settle down into a groove while doing my time, but I could never get comfortable with the idea of remaining in prison for most of my young life. Mentally, I rebelled, and it manifested in my actions toward the staff and other inmates. Everyday, I was consumed with anger despite how much I built with the brothers. I thought about my son and family constantly, and it tore my heart to shreds. The thought of my son growing up without my love and guidance tore patches out of my heart. I looked at his pictures daily and prayed that one day I'd be able to see him and hold him in my arms like I imagined my father held me when I was a baby. I thought about teaching him how to walk and ride his first bike, and how to defend himself in a fight. But I knew I wouldn't be able to do any of those things. I was comforted, however, by the fact that I knew my father would ensure my son's basic needs were met.

One day when I was returning from my work detail, an officer called out over the PA to let me know that I had a visit. It had been a while since I'd seen my father, and I was very excited to see him and talk to him about some of the changes I was making in my life. As I got ready for my visit, I didn't know what to expect because I had never had a visit at the Michigan Reformatory. I showered and rushed back to my cell to dress in some clothes I had borrowed from one of the brothers. I didn't have my own clothes yet and didn't want to go out on a visit in my state blues. Once I was dressed, I headed up to the control center to be processed through for my visit.

When I entered the visiting room, I was directed upstairs where my father and two younger sisters were sitting with my son Jay. My heart began pounding like an African drum as I studied my son from head to toe. His little fat cheeks just melted all of the prison hardness away like butter on hot toast. I greeted my father and sisters with a hug and smile before attempting to pick up my son. He pulled away from me, and in that moment, I wanted to die on the spot. It took all of the energy I had inside to hold back the tears that threatened to overflow like a swollen river. Before any depressing thoughts were able to take root, my father intervened with words of wisdom.

"It's okay. He'll come to you. It just takes him a little bit of time to warm up to people," he reassured me.

I listened to my father's words calmly, but inside I was screaming, "I'm not people, I'm his father!" I remained silent, however, and took a seat with my family. We had small talk about what was going on back home, but the entire time, my mind was on thinking of a way to break out of prison that day so that I could be with my family. I continued to interact with Lil' Jay as we called him throughout the visit, and finally after a half an hour or so, he allowed me to pick him up. I held him close to me so that he could feel my heartbeat and the undeniable love that I had for him. He smiled and laughed, and for the short time that I held him, he erased the prison walls that held me captive. I could see my features and Brenda's features in him. He was a beautiful baby, and I wanted nothing more than to protect him from the cruel, ugly world that he was born into.

After about an hour and a half, Jay started to fuss and get a bit cranky. My father said that he was probably ready for a nap, so they were going to leave. I hugged Jay tightly before handing him over to my father. I then notified the officers that my family was ready to go.

We were escorted downstairs and I stood silently as my family left the visiting room. A few minutes later, an officer came to get me so that I could return to my cell. When I exited the visiting room, my father called out my name, and when I turned around, my family was standing on the other side of the bars. I smiled and waved, and then Jay lifted his arms up like he wanted me to pick him up. In that moment, I felt like biting through the bars like a wild lion to get to my son.

"Mr. White, it's time for you to return to your cell," the officer said, jarring me from my fantasy world. I turned and looked at him with hatred in my eyes. Even though he wasn't responsible for me being in prison, I felt a hatred for him in that moment that raged and threatened to boil over. He lowered his head as he led me into the strip search room. I felt numb as I stripped out of my clothes. All I could do was think about the look of disappointment that crossed Lil' Jay's face when he realized that I wasn't able to pick him up, or leave with them.

With each visit, our bond grew closer, but the sense of heartbreak that I felt each time my family left the visiting room never left me. When I returned to my cell from my first visit with my son, I climbed into my bed fully dressed. I turned on my Walkman and listened to Sade until I dozed off. It was nearly three o'clock in the morning when I finally woke up, and all I could do was sit on my bunk and stare at the photos from the visit as I thought about ways to escape from prison.

Thinking of how vulnerable my son was without me out there to guide and protect him caused me to sink deeper into anger and depression. I found myself on edge everyday because I didn't know how to process all of the emotions I was experiencing. Deep inside, I was sad and emotionally broken, but the only way I knew how to express what I felt was through anger and violence. I developed a serious "wish a motherfucker would" attitude. Daily, I wished a motherfucker would get out of line so that I could release my pain by inflicting pain on them. It didn't take long before I was able to get some of this frustration out of my system. A week or so after my visit, an inmate, who I had had an encounter with at Carson City, transferred in.

While I was at Carson City, this guy accused me of stealing his vending machine card, and then went and told the officer working our unit. The officer called me down and told me to empty my pockets, his eyes lighting up when I pulled my card out of my pocket. When he discovered that it was mine, he apologized and sent me back to my cell. I knew if I were to beat the inmate's ass, they would know I did it, so I let it go, but I didn't forget. When he arrived at the Reformatory, I had made up my mind that I would get him whenever the opportunity presented itself. After two weeks or so, I caught him slipping. We had a substitute officer working the unit so it was the perfect time to act. When they broke our cells for chow, I waited for the guy to walk down the tier, then approached him swiftly. I had already given my neighbor the heads up to walk in front of us, blocking the officer's view.

"I told you I was going to get your rat ass," I said as I seized him by the neck and pushed his head through a nearby window, shattering the glass with his face. He screamed loudly as the glass tore through his flesh, causing a river of blood to flow down his face. I blended in with the rest of the crowd and went to eat chow as he was rushed to the infirmary to have his face stitched up. This was only the beginning. That brief adrenaline rush soothed the pain for a moment, but it wasn't enough. I needed to hurt someone whenever I could to stop my own hurting. It was as though I was an emotional vampire thirsting to drain the emotional blood from unsuspecting victims in order for me to stay alive. I was quickly earning a reputation as an extremist. Though I got away with most of the assaults, it wasn't long before I found myself heading back to solitary confinement.

I was working as the foreman on the chow line when my side of the line got backed up because of a disgruntled inmate who complained that he hadn't gotten enough gravy to go on his mashed potatoes. The brother working the window where the trays were passed through was doing his best to satisfy him to no avail. All the while, our line was backing up, which meant we would have to stay at work longer. As the foreman, it was my job to keep the line flowing, so I approached the window and asked the guy what the problem was. He responded with a verbal attack, going on and on about our ineptitude, so I offered to fix his tray. I scooped up a heaping mound of steaming hot mashed potatoes and drenched it with several ladles of scalding gravy. It was a double portion, which was more than he was entitled to, but I wanted to make sure that he was satisfied because I understood for some inmates, that was the only meal they'd have that day.

When I brought the tray to the window, the inmate started complaining that there was too much damn gravy. At that point, I had been pushed to the limits of my patience. I asked him to come closer to the window so that I could hear what he was saying, and when he leaned in closer, I slapped him in the face with the tray full of hot potatoes and gravy, causing him to yell and holler. My supervisor had seen the whole play, but he was cool so I wasn't worried about him doing anything. What I didn't anticipate was the inmate running to the officer who was patrolling the kitchen. When my supervisor saw the inmate take off toward the officer, he ordered me to the back of the kitchen.

I took off my hoodie, which I wore beneath my kitchen whites, and hid behind a large stack of pots and pans. Within two minutes, I heard the rush of boots slapping the ground along with keys jingling, as the officers rushed to the scene. My heart began beating fast as I held out hope that they wouldn't discover me. Much to my dismay, they had the inmate in tow when they reached the pots and pans room.

"That's him," the inmate called out as the officers found my hiding spot.

I stared the inmate down as the officers cuffed me up. His face was red and he still had remnants of mashed potatoes and gravy on his face and in his hair. In a matter of seconds, my anger had gone from 0 to 60. In that moment, I didn't care that my actions could have caused serious damage if the gravy or potatoes had gotten into his eyes. All I was concerned about was the pain I was feeling.

When I reached the cell in solitary confinement, I paced back and forth like a caged beast. With each step I took, I felt the callouses on my heart and mind thickening. I reinforced my anger by blaming the other inmate for snitching, when in reality no one was responsible for the way things were turning out in my life but me. I had allowed past hurts, disappointments, and betrayals to infect my soul with the worst and deadliest illnesses to invade our community – self-hate. At the end of the day, I was emotionally retarded, an angry boy in a man's body. It would be a few days before I'd learn my fate, but in the mean time, I laid in my bed, reading daily and feeding the rage.

Chapter 17

"I don't care what anyone calls you. There is never an excuse to allow someone's words to stand in the way of your success," my father said as we drove away from the Greyhound bus station. I knew he would be disappointed when he learned I had been kicked out of Job Corps, but I was just as disappointed in his words. I wanted him to understand why I lashed out. I wanted him to understand how I felt being demeaned and treated inferior because of the color of my skin. I wanted him to know what it felt like to have someone trample on my humanity and my right to freedom of speech. I wanted him to know that I had a responsibility to myself, and those who came after me, to voice my displeasure with how we were treated in Kentucky. More importantly, I wanted him to respect my right to fight for what I believed in.

What I hadn't accounted for was the fact that my father understood in ways that I wouldn't grow to appreciate until I was an adult. See, my father entered the military when he was 17 and grew up during the turbulent sixties and seventies. He lived through things that I had yet to discover, but as a 17-year-old, I couldn't relate to his lack of anger at the racism I had experienced.

When we got home, I basked in the familiarity of my surroundings. I was excited to be at home with Vanessa and my nephew Megale. Within a few days, I was back into the groove of being home. It was the dead of the winter, so there wasn't much activity on our block and I started getting antsy. Within a week or so, I found myself back down in Brightmoor hanging out at Tamica's house. I reconnected with Mark, Jimmy, Mack and Coop and started hanging out on the corner selling drugs and drinking 64 ounce bottles of Old English 800. The fellas were happy to see me, and I was happy to see them. I had missed hanging out, fighting dogs, hustling, and chasing girls with my homies, so it was refreshing to be standing out on the corner with the crew.

One day, we were on the block chilling when a customer I had never met approached us. It was a crisp, mid-January afternoon, and when he walked up, we were sipping Old English 800 to keep warm. The guy was more aggressive than I was accustomed to, and I immediately developed a dislike for him. His energy reminded me of Tiny, the dope fiend who robbed me when I first started selling drugs. Coop introduced him to me and I gave him a dry nod as they completed their business. When he walked off, I told Coop there was something about him that I didn't like. Coop said he had recently moved into the neighborhood and was good business. I chalked it up to me being gone for a minute, but my street sensibilities wouldn't allow me to completely discard the ominous vibes I was getting from him. I watched him walk away and reiterated to Coop that I didn't like the vibes I was getting from him. Coop laughed it off and joked that I didn't really like anyone outside of the crew. We got a good laugh and continued about our day.

Over the next few weeks, I found myself struggling to get back on my feet. Things were slow and I spent most days hanging out with the crew on the corner. I was tired of struggling, however, so I started thinking of different ways I could come up. I was staying with my sister most of the time, but it was a strain on her because she had three boys and a husband to look after.

Despite having a full plate, Tamica never hesitated to take me in and allowed me to stay at her house for as long as I needed to. She had basically raised me and was always by my side when my mother wasn't around. Though we were only a few years apart, she was like a mother to me. We stayed up talking most nights about making it out of the 'hood and how things would be better for us. She had been forced to grow up at an early age and endured the pains of being in love with an older man who physically abused her.

My sister and her husband argued daily, and whenever he got drunk, he would hit her and they'd start fighting. As good as my sister was at fighting, she was no match for a grown man, and neither was I. Later on, when I was about 16, I pulled a gun on him and threatened to kill him if he ever put his hands on my sister again. Tamica promised to leave him if I didn't shoot, so I didn't, and she eventually left him.

Things started to pick up slowly and I was able to get ahold of half an ounce of cocaine, which I cooked and cut up to sell. Mack and

Coop had built up the clientele on the block and neither had a problem with me making a few dollars. The reality was, no one wanted to roll all day, but we didn't want the clientele to go anywhere else, so we shared the business.

As we moved into the first week of February, things began really picking up on the block and I found myself staying up all night selling out of a spot a few doors down from Tamica's house. Then, on one fateful night, I happened to be lying on the couch at Tamica's house when Coop tapped on the window.

It was about two o'clock in the morning when Coop came by. I got up and went outside to see what was up. Coop asked if I had a few rocks because he was out and had a customer. I told him I did, but I needed to get them out of my stash. I went back inside the house to get my sack, which was stashed in the freezer to ensure my nephews didn't get to them. I came back out, gave Coop the rocks, and told him to tap on the window when he got done making the transaction.

Five minutes after he left, I was back on the couch knocked out. Moments later, I heard the faint sound of someone screaming my name. For a minute, I thought I was dreaming, but the sound grew louder, jarring me from my sleep. I jumped up from the couch and snatched the door open to see what was going on. When I looked outside, I didn't see anyone in front of the house. Just as I was about to turn and go back in, I heard Coop's baby's mother calling my name out of a window from across the street at Ms. Cooper's house. The first thing that crossed my mind was Coop was about to beat her up or something like that. Though I had never seen him hit or abuse her, I had been around enough domestic violence to trigger those thoughts. Before I could make sense of what was going on, Coop burst through his mother's front door holding a .357 Magnum in his hand.

"This bitch tried to rob me! This bitch tried to rob me!" he shouted as I approached the house. My initial thought was that a female, possibly his baby's mother, had tried to rob him. This wasn't uncommon in our line of work. The streets were cutthroat, and anyone involved in the lifestyle was capable of any level of disloyalty, betrayal and treachery. Before I could collect my thoughts, Coop went back inside his mother's house. I climbed the porch steps slowly as I tried to process what was going on. Was Coop trying to pull off a classic cover up to justify not having my money? I didn't know what to think as I entered the house, but when I stepped through the threshold, I wished I could have turned around and walked right back out; however, my sense of loyalty and dedication to my friends wouldn't allow me to walk the short distance back across the street to the comfort of my sister's couch. It was too late. I had already committed myself, and there was no turning back.

"Please, I'm dying," were the first words I heard before it hit me that the man lying on Ms. Cooper's living room floor was the same man I had met on the corner with Coop a few weeks earlier. He was dressed in dark pants and a dark sweater, which was saturated with blood. His breaths were labored and I could hear the gurgling of blood coming from his chest.

"I'm about to shoot this bitch in the head," Coop screamed as he stood over the dying man. "He was going to kill my whole family. My mama, my sisters and my baby is in here," he continued.

It took me a few minutes to calm Coop down. I begged him not to shoot the man in the head in his mother's house. By this time Ms. Cooper had come out of her bedroom, so I went to talk to her and calm her down.

As the man lay on the living room floor taking his last breaths, Coop explained to me what was going on. The man had come by earlier and bought some rocks, and then returned carrying the .357 and a pocket full of ammo. Coop let him in, then came and got some rocks from me to sell to him. When he returned, the man pulled the gun on him and told him to get on his knees. He removed a bullet from his pocket and told Coop to bite it to show that he wasn't playing. He told Coop that he would kill everyone in the house if he didn't show him where the rest of the dope was. Coop said that all he could think about was his daughter, mother and sister as he sat on his knees staring down the barrel of the .357. It was these thoughts that gave him the courage needed to attack instead of becoming a victim.

In a burst of adrenaline, Coop rushed the man, picked him up, and then slammed him on the kitchen floor. The force of the body slam dislodged the gun from the man's hand. Coop scrambled to get the gun, and in one motion, fired into the man's chest. The man then crawled into the living room where he collapsed and laid dying.

Once I got Coop calmed down, I told him to have his mother call the police and report the robbery attempt so that he could avoid getting charged with anything. Unfortunately, however, knowing that his family could have been murdered was clouding Coop's judgment. He said that he wanted to take the body across the street and dump it in the backyard of the vacant house next to Tamica's. I tried to talk him out of it, but he was determined to move the body from his mother's house. I knew it was a mistake, but there was nothing I could tell him to convince him otherwise. All I could do was try to be a friend according to my understanding of what friendship meant in my seventeen-year-old mind.

As we stood in the vacant yard staring down at the man, I was devoid of feelings. I didn't care that the man was lying dead. I rationalized my feelings by saying that it could have easily been Coop and his family. Looking back, it sickens me to think that at such a tender and fragile age, I had already developed a callousness around my heart that would prevent me from having human compassion and empathy. I was lost in thought about how the night could have ended when out of nowhere, Coop fired several more shots into the man's body. To this day, I think those last few shots masked what Coop really wanted to do, which was cry. His family had been threatened and he had been made to bite a bullet, and no man wants to live knowing that his actions or lack of action caused the death of his family.

Coop left and went down the street to his girlfriend Nita's house, then came back and told me to tell Tamica to call the police in the morning and let them know that the dog had found a body in the backyard next door. In the meantime, I told him to go to a family member's house and we would take care of the rest. Instead of leaving, however, he went back down the street to Nita's. The next morning when the police arrived to investigate, Coop came and joined us in the backyard. Once the homicide detectives investigated the scene, they concluded that the body had been carried from Coop's mother's house because of the trail of blood left behind. They questioned Ms. Cooper and arrested Mack, thinking he was Coop. The detectives said there would have been no charges had the body not been removed from the house.

Coop eventually turned himself in and was given a bond for $5,000, which his brother Boe paid. When he got out, we celebrated, but it was short-lived because we knew that he would be going to prison. It was during one of these celebrations that Coop told Boe, if he could trust anyone to hold him down, it would be me. From that night forward, Boe and I began building a bond. He had just lost his best friend, and now his brother was being sent to the joint. While Coop was out on bond, he hung out with the crew and enjoyed the rest of his freedom until he was sentenced in May of 1990 to five years in prison.

Over the next few months, I started selling drugs exclusively for Boe, which cemented our bond. The spring was upon us, and with the warm weather, it felt like our clientele was growing by the day. Mark, Mack, Boe and I stayed on the porch from sunup to sundown selling drugs and drinking. Blackstone was off the hook, and everyday there was something going down, from fights to parties. Despite the fact that we were selling drugs, most of our neighbors loved us, especially the neighborhood girls. They all wanted to be down with the guys from Blackstone. There were other crews in the area that we played ball with, and sometimes did business with, but Blackstone was the heart and soul of Brightmoor at that time, and for years to come.

Things were going pretty well until March 8, 1990 when the last remnants of my childhood were shattered by a rapid burst of gunfire. Like a crystal decanter exploding into a million shards of glass, my life was broken into pieces when an argument over a girl turned to gunplay. I was seventeen years old, and almost twenty-three years later, I can still feel the frosty winter air dancing over my teenage flesh as the gunshot wounds to my leg and foot sent waves of pain through my entire body. I remember where I was standing when the gunman drove by, what I had on, who I was with and where we were headed; but more than anything, I remember the intense heat that raged through my body as the first bullet met its mark.

When the first of three bullets tore into my flesh, I felt my shinbone cracking from the force of the bullet. Immediately, my shoe filled with blood, which sloshed around as I fled the scene trying to escape my assailant. One bullet still remains lodged in my foot as a reminder of how fragile life can be in the 'hood.

As I recall that fateful day, the scene of my shooting plays out in my mind vividly in slow motion. I can see the car pulling up to the corner where I stood talking to Boe. When I looked up and saw the driver, I knew something was wrong. We exchanged angry glares before I invited him to get out of the car to fight. Something in his facial expression told me that he had no intention of fighting. A smirk crossed his face as he reached down and retrieved his pistol. My response told him that I wasn't armed, and he took advantage of that fact. My reaction time was slow, and before I could turn and run for shelter, he squeezed off several shots, hitting me with the first two in the leg while the third bullet hit me in my foot as I fled for safety.

My heart pounded in my chest like a jackhammer as adrenaline flooded my system, and my legs pumped like pistons as I zigzagged back and forth, dodging the fusillade of bullets that the shooter unleashed in a fury. As I ran, I prayed that none of the bullets hit me in my spine, or even worse, in the back of my head.

I ran around the corner into this young lady named Lisa's house. She had witnessed the whole incident play out and was mortified as I approached her. She begged me not to come to her house, but I ignored her requests. I ran right past her and through her front door. I gathered myself in her kitchen, then exited the side door. When I opened the door and saw that the coast was clear, I ran back around to my block. My emotions boiled and raged like a violent sea storm. My initial fear was replaced by a deep feeling of loneliness. I couldn't comprehend why someone would attempt to kill me over a meaningless argument.

When I returned to my block, I saw my sister, friends and nephews standing outside. As I approached them, I started to feel dangerously angry. I was experiencing an amalgamation of emotions that began festering with the poison of revenge. I wanted someone to feel the pain, fear and sadness that I was feeling.

Tamica was the first person to reach me. She ran down the block and embraced me when she saw that I was still alive. Her eyes filled with tears as we walked back to the house. I took off my jacket and shirt, checking for bullet wounds. I was sweating profusely and my mouth was so dry it felt as though someone had stuffed a handful of sand in it. I ignored Tamica's request to put my clothes back on and pulled out a pack of Newports. Before I could light one up, I jumped up to go in the house and get a gun. I wanted to shoot someone so bad, it was killing me inside. I hated being a victim, and the only thing that would restore balance was getting revenge.

Tamica and Ms. Cooper did their part to calm me down. I lit up a crumpled Newport and sat on the porch sulking as I waited for an ambulance that never came. It wasn't a surprise to us. We were used to ambulances and police who never came to the rescue of Black children. This was the reality of living in the 'hood. Finally, after waiting close to half an hour, Boe drove me to Mt. Carmel Hospital. He reassured me that everything would be alright; my wounds weren't that bad. Boe and his best friend had been shot the previous year, and his best friend died on the scene. Knowing what he had been through helped me cope with some of the thoughts that began flowing through my head.

When I arrived at the hospital, I felt like I was being moved through an assembly line manned by robots. In Detroit, a child getting shot was business as usual. There was no compassion shown to me by any of the staff. I was given a shot of Demerol before being rushed to get an x-ray. When I awakened from my drug-induced sleep, the room was full of police officers. They asked me a barrage of questions about the shooter. Their demeanor was callous and confrontational, as though I was somehow the cause of my own shooting. I told them that I didn't know who shot me. My response incensed one officer to the point that he told me, "That's why your lil' Black ass is lying in the bed suffering from a gunshot wound." Somehow my ignorance and refusal to give him an answer upset his sensibilities. He hurled a few more invectives at me, then exited the room. I felt victimized all over again, but this time by an officer who didn't give a damn about kids like me who had to live in neighborhoods that were virtual war zones. There was a code that we lived by, and there was no way I was going to violate that code.

When the doctor arrived, I felt a sense of relief. For the first time, I felt like I could be a child and express my fears, but I was quickly reminded that we live in a cold and indifferent world. The doctor looked at my chart and left without saying much to me. He returned moments later with a pair of needle-nosed pliers. He dug the pliers into my flesh and wrenched the bullet from my leg, pulling bits of meat and bone with it. He irrigated it, then left to write a prescription for some antibiotics. I dozed back off and was awakened by my father, stepmother, and mother standing in the room.

In my father's eyes, I could see a sense of hopelessness while my mother stood paralyzed by fear, a fear that one day one of her children would be killed. Sadly, I was the third one of my parents' children to be shot. They were clearly at a loss for words. What could they really say to me? There were no parenting manuals to explain how to handle your child getting shot in the streets like a rabid dog. So we talked briefly, then they all left. I could sense their anger and frustration with me because they knew I would return to the scene of the shooting. I had long ago given up on going home to either of my parents and had accepted that the streets were my home. If not before, I surely felt this way after the shooting.

No one hugged me or told me that everything would be okay. No one came to talk to me and explain all of the emotions I was feeling. No one told me that I was programming myself to be a killer in response to my fears. In my mind, I would rather victimize someone else than to be a victim. No one explained to me that cars weren't death chariots carrying the grim reaper. So I became hyper-violent in order to restore a sense of emotional balance. If I shot first, I would no longer have to fear getting shot. It was a distorted way of looking at the world, yet it was the only way I knew how to cope.

When I left the hospital, I returned to my block deadlier than the man who had shot me, killing what remained of my childhood innocence. The anger I felt combined with the alcohol I regularly consumed cast a dark shadow over me. I wandered the streets blind to what was going on inside of me. Instead of crying tears, I cried bullets, screaming in semi-automatic bursts every time I found myself in conflict. Anger became my shield and the mask I hid behind as I navigated my way through the streets. This was the sad reality of the city I lived in.

Black children get shot and killed everyday yet very few receive psychological treatment or emotional counseling, so we grow up living in fear and anger, which eventually manifests into violent behavior. Everyday, I ask myself why we are considered the dregs of society. Columbine-like violence has been going on in the 'hood for years, but very little is done about it. Sometimes we march or hold candlelight vigils, but this does very little to solve the problem. No child should ever fear being the victim of gun violence. No child should ever feel that they must victimize someone else's child in order to survive. But that's exactly what happened with me.

Over the course of the next fourteen months, all of the violence that had been poured into my young life overflowed, leaving a trail of carnage in it's wake like a 'hood version of Desert Storm. The little compassion and empathy that I had left shriveled up like a prune, leaving a cold, hard lump of apathy behind. I had officially crossed over to the world of heartless killers who were legendary in the 'hood, young men who squeezed triggers out of desperation. I became obsessed with carrying a gun like a crackhead carries his pipe. I went to bed with my pistol, woke up with it, and took a dump with it in my hand or nearby. At the first sign of beef, I was ready to shoot it out. My mind became fixated on the ghosts that lay in the shadows ready to shoot or hurt me, so I made up my mind to shoot first. I knew it was only a matter of time before the cumulative effects of my paranoia ended with me shooting someone.

Chapter 18

It was my second time in the hole, but this time around, I was a lot more aware of what to expect caged up for 23 hours a day. I quickly developed a routine – sleep through the morning and read late into the night amidst the chaos – and made the necessary mental adjustments to survive the chaos of solitary confinement at the Michigan Reformatory.

When my father came up to see me, I had been in the hole for about 30 days. I was shackled and handcuffed, then led up to the visiting room where my father awaited me. They put me in a non-contact visiting booth where my father and I sat talking through a three-inch thick Plexiglas window for a couple of hours. We tried having a normal conversation, and my father did everything in his power to comfort me with warm words and thoughts from home. Though his words were well intended and I smiled in response, deep inside, they wreaked havoc on my emotions as I thought of the things I would never witness on free soil. I knew the little sisters that he spoke of would be women when I got out of prison and life in the 'hood would continue on without me. I knew my son who they were caring for would never get a chance to throw a football with me, or have me teach him the basics that fathers teach their children. These were thoughts I didn't want to face, so I pushed them deep down to the bottom of the rock that had become my heart.

When my father left, I went back to my cell and lay on the bed thinking deeply about things from his perspective. I could see that he was tired and hurt from seeing me caged up, so I wrote him a letter. I told him that he wasn't responsible for the choices I had made in my life and he shouldn't feel guilty about how my life turned out. I didn't know how he would receive my letter, but I wanted to be sure that he understood he was not the cause of the decisions I had made.

After about six months in the hole, I was released back to general population and assigned to the kitchen. When I found out I would working in the kitchen, I was very excited to reconnect with the brothers I had been building with. Unfortunately, however, I was assigned to the morning detail, which I hated with a passion. I have been nocturnal for as long as I can remember, so getting up in the morning has always been a struggle. I managed to overcome my disdain for the morning shift and ended up working in the kitchen commissary. It was a cool spot to work because I had access to all the food, which I smuggled out through other inmates. On the flip side, only a few inmates had access to our area so I couldn't build with the brothers the way I wanted to. After awhile, I requested to be transferred to the midnight bakery where I worked with two of my comrades Simba and Mallon. Every night when we were done with our work, we would kick it in the bakery, eating and reading whatever books we had smuggled over to the chow hall, which we discussed at length with each other. Things were going well and I was enjoying being able to build with my brothers, until I got called in early one morning for overtime.

We had gotten off the night before at about two o'clock in the morning, so I was pissed when they told me to report to work at 6 a.m. We discovered that a bread run had been messed up, and one of the morning supervisors wanted us to make some more. I told him that I wasn't baking shit and wanted to go back to my cell, so he fired me and wrote me a misconduct. I decided right then that my days in the kitchen at the Reformatory were over. I had grown tired of slaving in the kitchen and dealing with supervisors who acted like modern day slave masters. Although I'd miss building with Simba and Mallon, it was time for me to do something else with my time.

Getting fired gave me more time to build with the brothers on the yard. We formed coalitions and had intense study groups with other organizations and a few curious brothers. Our organization was undergoing continuous changes as spiritual advisors and security heads were transferred or voted in and out of positions. I continued to be a disciplined and dedicated leader, and the rest of the brothers looked to me for guidance. I had never considered being a spiritual advisor and preferred supporting brothers like Tommie X and Simba, who I felt were more spiritually inclined. However, when it was my time to assume the position, I rose to the occasion. I started challenging the Board of Directors to think of different ways to educate the brothers. With the help of brothers who had inspired me, I tried to change the culture of the organization to a more revolutionary and militant one. Instead of the Bible and Quran, which we used for spiritual development, I encouraged the brothers to read books by Assata Shakur and George Jackson for revolutionary inspiration.

Not long after leaving the kitchen, I was given a job working in the recreation center. It was the perfect place for me as the spiritual advisor because it gave me access to every yard, so I was able to talk to my assistants and security staff on a regular basis, which allowed us to forge a stronger bond. I was now in control of the callouts and could set up meetings whenever I wanted under the guise of a basketball or weightlifting callout. Whenever we had a beef on the yard, we were able to coordinate and strategize in a way that allowed us to attack with stealth. Whenever an inmate outside of our organization did something in J-Block, it was easy for us to have someone placed on a callout from I-Block to take care of it.

As our battles with other inmates intensified and hits were ordered, I found myself battling contradictions in the way I did my bid. On one hand, I was teaching the brothers that White supremacy and fascism were the enemy, and in the same breath, I was ordering the stabbings of other inmates – inmates who had brown flesh like me, and were therefore being smothered by the same blanket of oppression that smothered me.

I started growing tired of the countless and fruitless beefs that I either intervened on or had others stabbed over. I could feel the weight of the crown hanging heavily on my head yet I understood these were the rules of engagement at the Gladiator School. Eventually, the weight became too much for me to bear, and I resigned from my post. I was starting to feel like a fake ass hypocrite, and this was something I was uncomfortable with. I turned over the position to Simba and stepped back to reassess where I was heading in life. I was growing in my consciousness, but the gravitational pull from the negativity and violence of prison life was overwhelming. I found myself constantly battling my thoughts and everyone around me. The only peace I found was when I was in the recreation center working out.

I hit the weights with a vengeance and honed my pool skills two or three times a day. The weights helped alleviate some of the stress, and being around good people helped with the rest. We worked for the coolest staff at the Reformatory, and we had one of the best crews. My homeboy Mo Bounce worked in the rec center with me along with E Love, Roland X and Deombre X. In between yard breaks, we worked out and played basketball. We also took time to study and build. It was around this time that I wrote my first article for the prison newspaper. I hadn't given it much thought after I wrote it, but a month or so later, it was the source of a conversation that would change the course of my life.

When I arrived at work one day, I found our supervisor Tom, who was the coolest staff member at the Reformatory, sitting in the recreation center reading the paper. He kept looking up from the paper and at me with a curiosity that I hadn't recognized before. After reading my article in The Hilltop News, he asked me if I had really authored the article. I assured him that I had, and he told me that I was a good writer. In fact, he wanted to share the article with his wife who was an editor for a magazine. I didn't think anything of it, until he returned to work the next day and told me that his wife thought I had a future as a writer. I had never really thought of writing as something to take seriously, nor did I have an inkling to be an author. I simply wanted to get out of prison and go on with my life. I never thought of being anything other than free.

Though in that moment I didn't realize the impact that conversation would have on my life, Tom's words resonated with me. I went back and reread the article, trying to pick out of it what Tom and his wife had seen, but I couldn't find it. In my mind, it was just a simple story about something that a member of my family was experiencing and how I felt about it. Even still, I found Tom's positive reinforcement encouraging; he made me feel good about myself and my writing. It had been a long time since someone said something celebratory about me that wasn't connected to street or prison violence. I was actually being told that I was good at something other than hustling drugs and hurting people.

When I went back to my cell, I pulled out a notepad that I had been using to jot down my thoughts. It was then I realized that I was a

206

budding writer. It hit me in that moment that I needed to get a typewriter. I didn't know when, but I knew at some point, I would have to get my own typewriter, which became a tool of liberation for me.

I continued working in the recreation center, which was the heartbeat of the joint. Every hustle imaginable took place there, from drug trafficking and loan sharking to gambling and playing pool for money. To some degree or another, our recreation crew was at the center of it all. I had several hustles that allowed me to take care of myself. I loaned money at 100% interest and enforced a strict code of payment. If you were short with my money, then I doubled it again for the next draw day, which is what we called the days we were allowed to get money out of our accounts. If after two draw days you still didn't have it, you may as well had checked into protection because it was guaranteed you would be getting stabbed or hit in the head with a lock and sock. It wasn't personal; it was simply the business model that had been established in prison long before I ever committed my first crime.

Within six months, I had firmly established my position in the prison and was well revered by those who knew me or came in contact with me. The inmates could always count on me to be fair, and one of the things that separated me from others was my diplomacy. In the midst of conflict, I always tried to find a way to ensure that we all got what we wanted in the end. I wanted my money and they wanted their lives, so I was willing to work with them. However, if they were unwilling to work with me, they undoubtedly knew that I was coming to get what was mine.

During the summer of 1996, things between several of the organizations and their officers started heating up. Two officers who ran the yard at the Reformatory and a few officers in the units had become more and more brazen with their abuses, and we were tired of dealing with it. We organized silent protests, unified workout regimens, and other tactics to let them know that we were uniting together. The officers retaliated by setting up some of the leadership, and I found myself on the receiving end of one sergeant's harassment.

With the escalation of stabbings in the recreation center, the officer started shaking me down every chance he got, destroying my cell on a daily. I never got caught slipping, however, so there was very little he could do. Eventually, he got me transferred to Carson City Correctional Facility, but the war waged on. Not long after I transferred, several officers were jumped, and one was nearly stabbed to death. While it was good to hear about the officers getting what we felt they deserved, it was the stabbing of an officer that would send my life on another sharp turn down the drama-filled prison streets.

I was transferred back to Carson City for the second time and had no idea what was going on at the Reformatory, or how it would impact me. The eleven or so months that I was at Carson City, there was constant tension in the air between the officers and us. I had returned to my post as a Melanic and was eventually voted to be the spiritual advisor. I hadn't been in the post long before I ordered a hit on a known informant that tried to come to our service. It was business as usual, but I was able to justify my actions because he was a known rat who we all despised. Even though the officers' investigation came up short, me and the head of our security were placed under a cloud of suspicion. This created another wedge between our organization and the staff. They did everything they could to break us down, and we did everything we could to antagonize them.

In addition to my Melanic brothers, I had been reunited with several of my comrades from the Gladiator School. Tommie X, Mo Bounce, E-Way, Yella and my homeboy Boise were with me at Carson City along with a few more solid brothers. It made our time more bearable as we were able to support each other and keep each other hopeful. It was tough, but we continued to share books and information whenever we could. As time went on, I found myself emerging as a true leader. I read everyday and challenged my comrades to grow with me. Instead of preaching to them about doing right, I challenged the contradictions we were all guilty of from time to time. We shared information, worked out and studied together. We went back and forth daily as we worked out in an effort to harmonize bodies with our minds and spirits.

One day while we were outside working out, I noticed a few officers going in and out of our unit. They looked like they were preparing for something, but I didn't know what was going on. There hadn't been any beefs brought to my attention, and all of the brotherhoods seemed to be relaxed. I went back to doing push-ups, and just as I was coming up from a set of push-ups, an officer approached me and asked for my ID. I gave it to him, then braced my body for what I knew would be an invasive body search. I hated for the officers to touch me, but he surprised me when he handed my ID back and walked toward the unit.

When I finished working out, I went in and hit the shower, then headed back to my cell. I joked with my bunky Timmy about a shakedown we had received a few days before. Timmy was from the 'hood and was a good kid who was serving time for a murder that no one in the neighborhood believes he committed. He was a church boy, and the rumor was, he took the fall for a family member who refused to come forward. He was a phenomenal basketball player and everyone respected him for his game. We were different in many ways, but those differences allowed us to co-exist peacefully. Timmy wasn't a troublemaker, so when they snatched us out of our cell for a shakedown the first time, he was a bit shaken. We continued to joke about it, until we heard someone hollering down the tier that the police were coming down the tier.

Before I could get to the door to see what was going on, our cell door was banged open and I was asked to step out of the cell. As soon as I stepped out, several officers surrounded me and told me to get against the wall. They searched me violently before placing me in handcuffs, then escorted me to the hole. They talked back and forth between each other as though I weren't there. Though they tried their best to speak in code, I picked up that there was something going on about an officer at another prison getting stabbed, and somewhere in the midst, my name had surfaced. I knew nothing about the stabbing that they mentioned, so my mind started racing. The last thing I needed to add to my prison file was my involvement in the stabbing of an officer. I was escorted over to the hole, and before I could collect my thoughts, I was shoved into a dingy cell. It dawned on me that I would die in prison if I were found guilty of putting a hit out on an officer.

When the officers left my cell, I came to the door to see if there was someone else around me that I knew. I called out a few names of the brothers I knew had been taken to the hole over the last few days. My homeboy E-Way was the first to answer the call. We stood at the cell door talking as I tried to figure out what was going on. Our conversation was interrupted when an officer returned and told me I would be transferring in the morning. E-Way had already been told he was transferring as well, so we assumed we were going to the same prison. We ended our conversation with the understanding that we would be able to talk on the bus in the morning. I didn't realize it would be the last time I'd see him; we were sent to different prisons, and years later, after he was released, he died in a fatal shooting that is still unclear to me.

The following morning, I was transferred to Oaks Correctional Facility. It was my second stint in a maximum security prison in less than five years. Instead of moving forward as I walked the years off of my sentence, I was going backwards and making a bad situation worse.

Chapter 19

When I looked in the rearview mirror and saw the Michigan State Troopers behind us, I knew they were going to pull us over. It was the first time since we had fled Warren, Ohio that I had given any thought to whether the plate on the car we were driving was legit. Before the thought could fully register, I saw the red and blue lights bouncing off the back window of our car like a disco ball. I looked in the front at Frank, who was driving, and his eyes were calm as he pulled over to the side of the road. His father Punchy, who sat in the front passenger seat, told us to let him do all of the talking as the trooper got out of his vehicle and approached our car.

Punchy was a slick-tongued hustler from the era of notorious drug crews who ruled the streets of Detroit in the eighties like the Pony Boys and Young Boys Incorporated. His street pedigree was as thorough as they came, and I was confident that the officer would send us on our merry way, or maybe I was just crazy enough to think that our luck would never run out.

The trooper had a pleasant disposition when he approached the car and asked if we knew why we had been pulled over. We told him no, and he explained that we were driving over the speed limit. He quickly asked for license, registration, and proof of insurance, none of which we had. Punchy began talking, but before he could get out a complete sentence, two unmarked police cars pulled up alongside us. Within minutes, we were spread eagle on the side of the road as the officers tried to figure out where the key to the trunk was located. They searched us and relieved us of the money we had before their sergeant radioed in that they were clear to break in the trunk. When the trunk popped open and the M4 semi-automatic was exposed, the officers went into overdrive with their searches and questioning. They quickly separated us and began interrogating us one-by-one before hauling the three of us down to the station. They threatened us with charges that far exceeded what we ended up getting charged with, but we all refused to make any statements.

When the officers finally informed us that we were being charged with receiving and concealing stolen property over a thousand dollars, we were relieved because we knew we would be getting out on a low bond, or so we thought. The following day, we were charged for the four guns that they found in the trunk and given a bond of twenty thousand dollars. The prosecutor told the judge that he felt we were a flight risk so he requested a higher bond. The bond itself was the least of my worries, however; I was more concerned with what they might discover while I was in custody.

A few months earlier, Frank had come to me with an offer to set up shop in Ohio. He told me that his uncle had a house for us in Warren and it would be a very lucrative venture with great growth potential. I had only known Frank a short time, but he appeared solid so I told him I would consider it. I ran things down to Boe, and Boe agreed that it was a good business opportunity. He suggested that I do a trial run, so a week or so later, I got on the Greyhound bus with a .38 revolver tucked in my waistband and a family-sized bag of Frito Lays with about two thousand dollars worth of rocks in it. Punchy and Frank sat in the back of the bus and I grabbed a seat in the middle. My palms began sweating as more passengers boarded the bus. I surveyed each person's face to see if any of them looked like police or were suspicious of what I was up to. When the bus finally pulled off, I exhaled deeply and re-shifted my focus to the task at hand.

After a bumpy three-hour ride, we arrived in Warren, Ohio and went to work immediately. I gave Frank's uncle T-Bone some sample bags of rocks to take to the strip and pass out to other smokers. When he returned, he told us that some people would be stopping by. I was a bit skeptical, but chose to roll with the flow. We sat around drinking brews for a couple hours before we decided to call it a night. I dosed off on the couch, and within an hour or so, Punchy came to me and told me that he had a customer who wanted to buy some rocks. I got up to serve him, and it was then that I discovered we could mark the prices up three times what they were in Detroit. Rocks that we normally sold for ten or twenty dollars were being sold for forty and fifty dollars. Before the night was out, I had made nearly fifteen hundred dollars.

Within two days, I had sold everything I brought with me, so we went back to Detroit to get more dope. When we returned, I told T-Bone that I needed to find another spot because him and his wife had three young children staying there in addition to their teenage daughter Nycci. He told me that he would find another spot in the next day or so.

I wasn't comfortable selling out of T-Bone's house, and Nycci made it known that she wasn't happy with our presence. Whenever she came home, she gave me the evil eye and barely spoke to Frank or Punchy, even though they were family. Back then, I didn't fully comprehend the hell that we were putting her and her younger siblings through. We had people running in and out of their house at all times of the night, and stayed up late drinking and talking shit while they were trying to sleep. Worst of all, we kept their parents high all day. Despite the fact that I knew Nycci didn't care for my career choice, I knew from the moment I met her that I wanted her to be my girl, and I made it known.

One day, a young man came to the house and asked if Nycci was there. I told him that I was her new man and it wouldn't be wise for him to come over anymore. When Nycci found out what I had done, she was livid, but I didn't care; all I cared about was making her my girl. About a month or so later, her mother told me that her birthday was coming up, and I saw that as an opportunity to show her how much I was interested in her. While she was at work, I went shopping and got her a gift and a card. When she returned home and saw that I had thought enough about her to celebrate her birthday, it melted the frost she had around her heart. I asked her what she wanted to do for her birthday and she said she wanted to go to Youngstown. We made an effort to drive up there, but their was a problem with the car, so we spent the night talking to each other and getting to know each other. Before the night was over, Nycci was officially my girlfriend.

Once we became a couple, Nycci did her best to encourage me to get a regular job and leave the streets alone, but what she didn't account for was the fact that I was too entrenched in the streets. Though I knew she was well meaning, her words fell on deaf ears. I was more committed to the grind than I was to building a relationship with Nycci, but I made an effort to keep the streets away from her as much as I could. Within a few weeks, we had a spot across the street, so I spent the days over there making money and spent the nights getting to know Nycci.

It didn't take long for me, Punchy and Frank to build our clientele in Warren, and before long, we were travelling back and forth between Detroit and Ohio every few weeks. The money was flowing fast and I felt like I was on top of the world, until one day a bag of rocks came up missing. I had been stashing rocks at Nycci's house and some of them came up missing. Nycci's mother blamed Nycci's godfather, and when he came to the house, we beat him severely until he lay slumped over by the back door in the fetal position. I was in a drunken rage, grabbed a gun out of our stash, and attempted to shoot him, but Punchy talked me down. My determination superseded his wisdom, however, and before I knew it, I had pulled the trigger, shooting Nycci's godfather in the side. We all froze in place because we didn't know whether I had killed him. Thinking of the worse case scenario, Punchy hopped into action and started setting everything in motion so that we could wrap him up and toss his lifeless body in the river. But to our surprise, he was still alive.

Punchy decided it was best for us to rush Nycci's godfather to the hospital. I was unsure what the outcome would be when the hospital staff saw that he was brutally beaten with a gunshot wound in his side, but one thing I knew for sure, I wasn't sticking around to find out.

While we tried to figure out how and when we'd head back to Detroit, Nycci grabbed her brother and sisters and fled the house. Once we got Nycci's godfather in the car and Punchy took off headed for the hospital, I tracked Nycci down at her friend's house. She was so distraught that she refused to talk to me, so I left her alone and walked back down to the house. With each step that I took, the gravity of the situation sunk in deeper. The look on Nycci's face when I told her to come back to the house was a wake-up call. In her eyes, I was no longer the slick-talking dope boy from Detroit; I was a monster with a severe penchant for violence.

Prior to looking in Nycci's eyes, I had never given any thought to how my volatile behavior impacted anyone other than the intended target. In fact, the damage I had caused her and her younger siblings was much more severe; they were innocent bystanders. They hadn't agreed to the rules of engagement that come with living life in the streets. However, we had, and we understood the consequences. Even the man I had just shot understood how the streets worked – we could get shot, killed or end up in prison the longer we played the game. We all knew that no one got out of the game without their fair share of scars and losses; it was the cost of doing business in the streets.

An hour or so later, Punchy returned to the house as cool as an icicle in Alaska. He told us that he had concocted a story to tell the hospital staff when he dropped Nycci's godfather off. He then told us that the beating had done more damage than the gunshot, and Nycci's godfather was in critical condition. Although he had assured Punchy that he wouldn't say a word to the police, I wasn't ready to take that risk, so I told them we needed to head back to Detroit as soon as possible.

We tracked down one of our customers who had agreed to take us back to Detroit in exchange for some rocks. We gave him a few rocks and he gave us the keys to his car as his guarantee that he would be back in the morning to take us back to the city. We stayed up the rest of the night talking, smoking, and drinking. Before daybreak, Nycci returned home and got dressed for school. She was quiet and reserved, and I could sense that she was hurt and still angry. After awhile, we talked and she agreed to let me take her to school. I had no idea that that would be the last time I'd talk to her for a month. In that moment, I knew what I felt for Nycci was different from what I had shared with any of my girlfriends before her. Her opinion really mattered to me. Knowing that she was hurting tugged at my heart, but the allure of the game wouldn't allow me to fully embrace my feelings. I knew she wanted me to quit the streets, but I wasn't quite ready to let it go.

When I returned to the house, Frank and Punchy hopped in the car and we left in search of our driver. After driving around Warren for half an hour with no success, we made the decision to drive ourselves back to Detroit. We stuffed all the money we had made in our shoes, stashed the guns we had acquired in the trunk, and took off headed for Detroit.

When the State Trooper pulled us over, the events from the night before cartwheeled through my head like a gymnast; we didn't know if Nycci's godfather had made it through the night or if he had reported the shooting. The troopers took us to Flatrock State Police Post before taking us to Monroe County Jail. The Sheriffs stared at us with grim looks, and within moments, there was a quick buzz circulating through the jail. Rumors quickly superseded the truth, and within hours of being in the bullpen, we learned that we were being investigated for everything from dumping bodies on the freeway to high-level trafficking. Of course, we knew none of it was true, but it didn't take away our fear of them discovering that a crime had been committed with one of the guns they took from us. Each of us knew guys from the streets who had gone out of town and gotten caught up on all kinds of charges, so we knew it was possible for us to be charged with something we hadn't done.

Thoughts of trumped up charges haunted us as we sat beneath the glare of guards, waiting to find out what they had in store for us. Monroe County had a history of racial tension and it hung in the air like Jordan in his prime.

With every shift, we encountered thick-necked, backcountry, good ol' boys who looked forward to letting us know who was in charge. As much as I would have preferred being around Black guards and closer to home, being sent to Monroe County Jail turned out to be the best thing to happen to us.

Chapter 20

Oaks Correctional Facility was sterile and bland like unseasoned mashed potatoes. The exterior of the building was similar to Carson City and all the other prisons built during Michigan's prison boom. When the van pulled into the back of the prison, we were met hy several thick-necked White officers clad in black and grey uniforms and grim faces. Their presence was meant to intimidate and establish dominance, but I had long ago grown beyond the point of being intimidated. I had grown up in one of the toughest cities in America and the things I had experienced in the streets were far more frightening than any cellblock I had ever been in. When I got out of the van, I could feel the tension as the captain made his way through the group of officers.

"So, you're the bad ass who thinks it's okay to order hits on officers," he said as his mouth curled into a tight knot.

I had no idea what he was talking about so I didn't respond. My lack of response seemed to bother the rest of the officers who stared at me as if they wanted to take me out back and lynch me. I returned their glares with a glare of my own to let them know that I wasn't afraid. I was ready to die if necessary and felt like I had nothing to lose, so I held my ground like a dead-game pit bull. After a few tense moments, I was escorted inside the building and placed in one of the visiting booths while they tried to figure out what to do with me. Two hours later, the captain returned and told me that it was my lucky day. It turned out that the Notice of Intent form, which was required to keep me in solitary confinement, hadn't been filled out in a timely fashion so they were forced to release me into general population. At that point, I was still unclear why I had been placed in the hole, and transferred to maximum security.

When I finally got to general population and was able to talk to my counselor, I was told what was going on. My neighbor at the Reformatory had gotten into a conflict with an officer and brutally stabbed him. He was a loner in prison, but I was one of the few guys he walked the yard with. We had met in the county jail while he was on trial for killing his mother and eventually developed a bond. When I first heard that he had killed his mother, I didn't want anything to do with him. I lived by the code of the streets and you were never to harm women or children. The thought that he could kill the woman who gave birth to him just didn't sit right with me, but when he opened up to me about what happened, I understood.

He had just returned from Desert Storm and was shell-shocked. He said that he saw his mother's shadow as she moved around the house one night and thought that he was under attack by the Saudi's. He fired his gun out of survival. However, in jail and in prison, most prisoners shunned him because they didn't understand Post-Traumatic Stress Disorder (PTSD), even though many of them had suffered from PTSD as a result of what they experienced in their homes and communities. Instead of judging him, I embraced him and helped him cope with the guilt that he felt about causing his mother's death. He had been sentenced to life in prison, but the real sentence was the feelings of guilt that he will carry with him for the rest of his life.

The more my neighbor and I talked, the more I realized how intelligent and well read he was. We often exchanged books and had deep dialogues about revolutionary theory, African culture, philosophy, political science, and the military's role in destroying the minds of young men. One day, he pointed out the contradictions in the American legal system. The way he saw it, US soldiers were being sent to war to murder others in the interests of the American government while young men were being sent to prison daily for murdering in their own interests. We continued to build daily, and eventually he started coming to Melanic service. At the time, I was the spiritual advisor and required security at all times. Even though he wasn't officially a part of our security staff, he was vigilant when it came to making sure that I was secured. He carried two shanks with him at all times, and I knew he wouldn't hesitate to use them.

When he got into it with an officer and decided to stab him nearly to death, the administration investigated all of his interactions. They talked to officers and confidential informants, and my name kept coming up as one of the only people he talked to. They knew he had attended our service and I was the leader at the time, so they tried to say that I had ordered the hit. Although they had no evidence to prove I had ordered a hit, they sent me to maximum security anyway.

When I got to the cellblock, I saw a few of the brothers I had spent time with at the Reformatory. When we broke for chow, I ran into a brother named Eric Shabazz who gave me the rundown on the joint. He told me that our Executive Deputy Spiritual Advisor was in the unit and was considering shutting down our service. The brothers hadn't been living up to their potential, so he wanted to shake them up a bit. When I was finally able to talk to the spiritual advisor, he asked me to help him stabilize the brotherhood. I agreed and shared with him some strategies that I felt would help sharpen the brothers. I had learned early on that you needed to challenge the brothers to think and study. I didn't believe in anyone getting a free ride and felt that that strategy would separate those who wanted to be a part of our organization for the right reasons from those who simply wanted the cloak of protection that we provided.

Within my first week at Oaks, I was added to the service callout and scheduled to speak at the next service. I gave a fiery speech about accountability and sincerity when it came to the struggle to liberate the minds of our people. I could sense that the Executive Deputy Spiritual Advisor was impressed and his actions bore witness to that fact. He promoted me to spiritual advisor and told me to clean house. He wanted me to build the brothers up at whatever joint I went to from that point forward. It was a major appointment that came with a lot of responsibility, but I was up to the challenge. From the time I joined the organization, I had set out to build the brothers up and challenge them to be the best revolutionaries that they could be. It was a serious undertaking, but the rewards were worth it.

The rest of my time at Oaks was spent trying to decrease my security level. My ultimate goal was to get transferred back down state, so I tried my best to stay beneath the radar. I was classified to work in the kitchen, which I hated, but I had to do what was necessary to get my security level down. I started off making seventeen cents an hour and eventually worked my way up to thirty-four cents an hour as a baker/cook.

Things were rolling along until another inmate sent a confidential statement to the inspector that said I was planning to take the officers in the kitchen hostage. I was in the midst of pulling a pan of cookies out of the oven when all of a sudden, I was surrounded by several officers who told me to place my hands behind my back. I complied and was taken into the supervisor's office where I was interrogated by the captain and the inspector. I was pissed when I heard why they were interrogating me. They knew that inmates who wanted to get someone else's job would make up shit, but they decided to question me anyway. Before I blew my top, two of my supervisors came into the office and rushed to my defense. They told the inspector that I was one of their best workers and they had never had any problems out of me. It worked, and the officers went on about their way.

I continued to work and stay out of trouble, and within a few months, I was transferred to Gus Harrison Correctional Facility in Adrian. Though it was only a little over and hour ride from Detroit, there was a lot of racial tension between the inmates and guards. In fact, not long before I arrived, a riot had erupted and they locked the prison down for about a month. By the time I got there, the prison was still in semi-lockdown mode so movement was limited.

It was late in the evening when I reached the cellblock I had been assigned to. When I entered the cell, I could see from his belongings that my bunky was White. That was the first time in my incarceration I had bunked with a White inmate. When it was time for the unit to lock down, I waited patiently for my bunky to come back to the cell, but he never showed up. When an officer came to pack up his belongings, he told me that my bunky didn't want to be in the cell with a Black person, and they had to take him to solitary confinement because he refused to lock up. Within a few days, they put another guy, who I found out was a rat, in the cell with me. He had snitched on a female officer who took care of business for a few of my guys. When I found out who he was, I told him that he had to move out of the cell or I was going to kill him. He left and never returned to the cell. I eventually got a bunky I could get along with, and we did our time in a way that didn't interfere with each other.

When I got to Adrian, I could tell the brotherhood wasn't as tight as it should have been, so I went to work organizing the brothers and getting everyone on the same page. As I had done at Oaks, my strategy was to get the brothers to read and study books that would inspire the best in them. I had learned early on that if our religion wasn't connected to our cultural reality, it was useless to our struggle, so I started introducing the brothers to more of the books I had read and had in my personal collection. I put a lot of emphasis on brothers reading Assata Shakur's autobiography because I believed hearing the truth from a woman would have a powerful impact on them. I also intensified our physical training to ensure that we were balanced in our development. We made what we called a "cook up" and ate together nearly everyday to make sure all of the brothers were eating and their basic needs were met. The cook up was a concoction made of Ramen Noodles, cheese, summer sausage, pickles and chili poured over nachos. It was our way of supplementing meals and breaking up the monotony of the prison slop that they fed us.

People started to take notice of how organized the brothers were becoming, but there was one brother who mentioned it every time he saw me. The first time he said something, I took it as a compliment. Then, I noticed that he kept talking about this one brother who he claimed had been acting different ever since I arrived. The second time he mentioned something, I told him that it really wasn't any of his concern how the brother had changed and he should keep his comments to himself. A few weeks later, the brother that he kept talking about got into a conflict, and he ran around the unit telling everyone what happened. He had been forewarned about speaking on our business, but disregarded the warning. I consulted with my security staff and we agreed that he was a threat to the safety and well being of our brotherhood. He was reckless with his mouth, and that wasn't something we could let go. If we did, then others would think it was okay for them to do the same thing.

As one of the leaders of the organization, I was supposed to go into my cell once hits were ordered and wait until the security staff had handled their business. On this particular day, however, I couldn't return to my cell because they were running chow. I was walking back from chow when I saw the guy running across the yard holding his face, blood pouring profusely from his wounds. He ran right by me, headed toward the unit. He had talked so much about so many people that he probably couldn't put two and two together. He went to the infirmary, and that was the last we heard of him. Unfortunately, however, it wasn't the last time I had to deal with conflict.

When I arrived at Adrian, I was just coming off of an ACL tear that happened while I was shooting hoop. The doctor had given me a big brace, and after a few months, I started back hooping. I loved and loathed basketball simultaneously. I loved the game, but hated the games that were played when it came to conflicts on the court. Over the years, countless stabbings had taken place over missed calls, fouls, and slick talking.

Despite suffering a serious injury to my knee, I still made my way back to the court. I found a crew of brothers who I could ball with, and every day when we were allowed out for our two-hour yard period, we ran half-court games. In a matter of days, I had developed a good chemistry with a few of the brothers so we kept the same team daily. We were nearly unbeatable, and after awhile, it became a big thing for anyone to beat our squad. Of course, there were more athletic players who played better than us individually, but none of them could beat us because of our chemistry and unselfishness.

We quickly became the bane of this guy named Tone's existence. Everyday, he came out with a different team of guys attempting to beat us, only to leave the court in defeat. It had gotten to the point that Tone started playing extra aggressive out of desperation. It didn't bother me, until one day he went too far. During our first game against Tone and his team, I came out on fire. I had a stretch where I hit several jumpers in a row. The guys on the sideline started talking smack to Tone, telling him that he couldn't handle me. He said the only reason I was scoring was because I was shooting all jumpers. I took that as a challenge and told my team to give me the ball in the post. They passed me the ball and I scored back-to-back, further frustrating Tone. In an effort to stop me from scoring, he started pushing me in the back and kneeing me in the same knee with the torn ACL. In the middle of the game, I told him to stop playing dirty. In return, he told me, "Play ball!" with a sneer on his face. I smiled to myself because I realized in that moment that Tone had mistaken my genuine concern for brothers as a weakness. He hadn't been in prison long and didn't have a clue about who he was dealing with.

We continued to play, and he continued to play recklessly and talk shit. A few of my guys who were standing on the sidelines watching signaled to me that they were ready to stab Tone as soon as I made the call. I waived them off and told them that I had it. The next time I got the ball, I went down to the post and was about to shoot when Tone kneed me again. I dropped the ball and smacked Tone so hard that it sounded like a gunshot. Before he could react, I choked him up and told him that the next time he disrespected me, I would kill him on the yard. Tears rolled down his face as he looked around for someone to rescue him. A few of the guys were laughing at Tone, saying that they had warned him he was playing with fire.

I knew Tone was a part of the Chicago-based street organization Gangster Disciples, which meant smacking him could lead to a bloody war on the yard, but he was in violation and I was ready to go to war to defend my honor. The code of the yard dictated that the head of the Gangster Disciples address the physical assault of one of his members. Anytime there was conflict between organizations, how the leadership handled it made all the difference in the world. A hotheaded leader could cause a riot to erupt, whereas a levelheaded diplomat could ensure that justice and peace prevailed.

Later that evening before I left my cell, I ensured that the shank I had was as sharp as possible. I packed my property up and threw on a sweathood and boots. The prison was tense as word about our altercation blazed through the compound like a wildfire. When I reached the end of the tier, my security personnel and a few of my homeboys were waiting on me. They knew, without me having to say a word, what had to be done in the event that the Gangster Disciples reacted violently.

When we exited the unit, I saw the Gangster Disciples walking down the walkway slowly. I could tell that they were waiting on me to come out. I gripped the shank tightly as I increased the pace of my steps.

As I got closer, I could see the concerned look on Chicago's face. He was a standup brother and the leader of the Gangster Disciples. We had developed a rapport in the short time I was there, and neither of us wanted to intentionally compromise that. He had been in prison long enough to know how small conflicts could turn into large wars that spread from prison to prison. I was also conscious of the responsibility that I had to my members.

When I approached Chicago, he stepped up and greeted me. I returned his greeting and we both gave a nod to our respective members to stand down as we stepped over to the side. Chicago told me that he'd heard about what happened from several sources and understood my reaction. He acknowledged that Tone was out of order and apologized on behalf of the Gangster Disciples. Like most organizations, the Gangster Disciples had a protocol its members were supposed to follow, and that included never creating unnecessary conflict. In response to Tone's violation, the security arm of their organization took him on the back forty and administered a severe beating.

Though the conflict had been resolved, the tension lingered in the air for a few days so we remained vigilant. We had been trained never to let your guard down once an altercation had reached a physical level. Under normal circumstances, I would have made sure Tone went into protection or visited the infirmary, but I followed the agreed upon protocol when it came to resolving conflict between organizations.

When things smoothed over, I took some time to think about the potential outcome of the conflict and decided to ease back from playing basketball again. I was tired of getting into conflicts with men who were suffering as much as I was suffering. I wanted to set a better example for the rest of the brothers as well, and I knew that would take a high level of discipline on my behalf. I loved playing basketball, but I loved what I was striving to be as a man more. I thought about how Malcolm and Assata would have handled the situation, and it hit me. They would have never been playing basketball in that environment in the first place. So instead of playing ball, I intensified my workouts and study sessions on the yard for the rest of my time in Adrian.

By this time, I was eight years into my sentence and beginning to see the light at the end of the tunnel. I was halfway through the minimum range of my sentence and my security level was close to being reduced. On a visit with my father, son and stepmother, I shared the excitement I felt in knowing that I would be in medium security soon and was steadily working my way through my sentence. Although I still had eight years until my earliest release date, knowing that I had made it through the first half gave me a good feeling. My father told me that he was proud of how I had begun handling myself and staying out of trouble.

My father's words meant a lot to me because I knew I had caused him so much pain and heartache. Whenever they came to visit, my father tried to remain upbeat and focused on us enjoying the brief moments we had together. Sometimes we would just sit and play cards, eat food out of the vending machines, and joke around. In that short space of time, I didn't think about the prison bars that kept me away from my family. All I thought about was their smiles and the laughter that we shared, until it was time for them to leave. That's when the emptiness started to settle in. Sometimes it happened while we were sitting in the visiting room. At that point, I would start feeling anxious and wished they would leave, but I never told them that. I would just sit and act as though I was enjoying their company, while inside I really wanted to be alone.

As I watched my son grow into a young boy and my sisters grow into young ladies, it tore at my soul knowing how much I was missing them. However, I knew that I had to keep my eye on the prize, but it was not an easy task. A few days after my family's visit, my discipline would once again be tested.

It was a brisk fall morning when the brothers and I hustled over to the chapel for our early morning service. When we entered the building, I heard the chaplain in a heated exchange with the officer who worked in the chapel. From the snippets of their conversation I could hear, I gleaned that the officer didn't want to sit in on our service, and it showed on his face when he opened the door to let us in.

Once inside, our head of security began assigning posts to the security personnel before the rest of our members and guests arrived. Whenever a brother was assigned a post, he couldn't move until the floor sergeant officially released them. One of the brothers was assigned the post by the entrance, but the officer told him that he had to get from in front of the door, and he didn't budge. I was in the front of the chapel and saw the officer in the brother's face telling him to get from in front of the door before he sent him to the hole. The brother wore a stoic expression as he held his position. I could see where things were headed, so I sprung into action to keep the interaction from escalating. I told the security head to relieve the brother of his post as I talked to the officer.

I explained to the officer that we had been given permission to hold posts by the administration, but he didn't want to hear it. He said he was canceling our service and sending the brother to the hole. I told him he was overreacting and explained that we weren't going anywhere until we concluded our service. The chaplain stepped in during our exchange and sided with me, but the officer wasn't having it. As we went back and forth, the tension thickened, and before I knew it, the officer had pushed his personal protection device (PPD), leading several officers to rush over. The brothers jumped to attention and stood ready to go to battle with the officers. The last thing we needed was another riot, so I acted quickly. I noticed that the sergeant who came over was our unit sergeant and the supervisor for my job in the unit. I approached her and began explaining what had occurred as the officers and the brothers stood nearly nose-to-nose waiting for someone to give the word.

The sergeant recognized the extreme nature of the situation and told her officers to stand down. The chaplain sided with me, but said he couldn't do anything about the brother who refused to leave his post. The sergeant told me that she had no choice but to place him in the hole, but said she would let him walk back to his cell to pack his property after our service. It wasn't the kind of news I wanted to hear, but I was wise enough to know that it could get out of hand if I reacted out of anger. I told the brothers what was going on and we agreed to continue service, then support our brother while he was in the hole.

When we got back to the cellblock, we had a meeting to discuss the next steps. We knew it was only a matter of time before the administration would try to break up the leadership and ship us off to different prisons. Several of us had been down that road before so we started preparing for a transfer of authority. I was saddened by the fact that our coterie of solid brothers was going to be broken up. We had developed a very solid bond, which made our time less stressful. I knew I could count on the brothers for anything, and they knew that they could count on me.

When the officers finally came to get me a few days later to pack up for my transfer to Muskegon Correctional Facility, it was heartbreaking. Through our battles, I had developed a genuine bond with the brothers who were there, and I felt like they were family. Before I left, the brothers rallied around me and bid me farewell, but promised to keep in touch. Little did we know, that would be the beginning of the end of our organization as we knew it. The next time we saw each other, we would have to operate clandestinely.

Years earlier, when I first read about J. Edgar Hoover and COINTELPRO, I had no idea that such tactics would be employed by the prison administration to dismantle the Melanic organization. But indeed, COINTELPRO was just as relevant and disruptive in 1999 as it was in 1969.

Chapter 21

As I lay on the cracked, wooden bench bolted to the wall in the bullpen of the Monroe County Jail, I started to think about where my life was headed. I had no desire to live my life in captivity, but all of my actions up to that point said something different. I lost count of how many times I had been arrested in my young life. Both of my brothers were incarcerated, so I couldn't say I didn't know any better. Despite their situation, I continued to walk down the same path that led them both to prison.

I was jarred from my thoughts by the sound of loud banging, which caused all of us to look up. Across from us, an inmate was having what turned out to be a psychotic episode. Within moments, a legion of officers rushed into the cell and pummeled him into submission before handcuffing him and leaving him on the floor. In that moment, all I wanted to do was wake up from what was turning out to be a nightmare.

Moments after the excitement died down, I drifted back into thoughts about my life. I made a small promise to change my life if I got out. Conversations that I had had with Nycci flowed through my head in a steady stream. She had encouraged me on several occasions to get a job or go back to school. She believed in me even when I didn't believe in myself, and that made me smile.

I wasn't on a tier with a phone, so I couldn't call Nycci. I missed her raspy voice and smile, and all I could think about was how overjoyed she would be to hear from me. The following morning, we were moved to a different tier, and the first thing I did was rush to the phone. I called Nycci collect and lit up like the sun when she answered. Sadly, my excitement was short-lived. Nycci broke down crying as she told me that she couldn't handle me being in jail. She then told me that she was through with me because she didn't want to jeopardize her safety or sanity. I promised her that I would change if she gave me a chance, but she had seen too much in her young life. She had been lied to and deceived by her parents, so she understood the pathology of the streets and how it manifested in people, even in those you loved.

When I got off of the phone, all I wanted to do was go to my cell and go to sleep, but I couldn't. The jail had rules that restricted us from returning to our cells during certain times of the day, so I grabbed a roll of toilet paper off of the ledge and lay on the floor, using the toilet paper as a pillow. I was super tired and had seen other inmates do it, so I followed suit. Before I could fall into a slumber, I heard a guard calling my name for court. We were being arraigned on charges of receiving and concealing property over a thousand dollars for the stolen guns.

For the next week or so, I fell into a routine, which consisted of sleeping as much as I could and playing basketball whenever they allowed us to go to the recreation. When our preliminary trial date finally arrived, I was tired and worn down. I was ready for it all to be over so that I could find out our fate. Boe had paid for two lawyers, and when we got into the courtroom, they approached us and told us how to conduct ourselves. I prayed that they would let us out, but I had no idea how things were going to go because they had caught us with four guns that had been reported stolen. Although I knew nothing about the legal nature of possession, I figured we were going to prison for awhile if we were found guilty.

The prosecutor called the arresting officer to the stand and asked him to describe the arrest. He started off explaining how he noticed us going above the speed limit and pulled behind our car. He then told the prosecutor that he pursued us to the Monroe and Wayne County border as he ran our plates, then followed us into Wayne County before hitting his lights and pulling us over. All the blood drained from the prosecutor's face as she realized that we had been arrested outside of her jurisdiction.

She shuffled through a pile of papers in front of her, then called a side bar with our lawyers. Moments later, our lawyers came over and told us that they were dropping the charges, but would continue to detain us to see if Wayne County wanted to pick us up on some outstanding warrants we had. Our warrants were for misdemeanors, so the sheriffs told us it was unlikely that Wayne County would waste the time coming out to Monroe to get us. They took us back to the tier where we stayed until nearly midnight.

When the midnight shift came on, the sheriff told me that we were being released and needed to call someone to pick us up. I called my sister Tamica and asked her if her and her husband could come get us. Within an hour, they were calling my name to be released. We changed out of our county blues and back into our street clothes. As I tossed the county blues, I discarded all of the promises I had made to Nycci, my father, and myself as I walked out of the door.

When we got back to Blackstone, Boe and the crew were waiting on us. I was excited to celebrate with my crew, but Boe had other things in mind. While everyone around me was celebrating and drinking 40 ounces of Old E, Boe asked me to step outside on the porch. He started checking me about some of the decisions I had made, and told me that I was being too reckless. The way he saw it, carrying guns interfered with us making money. That was a point of contention between us from day one. Boe understood that gunplay was a part of drug dealing, but he also knew that it brought a different kind of heat and attention to what we were doing. It was understood that you could sell drugs all day and make a lot of money before the police came searching for you, but the moment someone got shot or murdered, the heat was on.

I listened to him and didn't say a word because I knew he was right and had the best interests of our team at heart. However, I wasn't interested in putting the guns down. I felt like guns were the only way to establish and maintain our respect in the streets. I told him that I would chill with the gunplay, but I wouldn't stop carrying a gun. When we finished talking, we went back inside and partied with the rest of the crew.

Within a few days, Frank, Punchy and I decided to go back down to Warren. I couldn't wait to see Nycci and the kids. Even though she had told me that she never wanted to be with me again, all of that changed when I pulled back up in Warren. She fell into my arms and we continued our relationship as if I had never left. Our business had also picked back up so we started bringing other guys down there to help us expand our territory. It was always fun to bring the new dudes down because the girls loved guys from Detroit. For some of them, it was their first time feeling like a celebrity.

Things went smoothly for a few months. We were making more money than we had ever made in our young lives. Every week, we took trips back and forth between Detroit and Ohio. After awhile, we started getting into beefs with the locals who were mad because we were stealing their women and making more money than they were making. They started sending crackheads to our spot to steal, and one night, after they had pulled a jack move on one of my workers, I decided to come over and take care of it.

Earlier that night, a few crackheads rolled up to our spot and asked my worker to let them see the rocks before they made a purchase. When he pulled out the rocks, they slapped the rocks out of his hand, causing them to land in their car, then pulled off. When my worker told me what happened, I was pissed. I put on all black and stood in the back of the parking lot of the spot where we sold dope. When I saw the car pull over, I went over to serve them. I placed my hand in the window to show them a few rocks, and just as my worker had told me, one of the guys slapped the rocks out of my hand and tried to pull out of the parking lot. But before they could reach the end of the lot, I riddled the car with bullets, shooting the driver in the shoulder. I then slipped back into the darkness and headed back to the house.

It didn't take long for word to spread that a Detroit guy had shot what turned out to be one of the local dealer's uncle. Word around town was that the local hustlers didn't take kindly to the fact that I had shot another guy down there. Despite the gossip circulating about them seeking revenge, we continued to open up spots and make money. We were still bringing guys from Detroit, but had also started employing guys from Warren. I found that some of the guys I brought from Detroit were more focused on the girls in Warren and hanging out than they were on getting money, so I sent a few of them back.

One night, Frank and I went to check on one of the spots that we had a guy from Warren working. When we arrived, we knew something was wrong because the woman who lived there was acting strange. Our worker was also seemed kind of nervous when we asked him about the sales for the day. He said it had been a slow day so he didn't have much money for us to pick up. We had been selling out of the spot for a few weeks and had never had a slow day, so I knew something was amiss. I asked him to go get the sack we had given him, and when he returned, I immediately knew that he had messed up. The rocks were small and the bags looked like they had been tampered with. I asked him what happened to the rocks, and he told me that they were like that when I gave them to him.

I looked at Frank, and before the guy could begin explaining, Frank slapped him with a pistol, knocking him into the wall. As he bounced off of the wall, I delivered another blow, which staggered him, but before he hit the floor, he took off running up the stairs. Frank started shooting at him as he fled and he jumped out of the second story window as we gave chase. When we got back downstairs, the woman who lived there stood in the kitchen shaking and in tears. She begged and pleaded with us not to harm her and assured us that she had nothing to do with him messing up the sack. It turned out that he had shaved the rocks down and used what he shaved off to trick with women who came to the spot looking to buy drugs.

We didn't think much of what we had done because we had been in the cycle of chaos and destruction for so long that it was like another routine day. We hadn't accounted for the fact that we were in a small town and things that we saw as petty or insignificant were magnified down there. Within a couple of days, more rumors had been circulated, and before we knew it, people were saying that the police were looking for us and had given the locals the green light to exact revenge on us if they caught us slipping.

There was a lot going on in my head at the time. I was frustrated over a few drug deals that had gone wrong, and I was blowing more money than we were making. I also owed Boe a large amount of money. Instead of telling him that I had messed up, I decided to keep what we made and buy my own weight down there to sell until I made enough money to pay Boe back and keep my thing rolling.

We sought out a few guys from New York to see if they had something for sale, but no one seemed to have anything. We eventually ran into some guys from Detroit and decided to cop from them. What we didn't know was that they were down there to hit a quick lick and then leave. We bought what turned out to be two ounces of fake crack and that put us back considerably, so we decided we had to shoot back to Detroit and deal with the fallout from messing up Boe's cut of the money. I knew the onus of responsibility was on my shoulders because I was in charge.

Once we decided it was time to head back to Detroit, we gathered all of our clothes to take to the laundry mat. We had washed our things and was heading back to the house when a car rolled up on us and started shooting. We had left our pistols in the house, so we had to duck a fusillade of bullets without firing back. Once we made it back to the house, we figured out where the shooters had come from. It turned out that the guy who worked for us and was shaving down the rocks was the brother of one of the local dealers. It was set in our mind that the beef was on. Even though we were leaving out within a few days, we were set on getting revenge and leaving our mark on Warren, Ohio. Over the next two nights, we located all of the drug houses that we thought were associated with the shooters. For two nights in a row, we terrorized the local dealers. We kicked in doors and shot our way into several spots. One time, we caught one of them slipping. He was pulling up to a spot we had just robbed, so we shot up his car and robbed him and the lady he was with. When it was all said and done, we wanted them to know that Detroit had come through.

After our reign of terror, we packed up and headed back to Detroit. It was a bittersweet return because I knew I was going to miss Nycci and the money we were making. In that short amount of time, Nycci and I had been through a lot and I had started growing in love with her. The disease of addiction had wreaked havoc on her life, but she was determined to succeed. All I could do was offer her words of encouragement because I was in no position to take her and her siblings away from the madness, nor was I ready to leave the streets alone. Her spirit of determination inspired me and I wanted the best for her, even though I knew I couldn't provide it. I knew that she loved me and wanted the best for me as well, but I was hell bent on doing things my way. It was hard leaving Nycci behind, and I struggled with the decision, but in the end, I knew it was time to go home and get a fresh start.

Chapter 22

I had heard a lot of things about Muskegon Correctional Facility (MCF) throughout my incarceration. Over the years, it had earned a reputation as one of the best prisons an inmate could be transferred to. Ironically, it also had a reputation as one of the most dangerous prisons because guys got comfortable very easily. It was one of the only prisons in Michigan that allowed inmates to ride bikes, play golf, and hang out anywhere in the prison most of the day. However, a few incidents, including a couple of inmates who took a guard hostage over an unpaid drug debt, a mini-uprising and several brutal stabbings, had caused the administration to tighten things up a bit.

When I arrived, it was in the heart of the summer and the sweltering heat was nearly suffocating. My blues were drenched with sweat and I was ready to take a shower; however, before we were assigned a cell, we were taken to quarantine to be processed into the prison. I had gone through this same old routine with each transfer from one prison to the next. I hated every part of it because I never knew when I would have my own property, or be able to take a shower. I also hated the thought of adjusting to a new bunky.

Within a half an hour, I was assigned to a cell, which was occupied by a brother who was days away from going home. When he told me that he would be getting out in a few weeks, a small knot grew in my stomach. While I was happy to see a brother leaving, I was saddened by the reality that I wouldn't be walking out of those doors behind him. I had long ago blocked out thoughts of what it would be like to be released from prison – I knew that was the only way I could keep myself from going insane – so it was difficult to be in a cell with a guy who was only days away from reclaiming his life on the streets.

My bunky gave me the rundown on how the prison worked as we waited for count to clear. When count cleared, I went down to the day room to get a feel for the joint and see if there was anyone there that I knew from other joints, or if there were any Melanics. I didn't notice anyone who looked familiar, so I just sat back and observed the vibe of the unit. I could immediately see the difference between the higher levels and the lower levels. A lot of the inmates were laughing and joking as if they didn't have a care in the world. This was in stark contrast to being in close custody where the majority of inmates were serving sentences from ten years up to life.

There was also a difference in how the inmates interacted with the officers. In the higher levels, the relationship between the inmates and the officers was very antagonistic, but at MCF, every time I looked up, an inmate was in an officer's face. I knew right then that I was going to hate being there. I thought about everything I had heard about the facility and how nice it was, and that made me even madder. I had no desire to be in a beautified version of hell; I never wanted to be under the illusion that prison was okay. Whenever someone asked me how I felt being in a lower level, I told them that I hated it, and they immediately retreated to silence. No matter how manicured the lawns were or how many recreational outlets MCF had, it wasn't a substitute for freedom.

When they called us out for chow, I walked in the back of the crowd to get a sense of the joint and further explore who was around me. When we exited the unit, I marveled at how large the compound was. As we walked past each unit, I heard a few guys hollering my name out of the window. They asked if I needed anything and told me they would see me when the yard opened up. I felt a little better knowing that some of my guys were there, especially some I hadn't seen in a few years. When yard opened, it was like a Michigan Reformatory reunion. There were a lot of brothers there who I hadn't seen in years and it felt good to reconnect, even though our circumstances were what they were.

My homeboy Lorenzo Jewell gave me a rundown of the yard and introduced me to some of the brothers, I eased into my regular routine – working out and studying. I enrolled in school and everything seemed to be moving in a positive direction. I had a pretty good routine by the time my father, stepmother and son came to see me on a visit. I was proud that I had made it down to level three and couldn't wait to share the news with my family. My father told me how proud he was, and that increased my desire to get my level lowered even more. We had a good visit talking about life and all of the possibilities that lay ahead for us. My father reminded me that I was more than half way through my sentence so the worst was behind me. His words were encouraging and gave me a different perspective on where I was in my sentence.

I returned to the unit feeling good about our visit. It made my day to see my father and stepmother get excited and smile for the first time in awhile. After visits, I always thought about how my incarceration impacted my family and how much I wanted to get out. I not only yearned to free myself, I also wanted to free my family from the prison I had created around their lives.

The summer was moving along quickly and our Melanic brotherhood was preparing for the Day of Remembrance celebration where we honored the memory and legacy of the millions of Africans who were enslaved or died during the transatlantic slave trade. This was a time for us to reflect on our ancestors and see how we could make a positive contribution to the world on their behalf. We fasted for twenty-four hours in preparation for our annual banquet, which was held in the chow hall. I was one of the featured speakers and I talked about the sacrifices made by Nat Turner, an enslaved African who planned one of the greatest revolts on American soil in an effort to liberate our ancestors from bondage. I explained to the brothers that Nat Turner was a brave man who took up arms against his captors, but his greatest sacrifice was risking his life to learn how to read so that he might be a better leader. This was a point often overlooked by the brothers. It was easy for us to focus on taking up arms because that was the reality for many of us growing up in the 'hood, but not many understood that the written word proved to be Nat Turner's most powerful weapon.

It felt good sharing moments like these with the brothers, and when the ceremony ended, the younger brothers gravitated toward me. I represented the balance and integrity that they had been seeking. They told me that they were inspired to learn more so that they too could lead and make a difference when they were released. Feedback like this was one of the things that made the struggle worth it. Being a member of an organization came with many challenges, from battling the officers who hated what we stood for to battling some of the elder brothers who were stuck in the old prison mindset "might makes right." It was these conversations with the younger brothers that fueled my desire to teach them more about our glorious past and our personal responsibility to our community.

Once the buzz from the ceremony died down, it was back to business as usual. As fall arrived, I was feeling good about things. The chill of fall always made me feel optimistic. It was a symbol that the year was coming to an end and a new one was beginning, which meant I was one step closer to knocking another year off of my sentence. Freedom was beginning to feel more and more tangible, and I started thinking more optimistically about my future. I clung to anything inspirational as a sign of things to come, like Serena Williams claiming her first US Open title on September 17, 1999. All things considered, life was good, and over the next few weeks, things were smooth sailing. That is, until one fateful moment when everything I had learned came crashing down on me and I was put to the ultimate test.

On a crisp fall day in October 1999, my chances of ever getting out of prison were almost stripped away forever and I was once again returned to the hellish existence known as the hole for nearly five years. It all happened on a cold Friday morning. The day started off normal enough, or at least as normal as a day in prison could be. I went to breakfast, and then to school. I had been at MCF for two months by this time and was really feeling good about where I was in my transformation at that stage of my incarceration. That was the first time I had been placed in a lower security level, and I knew this was a step closer to going home.

When I initially arrived there, I decided to sign up for the Automotive Technology class that they offered. It was one of the better vocational classes in the system, and upon completion, the job prospects were good. The class was interesting and I was learning a few things about cars that I knew would be beneficial if I stuck it out. But I have to admit, I always looked forward to Fridays, which was the last day of class for the week. I really hated getting up early in the morning during the week, so when the emergency count siren began blaring, I was a happy camper; it meant I would be out of school early and we had the whole weekend ahead of us. The teacher dismissed us and we walked back to our respective units. As I entered my unit, my bladder was on the verge of exploding and I knew I had to make it to the bathroom we were locked down for count.

The sound of the siren pulsated throughout my brain; it was a sound that I had grown familiar with over the years. At some point each month, it was blown to signify emergency count, and we all had to drop whatever it was we were doing and return to our units. The only other time the siren was blown was when there was a serious assault, murder, rape, or an escape attempt. The frequency of the siren often depended on the joint. In prisons like the Michigan Reformatory and the State Prison of Southern Michigan in Jackson, it could be heard more frequently.

When I reached the top of the steps in my unit headed for the bathroom, I noticed several inmates scurrying in and out of the bathroom. It was their last ditch effort to relieve themselves before they locked the prison down for the next hour and a half. As I approached the bathroom door, I knew there was going to be a problem. The officer standing at the door disliked me because of an incident that occurred a few days earlier. It all started when I was released from class early because our teacher was absent. It was during our morning yard period, and when I returned to the unit, I approached the desk and asked the officer to write me a pass to yard. At the time, he was engaged in a conversation with a new female officer. He looked up at me contemptuously and refused to write me a pass. I was not moved by his refusal because I knew I was entitled to go to yard according to policy. My citing of the policy compelled him to write me a pass, but deep inside, I knew it would not come without a price. I figured he would, at a minimum, go and shake my cell down and throw my meager belongings around. However, I had desensitized myself to the value of property so I wasn't really concerned about the shakedown. I had grown to understand that in order to survive in prison, I could not afford to grow attached to anything or anyone.

He knew I didn't fit the mold for the complacent, subservient inmates he was accustomed to dealing with. I wasn't supposed to challenge his authority or quote policy, even though he was clearly in the wrong. As he saw it, I was supposed to walk away with my head lowered, mumbling to myself. But I refused to accept inferior treatment just because I was being held captive. To him, my refusal was the equivalent of a recalcitrant slave defying the authority of the plantation overseer.

That was not the first time I witnessed the superiority complex common among White officers rear its ugly head. In fact, this superiority complex is deeply embedded into the psyche of those White officers whose first contact with people of other races occurred when they were hired, and could be activated by what appeared to be a shallow victory by an inmate. There was just no way he could let a "nigga" get away with outsmarting him. This was something I had come to learn through observation over the years. Even the officers who professed to have no racial prejudices were prone to exact revenge on a Black inmate if they thought he had gotten over on them.

This dynamic is an indictment of the racial reality of America. Some White people cannot come to grips with the fact that Black people deserve to be treated with the dignity and respect that's due all human beings whether we are incarcerated or not. When I started my incarceration, I vowed never to be one of those who bowed down, and I intended to do my time with as much of my humanity intact as my circumstances would allow.

I had been working every day to better myself and learn all that I could in order to deal with my anger and bitterness, but I realized that this rubbed a lot of officers the wrong way. As long as I refused to joke with the officers, waste my time playing cards and sports all day, and spent my time cultivating my mind, body and spirit, I would be perceived as a threat. This was a reality that I refused to run from, and a reality that nearly cost this officer his life, and me, the rest of my life in prison.

As I approached the bathroom, the officer asked me where I was going in a sarcastic way, indicating that I would not be allowed to use the facilities. I told him that I was going to the bathroom, and he responded, "I don't think so," as he let other inmates go in and out of the bathroom. My choices had been narrowed down in a matter of seconds as the officer wasn't wavering. I could either accept a disobeying a direct order misconduct, or I could urinate on myself or out my cell window, neither of which honored my humanity. To this day, I would still choose my dignity over the prospect of a misconduct.

So, I brushed past the officer and entered the bathroom. The few inmates who were in there hurried out; they all knew about me and my previous confrontations. I had recently spoken at the Million Man March Anniversary Celebration in the prison auditorium and had used words and names that conjured up images of resistance. Words like revolution, self-defense, Black Panthers, Nat Turner, George Jackson, Assata Shakur, and Malcolm X. I used those words not to incite, but to share our historical legacy. I wanted them to know that not all of our people sat around twiddling their thumbs and tap dancing; that there were strong African men and women who took a stand for justice. But these were the kind of words that the prison administration held secret meetings about.

Unfortunately, there were a lot of inmates who talked the talk, but very few who were willing to take a stand for anything, and it was those cowardly men who ran off to the comfort of their cells when they saw me push past the officer in order to use the bathroom.

"That's an assault on staff," the officer barked as I used the urinal. As his words echoed in my ears, a brief view of the situation flashed through my mind. I knew I had a disobeying a direct order misconduct coming, but I hadn't assaulted him. If I had, he would have immediately pushed his PPD. I was vexed at the thought of a trumped up charge. As I washed my hands, the officer and I exchanged glances. There were still a few inmates in the hallway standing around trying to see what was going on. A few of them pleaded with him to let me out of the bathroom. He responded by ordering them to lock up.

"Give me your ID," he demanded, blocking my exit from the bathroom. I informed him that I didn't have it on me, then asked if I could leave. He smiled sardonically, which made me realize that this was a sick game that he was enjoying immensely. The whole scene reminded me of a schoolyard bully who continues to shake the life out of a kid even after he tells him over and over that he doesn't have any lunch money. In this case, no matter how many times the officer asked for my ID, I couldn't give him what I didn't have.

The officer continued to egg me on. "You'll produce an ID or you won't leave out of here," he warned as he stepped so close to me that I could feel his hot fetid breath on my face.

It felt like the whole world was closing in on me. I attempted to slide past the officer, and that's when I heard the word "nigger." The officer hadn't moved his lips, however, only his hands. He pushed me in the chest demanding that I produce an ID that I didn't have, and all I could hear was the harshness of the word "nigger" echoing in my head over and over again, telling me that I was less than and my personal space could be violated at anytime. I thought of all the Black men who had been dragged from their beds in the middle of the night kicking and screaming, their cries silenced by the thick rope that was wrapped tightly around their necks before they were hoisted into the air and left to hang from trees like strange fruit. I thought of all the Black women who had been raped in slave quarters while their husbands stood by helplessly, holding in all of their rage to keep his family from being brutally beaten or murdered.

A sense of calm came over me before I attacked with the fluid motion of a panther. I responded instinctually, drawing on survival skills that had been honed in the alleys and streets of Detroit. With each blow I landed, I felt a weight lifted. I felt free from all of the oppression I had experienced at the hands of racist officers and unjust prison policies. I now understood what Frederick Douglass felt when he whooped the overseer who sought to break his spirit. I was no one's slave, and I would rather die or live the rest of my life out in prison than allow anyone to trample over my dignity.

As I stood over the officer choking away the racism, the unearned superiority complex, the 400 years of violence and oppression that African people had endured, I felt liberated, even as another officer twisted my hands behind my back. Several officers dragged the officer, who was now unconscious, into the bathroom where they fought to save his life. Meanwhile, two other officers cuffed me and escorted me to the hole.

Before I left the building, I looked around at the inmates who stood by watching the whole scene play out, and I was deeply hurt. When I looked into their eyes, I saw contempt and anger, all directed at me. It was then that it clicked in my head. I had exposed the talkers for what they were, a bunch of "kneegrow" slaves who would kill each other at the drop of a hat, but refused to stand up for their own humanity. It was a sad and costly day for me, but it was also a moment of epiphany. I felt condemned by the brothers who I loved and wanted more for, and that was far worse than anything the State could have ever done to me.

As I sat in the hole that first day, I asked myself some very serious questions. I sat alone in my cell, staring out of the window at the inmates walking by below and wondered if Nat Turner had felt what I felt when two slaves turned him in to the slave master. I wondered if Malcolm X felt the way I did as he took his last breath, slowly dying from gunshot wounds inflicted on him by the very people whose lives he was trying to save. As I thought about all of my ancestors who had taken a stand for justice, only to have their own people turn their backs on them, I couldn't do anything but shake my head.

Within two hours, several officers came to my door and told me to back up to the door so that they could handcuff and shackle me – I was being transferred. I was then hustled out to a waiting van, which shuttled me to Oaks Maximum Correctional Facility. It would be my second time at the prison, but my first time serving time in the hole there. I would soon learn that it was by far one of the worst places a human being could find himself.

When I arrived in the control center, several officers stood around in a small circle holding handcuffs and shackles. The officers who brought me in had to get their cuffs back so they were forced to switch without freeing my hands and feet in the process. The switch with the handcuffs went smoothly; however, when they got down to my shackles, they discovered that the officer at MCF had placed the shackles on upside down in his haste to get me out of Muskegon, which made it difficult for one of the officers to get his key in the lock. He attempted to twist the shackles around so that he could see better, but that caused the shackles to bite into the tender flesh on the back of my ankles. After a few frustrating minutes, another officer took it upon himself to kick the shackles, causing them to sink deeper into my flesh. We exchanged glares, and I warned him if he put his feet on me again, he would find himself lying in a hospital bed alongside his co-worker. He glared at me without saying anything, but he didn't kick the shackles again. Once they made the switch, I was escorted down to 5-Block and introduced to Michigan's version of hell on earth.

I was immediately placed in a shower cage and strip-searched, then taken to a temporary segregation cell. As the officers opened the cage, they threatened to slam me to the ground if I made any sudden moves. I laughed inside because I knew they were cowards who didn't want any problems. It was quite amusing that people who were supposed to be responsible for our rehabilitation could be more criminal than those who they were supposed to be helping.

Over the next couple days, I felt like an animal in a zoo exhibit as officer after officer came to my cell to see what I looked like. They were all curious about the "monster" they had heard so much about and needed to see me for themselves. Over the next four and half years, a lot would change in how the officers perceived me and how I perceived them. In fact, that experience would mark the beginning of a very powerful transformation inside of me.

Prior to this last experience in the hole, I was a very bitter and angry young man. Like all the other guys who felt they were dealt a bad hand in life, I was vexed with the world. This attitude dictated how I responded to situations, and during the first couple of years of my incarceration, my anger and bitterness had intensified to a dangerous level. But the power of redemption allowed me to conquer my demons and quiet the negative thoughts that threatened to destroy my sanity.

One of the first things I remember when I was finally escorted to my cell was the unbearable smell of human despair, a smell that will forever be burned into the memory of my olfactory system. The smell of defecation, unwashed armpits, soggy toes and spoiled booties mingled in the air with the pepper spray the officers used to extract inmates from their cells. Within a few weeks, I was introduced to a whole new language and culture of madness. Indeed, being caged inside of a cell for 23 hours a day breeds an animalistic mindset within the inmates and the officers.

In an attempt to gain some semblance of control over their environment, the inmates waged battle after battle with each other and the officers, and the officers waged war against the inmates. For the inmates, the weapon of choice was what we called "Weapons of Ass Destruction." These feces-filled bottles were smuggled to the showers or yard cages like pistols. Inmates took deadly aim on anyone they considered an enemy, and once they squirted their shit pistols, the smell clung in the air for days. If they couldn't get you with a pistol, they would make shit patties and slide them underneath your door.

Everyday, I had to wage a war inside myself to ensure I didn't fall into the same mindset that allowed this environment to reduce some inmates to savages. I refused to sit up and play in my own feces, or subject myself to the feces of another inmate. The unfortunate reality, however, was that no one was immune to a misdirected attack. There were a few unsuspecting inmates who were mistakenly doused with someone else's bodily waste because they weren't paying attention when they walked to the shower or the yard.

In the hole, inmates devised every way imaginable to get to their enemies, and for every measure of prevention that the officers came up with, the inmates devised a way around it. After one incident, the officers placed bolts on all of our food slots.

One day, two inmates were arguing, and one of them manipulated his food slot open and waited for the one of the officers to escort his enemy to the shower. When they got in front of the inmate's cell, he kicked the food slot open and squirted a thick stream of feces from his colostomy bag on the inmate and the officer. No matter how many showers they took, the thought and feeling of being drenched in another person's defecation was not easily forgotten. The smell hung in the air like a miasmic cloud for the next couple of days, standing as a reminder for everyone else to be careful.

Once the bolts were drilled into the food slots, several inmates went into MacGyver mode trying to figure out a way to jimmy the locks open, and it didn't take long. First, they had to slide a comb, which they attached to a piece of string, out of the top of the door while their neighbor across the hall guided their movements. Once the comb was lined up with the bolt, they pulled the comb up until the lock came undone. After that, all they had to do was slide a cable cord beneath the door, twist it around the knob, then continue twisting until the slot popped open and it was business as usual.

Another weapon of war was sleep deprivation. Sometimes when inmates were in conflict with each other, they'd beat on the steel toilets or walls all night with a brush or some other hard item, which of course impacted the whole wing. Sometimes these wars lasted for weeks, or until one of them was moved to a different cell. There was never any regard for innocent bystanders, and this often led to others being drawn into their wars. Another method of getting even was to blow the power, which meant the other three inmates who shared the same breaker would be unable to watch the three channels of TV that we had.

Every day that I spent in the hole, there was something going on that challenged my humanity. After the first two years, I had grown tired of seeing grown men act like children; however, instead of complaining, I sought to gain an understanding of my environment and why other inmates reacted the way they did. But first, I had to gain an in-depth understanding of myself.

Though my reaction to the environment didn't manifest the way it did with others, it didn't mean that I wasn't as psychologically scarred as the rest. In fact, to some degree, the internal scars that I bore were far worse, and if I had allowed them to remain beneath the surface until I was released, the consequences could have been catastrophic. I knew that a complete change was needed, so I set out to transform my thinking.

The Honorable Elijah Muhammad once said, "In order for a man to completely change his conditions, he must be completely dissatisfied with them," and there was no doubt I was completely dissatisfied with my conditions. So, the first thing I started doing was keeping a journal. It was within the thin pages of my notepads that I found a peace of mind and was able to truly be myself for the first time in a long time. I got down to the root of who I was as a person and realized that I wasn't much different from those who used "Weapons of Ass Destruction." Inside of me burned that same rage, the kind of rage that nearly cost an officer his life, and me the rest of my life in prison. It was this same kind of anger that clung to my back while I was on the streets, leading me to take another person's life.

I was tired of living in a ball of anger and bitterness and tired of hurting people, including myself, but I didn't know what to do or where to turn. As I sat back listening to the chaos on the wing, I knew I could never leave prison the same way I came in. I had to change. Prison had nothing to offer me other than more anger and violence. The officers had no vested interest in seeing me turn my life around; to most of them, I represented job security. Furthermore, the State had long ago given up on rehabilitation, so in order to be the man and father that I was destined to be, I had to take a long and painful look at myself.

I began charting my anger by writing my thoughts down whenever I got angry. One day, my neighbor blew my power while trying to get a light for his cigarette. When I asked him about it, he lied, and my immediate reaction was to kill him. To me, his life was worthless and he deserved a swift and painful death. A few days later, after I had calmed down, I returned to my journal and read what I had written in response to my neighbor blowing the power. I found it quite disturbing. Despite his inconsideration and blatant disrespect, I knew what he had done wasn't worth me killing him or inflicting any physical harm on him.

Throughout the remainder of my time in the hole, I continued to chart my anger and document my thoughts when I got angry. Through this process, I slowly realized that I had some deeper issues that I had never addressed. I started writing about how I felt about my relationship with my mother and how I felt as a child when she beat me for minor infractions. I wrote about my parents' divorce and how the dissolution of their marriage impacted me. There were so many things that came to the surface as I wrote in my journal, and it felt like a great weight was being lifted off of my shoulders with each page that I wrote. No longer did I feel the old familiar bitterness that I had carried around inside of me in a tight little ball, keeping me one provocation away from exploding.

I also wrote about all of the physical violence I had suffered in my life and how it made me feel towards people. I discovered layers upon layers of scars, and eventually realized that I was like a whole lot of other young males who suffered from Post-Traumatic Stress Disorder. Like them, I had been forced to suppress my feelings for years. There was no one I could share my pain or my fears with, and this silence began manifesting into anger and violence toward others. The way I saw it, no one had ever felt anything for me, and so I didn't feel like I had to care about anybody else.

When I went back and read page after page of my journal, I could feel myself growing stronger and stronger as each day passed. As the pain from years of abuse and neglect began to dissipate, my feelings toward my fellow inmates began softening and I started becoming more compassionate toward them.

To a certain degree, I already knew how the hole was supposed to impact me, and that helped me avoid falling into the abyss of despair and insanity that has claimed so many. I knew I would leave with some indelible scars to my psyche, but I had to do everything I could to minimize the damage if I wanted to be the father that I needed to be to my children. Everyday was a test of my will to survive as I watched the insanity all around me. I continued to write about the things I saw and experienced, and by doing so, it felt as though I was taking the power away from them.

One of the experiences I wrote about in my journal was the night a Latino inmate set himself on fire. He was so desperate for escape from the pain and misery of solitary confinement that he chose to end his life through immolation. His ordeal began weeks before when the officers began harassing him constantly because of his sexual orientation. After days of harassment, he woke everyone up in the middle of the night with a loud and chilling rendition of the Lord's Prayer. The next day, he set the cell on fire while he was in it. The officers rushed onto the wing and sprayed him with a fire extinguisher before taking him to a suicide watch cell. Within two weeks, he attempted the same thing again, after which they removed him from the cell and never brought him back.

The depth of the psychosis that I witnessed every day was terrifying, but the staff psychiatrist downplayed it. He claimed that these inmates were just "acting out." However, I know from living in the hole around hundreds of inmates for nearly five years that isolation causes a disconnect in the deepest part of the human psyche. There is nothing humane about being caged in a cell for twenty-three hours a day. Add to this, all of the other stresses that inmates face day-to-day, including being neglected and abandoned by their family members, and you have a recipe for disaster. Extended isolation is enough to cause a significant mental breakdown. I witnessed guys who I had known for years as solid people have mental breakdowns after ninety days in the hole.

As the months passed by, I documented the wars that were waged between the inmates and the officers. Whenever the officers did something that we felt was unjust, we flooded the wing with water from our toilets until they cut the water off. On one occasion, as I stood by my door watching the two-inch deep pool of water ebb and flow outside of my cell, I couldn't help but think about of the people in Third World countries who were dying because they didn't have clean water, and here we were forced to use water as a weapon of war. But sadly, this was the only way we had to voice our grievances and get an immediate response. The officers knew if they didn't pass out our mail in a timely fashion or served our meals cold, they would have to wade through water until they got porters to clean it up. And if they played with the showers, we would beat on our doors relentlessly until they corrected their behavior. The way we saw it, if we didn't fight back, they would continue to run roughshod over us.

So with pen and pad, I clung to my sanity; between that, writing letters to my family and reading their letters to me, I redeemed my soul. There were plenty of days when I felt like the hole would consume my spirit, but I fought tooth and nail to stay strong. There were days when I swore I couldn't take one more day smelling another human being's bodily waste, or one more rejection from the prison's security classification committee regarding my release from administrative segregation, but then I would sit down and write out my thoughts or read an inspirational book, and I knew I had to keep on keeping on. My community and my family, including the brothers who had become my family in prison, were counting on me to be strong, so I fought for my sanity until the day of my release from the hole. It was then that the true test began.

Chapter 23

When we were finally released from Monroe County Jail, I returned to Detroit ready to pick up where I left off, but things had cooled down on the block. If I wanted to make any money, I knew I had to figure out a way to turn the heat back up on Blackstone.

While I was in Ohio, things had changed a lot. Boe had moved his mother off of the block and business had slowed down a lot. My relationship with Boe was strained, but we had started talking again. He was out on bond for a dope case and was focused on how he was going to get from under the charges. My sister was in the process of moving on with her life. She had separated from her husband and moved off of Blackstone.

I reached out to some of our old customers and told them that we were going to crank things back up, and slowly but surely they started coming back. Things were going slow, but I was making enough money to stay fresh and take care of the basic necessities, but it didn't compare to the money I was making in Ohio, or the money I was making on Blackstone before I left for Ohio. However, I had faith that Blackstone could rebound and I'd be making money again soon.

I had been back a week or so when I took notice of our new neighbors, who had moved into the house next door to Tamica. The house once belonged to her friend Lashawn. She had moved on and a new family had moved in. I didn't know any of them, but it wasn't long before I started seeing a bunch of young ladies going in and out of the house. From all appearances, it was mostly females living there, which was right up my alley. Our crew had built a reputation for hooking up with all the females in the neighborhood, and I knew it wouldn't be long before I was in hunter mode.

One night, I was standing outside kicking it with Mark when one of the females from next door asked if we could help them get their car started. She was really pretty with long hair and I was drawn to her. I later learned that her name was Michelle and her man was one of two guys who lived in the house. We laughed about me hitting on her while her man was in the house and I thought nothing more about what was going on over there until a week or so later when I started noticing a few of our old customers stopping through. That's when I realized someone over there was selling dope. My thoughts were confirmed when one of our old customers stopped by our crib and asked me if that was our operation. I told him no and kept it moving. Later that same day, one of the girls from next door came outside and approached me. She had on a sweatsuit with her hair pulled back in a ponytail. I watched her demeanor as she walked up and laughed inside at how confident she appeared to be.

"Do you have a pistol I can borrow," she asked with the ease of someone asking to borrow a cup of sugar.

My initial thoughts were, what did she need a gun for, and why would she approach a complete stranger? Then, I thought about the activity next door and some of the things I had seen over the years. I considered her request and thought about a small .25 caliber Raven I had purchased from one of our customers. I told her that she could use it, but she had to return it. She agreed, and I gave her the pistol. I didn't even think about the fact that I was a teenager giving another teenager a gun, nor did I think about how easily guns fall into the hands of young Black youth in cities like Detroit. All I thought about was what I would want someone to do if I needed access to a pistol.

Later that night, she came back to the house and I learned her name was Brenda. She asked me if I wanted any money for use of the pistol, and I told her no. We talked for a minute and she told me why she needed the pistol – she was at the other end of Blackstone selling crack. She then asked me if I wanted her to take some rocks down there the following day. That's how my relationship with Brenda began. It wasn't the traditional boy meets girl and fall in love type of thing. However it was defined, this is how we were brought together. At the time neither of us knew where things were headed because Brenda was in hustle mode and wasn't looking like the attractive young lady that I would later discover.

Over the next couple of weeks, Brenda and I spoke whenever we saw each other, but it wasn't until I was coming down the block one day that I noticed Brenda in a different way. She had her hair done, a little makeup on, and was dressed up like a young lady. She had piqued my interest and I had obviously piqued hers according to one of my homegirls. Within a few days, our brief conversations grew in length and we started hanging out together.

On the exterior, Brenda had been hardened by the streets of Brightmoor and a rough upbringing. It didn't take much for her to fight and she rarely backed down. However, the more I got to know her, I saw a young lady with a heart of compassion who was loyal to her family. Sadly, like many Black youth growing up in dysfunctional homes, her golden heart had been calloused by neglect, hurt and heartbreak. Together, we were like two birds with broken wings trying to find solace in each other.

Our relationship started off cool and we enjoyed each other's company. We laughed and joked most of the time or just sat in the back room of their house kicking it. It wasn't long, however, before the mercurial nature of our personalities began clashing. Brenda didn't believe in holding her tongue whether she was right or wrong, and I refused to be spoken to in a disrespectful manner. When we had our first argument, we nearly came to blows, and at that point, I should have known that it wasn't going to get any better. I was raised not to hit women and didn't believe in demeaning or degrading them either, but nothing in the father/son handbook had prepared me to deal with a girl as volatile as Brenda.

I had been around men who thought nothing of hitting women who they felt were out of line, and I always despised their behavior. To me, hitting women was a sign of weakness and an indication that they were out of control; however, I never condemned any of them. I knew so many guys who dealt with conflict that way that it wasn't out of the norm. Personally, I had no desire to travel that route, but one day I found myself faced with a girl who wouldn't back down.

It all started with the fellas chilling next door kicking it. Brenda's cousin Michelle was eavesdropping and overheard her man JB saying something she disapproved of. Before we knew it, Michelle burst through the door cursing him out. JB made her go next door, then followed her over to the house while the rest of us lingered around drinking and talking. After awhile, I went next door to check on JB and discovered him and Michelle in the room fighting. When I knocked on the door, Michelle started cursing me out, telling me to get the fuck off of her porch. I had never disrespected her, so I told JB to check his girl because she was out of line. I didn't know he was going to start beating on her, otherwise I would have left it alone.

I stepped off of their porch and all I could hear was screaming and banging. I felt bad for Michelle, but before I could even process what was going on, Brenda burst out of the house accusing me of starting the whole thing. I told her to calm down, but she kept cursing and talking shit. Her verbal assault continued for several minutes before I told her to shut the fuck up before I beat her ass. That was the first time she had seen me that angry, but instead of seeing that she had gone too far, she continued to egg me on. I ran up on the porch to get to her, but she ran into the house and locked the door. She then proceeded to curse me out even more, joined by her sisters and cousins. I had been drinking and my anger was boiling and raging hot like lava. I told them that I was going to beat all of their asses when I got in the house. They laughed and mocked me as I stood outside of the window. After awhile, I said to hell with it and went back inside my crib.

Moments later, one of our friends named Derrick came over and we started to talk. He asked where JB was and I told him next door. He had made his way over to the house and was standing on the porch when I came back outside. I walked over and stood behind him so that they couldn't see me, and when they opened the door to let him in, I rushed through the door. Without giving any thought to my actions, I hit Brenda in the face and grabbed her up. Derrick attempted to grab me and calm me down, but by then, I was too far-gone. I hit her a few more times and threatened to shoot her sisters and cousins for getting in my business. I was in a rage and was determined to make her respect me. I didn't realize that I was losing it. I had crossed lines I said I would never cross, and did so with relative ease. I had intentionally hit Brenda and threatened to shoot her family members. Sadly, when we made up a few days later, it became a long running joke between us.

While that incident was the first, it was certainly not the last time Brenda and I would clash. Like me, Brenda and her sisters had seen so much violence and heartbreak that fighting each other had been normalized.

Over the next few weeks, Brenda and I continued our relationship and eventually moved in together. We sold crack together and did what we felt was necessary to survive at the time. We had customers coming to the same place we laid our head, so we were extra vigilant. We had several guns in the house and I never doubted whether Brenda would use one, if necessary. We had both seen enough to know that no one was to be trusted, and at any given time, a customer could become an enemy, or a rival dealer might try to set us up.

It was a fast, hard life characterized by desperation and hopelessness. With each day, I drank more and more in an effort to numb myself from the madness around me. I wasn't happy, and no matter how much money we made, it wasn't enough to heal the deep wounds that I had on my heart and soul.

Our days and nights started merging into a blur of shopping trips to Northland Mall, eating at restaurants, and throwing impromptu parties at cheap motels. We spent money recklessly and found ourselves always playing catch-up because as fast as we made it, we spent it. Like most dealers, we were living for the moment so we didn't have an investment or savings plan. We also had no long-term plans to get out of the game or do anything substantial with the money we made. The game was up and down, and for a minute, we found ourselves struggling to make ends meet. So, essentially we were risking our lives for what amounted to a minimum wage job.

After a few months, things were really picking up and I started doing business with Brenda's cousin's boyfriend. We went half on various amounts of crack and split the profits. We went from making a few hundred dollars a day to making a couple thousand every few days. It wasn't King pen status, but we felt like we were moving in the right direction. I started saving more money to buy larger quantities and felt like it was only a matter of time before I would be making a lot of money.

The timing couldn't have been better because Brenda thought she was pregnant. I was excited when she broke the news, but a little hesitant to embrace the fullness of her revelation. I had already suffered a devastating blow from a young woman named Sherita who played games with me about being pregnant with my child. When Sherita and I hooked up, she was living with her son's father, but when she found out she was pregnant, she told me that it was my child. I told her that I would do my part to take care of the baby if she was sure it was mine. She said she was sure, so we started planning for the baby's arrival. However, every time she got mad at me, she would tell me the child wasn't mine. Despite the growing doubts I had, when the baby was born, I embraced her in my heart as my daughter.

Unfortunately, I had no legal standing when it came to seeing my daughter so I was at the mercy of her mother. One night, I couldn't take being denied what I felt was my right to see my daughter, so I took her from Sherita. She told her son's father and he came over to the house where we were chilling. I had just left the house, but Mark was still there and the two of them got into a shootout that left Sherita's son's father and her sister shot. One of my aunts told me that I needed to take the baby back to Sherita, and that was the last time I had my daughter on my own. It would be twelve years later before my daughter and I would finally reconnect.

Over the next couple of weeks, Brenda started to show signs of pregnancy, including morning sickness and weird eating habits. At night, we laid in the bed kicking it about the upcoming birth of our child and what we wanted for him or her. The reality of bringing another life into the world changed our focus about hustling. We talked about saving enough money to move and get away from it all so that we could get a fresh start. At the core of our being, we both wanted better for ourselves and our child; we just didn't know how to get out of what had become a vicious cycle of dysfunction. At night when we were laying up talking, everything sounded good; however, when the morning came, it was right back to the cold reality of the dope game.

One day while we were sitting in the living room, Derrick came by and told us about this party around the corner. He said the guy needed a DJ and asked if I was interested. I told him that I was and we set up an agreement for me to do the party. The next day, Brenda and the rest of the crew went shopping to get fresh for the party. It had been awhile since we had all gone out to a spot to party, so we were super excited to cut loose for a minute. I think I was more excited than anyone else because I would be DJing for the first time in a long while. Music was one of my passions, and I loved nothing more than watching people dance to whatever symphony I composed.

When I arrived at the party, people had already started showing up, which was a good sign that the party was going to be live. Within an hour or so, the backyard was packed and the party was in full swing. Everyone was drinking and smoking, but I was chilling because I didn't want to get too drunk while I was spinning. That didn't last long because a few of my homeboys from my other 'hood came through, and before I knew it, they were passing around Old English 800 and Seagram's Gin. Once I started buzzing, I let someone else take over the turntables and went to drink with my crew. We had a table in the back of the yard and started dancing and acting silly with each other. That was the first time Brenda and I had been to a party together and we were having the time of our lives, until gunshots rang out.

People started running out of the backyard screaming and hollering. I pulled out my pistol and told everybody in our crew to follow me out of the party. When we got to the front of the house, I ran into one of my homeboys who told me what happened. When I learned that Derrick, who was in our crew, was the one shooting, I became very alert. I didn't know if the beef was with someone we didn't know who might come back and retaliate, or if it was with someone we knew. Derrick was nowhere around, so I had no way of gauging the situation. I told Brenda that it was best for us to head home, so we left and started walking back around the corner. Before we reached the house, a Jeep pulled up on the side of us and I slowly eased my finger around the trigger of a .380 that I had in my pocket. I didn't even pull the pistol out of my pocket because I had already planned to shoot through my jeans if I saw any sign that they wanted beef. It turned out that they were only looking for directions. I breathed a sigh of relief and continued talking to Brenda until we reached the front of our house.

Just as we were preparing to go inside, another car pulled up in front of the house and the car window lowered slowly. All I could think about was how vulnerable we were, but I was ready to go down in a blaze of gun smoke. Once again, I found my finger resting in the familiar comfort of the trigger and was prepared to shoot.

"Yo Jay, you on?" a familiar voice called out from the backseat of the car.

I told Brenda to go inside the house as I headed over to the car with Mark not far behind. When I reached the car, I noticed two White men who I had never seen before in the front seat, and Tom, who was one of my favorite customers, sitting in the backseat with a handful of cash. He was known to spend several hundred dollars each time he stopped by, but this time he had more money than I had ever seen him with.

"Yo, why you bringing people to my house I don't know. You know the rules over here," I responded with a bit of irritation in my voice.

Even though we were selling out of our house, we limited who we allowed to come over, and we never welcomed strangers. Too many guys we knew had been set up to be robbed or busted, and I wasn't about to take any risks no matter how much money they talked about spending. I conveyed this to Tom and we started arguing. I told him that I thought he was trying to make a deal for the police and I wasn't going to serve him. He continued trying to make the deal, and at that point, I was really suspicious so I told him to get off of the block. I took a step back from the car and was about to go inside the house when Tom called me back over and begged me to make the deal. I refused, and at that point, I was irritated and getting pissed off.

I told Tom that he had five minutes to get off of the block, and that's when one of the other passengers joined in the conversation. He told me that I couldn't make them go anywhere. I turned to Tom and told him again to get the fuck off of the block. His friend told me to fuck off; they weren't going anywhere. I asked them if they were the police because I had never seen any of my customers come in the 'hood and act so brazen. I asked them to leave for the last time and Tom's friend continued shouting out of the car. That's when I pulled out my pistol.

At that point, Mark was like, "Fuck them, Jay. Let's go in," and I started walking toward the house. I had taken about three steps when Tom's friend opened, or attempted to open, the car door. Thoughts of getting shot flashed through my head and I spun back around with the pistol in my hand. The guy said something else, which I can't remember to this day. All I recall is the feeling of danger that I felt, and in response, I fired several shots into the car before they sped off headed toward Fenkell.

It was nearly three o'clock in the morning and it was hard to see, so I never saw the guy's face or if he had anything in his hand or not. Although I didn't know where the shots I fired had landed, something in my soul told me that something terrible had happened. In that moment, I knew the guy had died, long before we found out for certain the following day. I had shot several people before, but this time was different. I felt empty, afraid, and alone. I knew I had fucked up and there was no reversing what I had done. I had allowed my anger and paranoia to consume me in such a way that I developed a reckless disregard for human life.

The gravity of the situation hit me as soon as I went back in the house. It's like everyone knew that the shots were fatal. For the first time, I saw a level of fear in the faces of my friends that I had never saw before. We all packed up, locked the house down, and headed over to Brenda's cousin's house. I told Brenda that I knew I had killed him, and she broke down crying in my arms. The consequences of living the street life had manifested in our lives in the worst way. Here it was, Brenda was pregnant and ready to welcome life into the world, and I had just robbed a family of their husband, father, son, and brother. In that moment, I prayed that it was all a bad nightmare, but sadly, it wasn't.

Brenda and I discussed going on the run together, but we were naïve and immature. A couple days later, the thought of living life on the run was dashed when I was arrested and charged with open murder.

Chapter 24

I was not having a good day – I mean, no day in prison was good – but I had seen better. They had just picked up the trays from lunch and the unit was loud as usual. Normally, I would have just blocked out the noise with my thoughts, but I couldn't. I had too much on my mind. I was ready to get out of solitary confinement and the wait was unnerving. It had been nearly two weeks since my file had been sent to the security classification committee for review.

This was the fourth time my file had been reviewed by the security classification committee. The first two times, I knew I didn't stand a chance at getting released. It wasn't until my third year in the hole that I felt I had a real chance. When I was denied that third time, it nearly broke my spirit. The saying "three strikes and you're out" echoed in my head as I thought about the men I knew who had been in solitary for over twenty years. When the counselor finally stepped to my door and told me that I was being released to general population, I was beyond shocked. I had hoped that I would be released one day, but I had become cynical.

On the day I was released from the hole, I did a George Jefferson stroll down the tier and out of the door. I had made a promise with the other inmates that I would stroll out of the building with that infamous walk perfected by Sherman Hemsley. It felt good to step out of the building and walk without handcuffs and shackles. I felt like all eyes were on me as I walked through the compound, but in reality, I was just another brother released from the jail within a jail.

Once I got my typewriter, I went straight to work typing out the books I had written while I was in the hole. Day after day, I pecked away on my five-year-old word processor. When I had typed thirteen pages, the memory on my word processor would fill up and I had to print out all of the pages, clear the memory, and start typing again. It took several days of typing all day to get a manuscript finished. Despite this painstakingly slow process, I was determined to get it done. I was in a cell by myself, so I was able to sit for eight hours at a time typing, uninterrupted.

A couple months later, they reduced the prison's security level to close custody and made us double bunk. My bunky turned out to be a brother from Lansing who I had heard a lot about. BX and I were a part of the same brotherhood so we shared a lot of the same views about life. We ended up getting along like brothers. In addition to bunking together, we both worked in the law library and worked out together. BX was serving 52 to 75 years and spent most of his time researching law. We talked about our sons, and he constantly reminded me why it was important for me to focus on getting out of prison. The four years that I had left before my earliest release date initially felt like a long time until he told me to take his sentence into consideration. His words kept me motivated about getting out and using my testimony to make a difference in the community.

A few months later, I was transferred to Carson City, and shortly after I arrived, BX showed up. We laughed about the coincidence and agreed that there was a reason we were relocated to the same joint. We immediately went to work organizing the brothers and facilitating study groups. The impact of our efforts was felt immediately throughout the compound.

Carson City had a notorious reputation as one of the most racist facilities in the state and the tension in the air was thick enough to slice with a prison shank. The younger inmates were clueless about how to deal with the officers who went out of their way to trample on the few human rights we had left. BX and I discussed what needed to be done and went to work showing the brothers how to use the grievance system to address whatever issues they had. Daily, we trained physically and mentally and the younger brothers gravitated to us. We were doing what had been done for us when we first entered the system as teenagers and felt it was our responsibility to do the same.

That year, we organized a Kwanzaa program, and after a successful turnout, we were invited by the special activities coordinator to organize events for Black History Month. We convened a small group of brothers that included one of my guys from MR named Larry X. We agreed to do weekly events, and then do a males rites of passage program. I reached out to my comrade Yusef Shakur, who had been home a few years, and asked if he could come up to speak with the brothers. He said he and another brother named Kwasi would come through and support our program.

On the day we were to launch the male rites of passage program, I was filled with excitement. I couldn't wait to see Yusef as it had been nearly ten years since we'd been at the same prison. He was the first brother I knew personally to get released from prison and follow through on his promise to be an asset to our community. When I told Larry X that Yusef was coming up, he got just as excited as I was. We had all grown up in prison together, sharing books and ideas.

When I reached the building where our program was to be held, I was met with disappointment. The activities director informed me that Yusef couldn't get clearance to return to the prison. I was pissed because I knew that the younger brothers needed to hear his story; to see that it was possible to get out and do something with your life. He told me that even though Yusef couldn't make it, two other members of Helping Our Prisoners Elevate (HOPE) had been approved and would be attending our program. I knew Kwasi was one, but I had no idea who the other person was.

A few minutes later, the special activities director returned to the room with Kwasi and a beautiful sister named Ebony, who I would later learn was also a member of HOPE. We had exchanged correspondence related to HOPE before, but I had never seen her or spoken to her. She had beautiful almond-shaped eyes and a positive aura about her that made me smile inside. I welcomed the two of them into the room and opened up the program. We had a very candid conversation about what we needed to do in our community and the brothers agreed to be difference makers when they were released. We then went into a Q & A session before concluding the program. It was then that I developed an intense attraction to Ebony. She was very passionate about her views on Black men and their role in the community. She articulated her points with a fiery intensity that made me think of Assata Shakur, who to me epitomized the strength and resilience of Black women. I listened to the words that flowed from her mouth as I fought the urge to stare at her and drink in all of her beauty. I knew I had to tuck away my thoughts for my own sanity and the sake of the program. Over the years, I had quieted the desire to be in the presence of a beautiful woman, but those desires returned with a vengeance after meeting Ebony. Despite my deep longings, I refocused on the task at hand. No matter how beautiful Ebony was, I was unwilling to compromise the integrity of the program or my standing as an organizer.

During this time, BX had been corresponding with a woman he met through another inmate. She was very supportive and did her part to help him gain his freedom. One day while I was on a visit with my family, she came up to visit him. When my visit concluded, BX came out to the yard and told me that she had a sister who might be interested in corresponding with me. I told him that I wasn't interested in another superficial pen pal relationship. I had long ago given up on having anyone in my corner other than my father and stepmother. I had endured years of broken promises and fraudulent correspondence, so I wasn't interested in going through the emotional roller coaster ride. Even though I was down to my last four years, I realized that it was still a long time for anyone to wait for me or stand by my side, so I told BX that I had no interest.

A few days later, he came out to yard and asked me to give her a chance. I thought about it again and decided to go ahead and write his girl's sister. I thought about BX's situation and the distance his girl had to travel to see him. I figured the worst-case scenario was that she'd at least have someone to travel with her, so I wrote a letter and gave it to BX to send out. A week or so went by and I didn't hear anything back. I had told BX that it would go down like that, so I retreated back to my writing and focusing on my freedom.

A day or so after my conversation with BX, I was transferred over to level two. I had never been to level two, so I was a bit excited and nervous at the same time. I had grown mentally since my short stint at MCF; however, I was apprehensive about dealing with the newer inmates who were coming in fresh off the street and the officers who thought nothing of sabotaging our freedom.

When I arrived in the unit, there was a buzz due to my presence. There were a few guys in the unit who had either heard of me or knew me from other joints. They stopped by my cell to see if I needed anything, and I told them that I was okay. My bunky was a young guy fresh off the street. We talked briefly as I cleaned up my area. As we talked, the officers stopped by the cell and dropped off our mail. He called out my name and number, and when I acknowledged, he handed me a small stack of mail. Most of it was internally generated mail about my transfer to level two, but amidst it was a small envelope with some unfamiliar handwriting.

When I read the name, I realized that it was the lady who BX suggested I write. Her name was Lauren and she was from Flint, Michigan, a small city north of Detroit. I could sense from her 8-page letter that she was down-to-earth and genuinely interested in learning about me as a human. Once I settled in, I wrote her back and began what turned out to be a great friendship. She became my comfort as I adjusted to the level two. We wrote each other nearly everyday and I found a part of my heart softening toward her. She was very inquisitive, but not in an intrusive way, nurturing and kind. Whenever we talked on the phone, she always asked if I needed anything and if I was feeling okay. After a few weeks of exchanging letters, we arranged our first visit.

I didn't know what to expect on the visit because it had been some years since I had a visit from anyone other than my family. I made it to the visiting room first and was assigned a seat where I waited for Lauren to enter the room. A few moments later, she entered wearing a purple skirt set that looked like it was better suited for a church than a prison visiting room. We took advantage of the rule that allowed us to hug and kiss briefly at the start of our visit. It felt good holding her softness in my arms and feeling the warm caress of her lips. For over a decade and a half, all I had experienced was the hardness and harshness of the cold and indifferent world of prison, so having a little bit of humanity smuggled inside felt amazing. We spent the rest of the visit getting to know each other and eating processed vending machine food, which tasted like gourmet cuisine compared to what they served in the chow hall.

We agreed that she would come to see me as often as she could. The more we visited, the more comfortable we got with each other, so much so that we started taking risks like copping illegal feels whenever we could and extending kisses and hugs until the officers said something. As much as I looked forward to our visits, they were very challenging, however. It had been years since I touched a woman intimately, and our visits only intensified my hunger for sexual intimacy. I allowed my hands to roam whenever I could, but it wasn't enough. Lauren was also fighting her urges to touch me the way that she wanted to. The more I thought about what I was missing out on, the more frustrated I became. Physical intimacy was one of our most basic human urges yet it was discouraged in the visiting room.

When I entered prison, I thought not being able to have sex would drive me insane, but I learned to channel that energy into other things. There were some, however, who couldn't channel their energy and turned to homosexuality instead. My personal view is that these inmates already had those tendencies and prison simply created the platform for them to explore their longings.

Lauren and I had been visiting for a few months when our sexual frustrations came to a head. We had been sitting on a visit for an hour or so when Lauren began stroking my hand. I slid my hand over her thighs and stroked them lightly, then caressed one of her breasts with the back of my hand. We knew the visiting room had a camera and an officer who were constantly on the lookout for any misconduct between couples, but we had gotten away with it in the past so we continued to sneak feels whenever we could. I placed my hand back down on my lap and we continued our visit. Lauren then put her hand on my lap beneath the arm of the chair and caressed my manhood. We went back and forth sneaking touches and gropes until the visiting room door slid open. When I saw the sergeant making a beeline toward us, I knew it was over. He told Lauren to grab her belongings and exit the visiting room. Sadly, that was the last time I'd see Lauren face-to-face for a couple of years. Our visits were terminated, and I was written a sexual misconduct for touching her breast with the back of my hand. That was the beginning of the end of our short-lived romance; however, our friendship remained for some time. We continued to write each other on and off throughout the remainder of my incarceration, but things were never the same.

About two weeks later, I was transferred to Riverside Correctional Facility, which was the first joint I had been sent to after I went through quarantine in 1991. Things were different and it took me a minute to adjust to the prison, which was a bit run down. I followed a similar routine as I had at previous joints. I joined the brothers for Kwanzaa and became a member of the National Lifers Association. Even though I wasn't serving life, I wanted to use my organizing skills to assist the brothers who were.

I had also gotten classified for the Business Computer Technology class and was excited to start. I knew I needed to learn all that I could about computers in order to pursue my dreams when I came home, so taking the class was a no-brainer for me. The class was very interesting because I didn't know much about computers. Outside of taking Data Business Processing when I was at MR, I hadn't been exposed to new technology. This is one of the great tragedies of being locked up; we were basically being left behind by the world. In class, we learned the basics, but weren't allowed to access the Internet so all of the information we were getting was outdated. It didn't matter to me though, because it was all new to me and I wanted to do my best regardless of how old the information was.

Once I got settled in, I went to class in the morning and worked out in the evening with the brothers. When I was in the unit, I spent my time writing and working on ideas for getting my work out there. I met a brother named Anthony Moorer who was very knowledgeable about urban literature and self-publishing. He had started a publishing company before returning to the joint and was able to give me a lot of pointers about the book game. We walked to chow everyday and talked about the future and how we would work together when we were released. Our conversations kept me inspired and motivated.

While I was at Riverside, I realized how much of the prison experience I needed to shake out of my system. I no longer cared about what was going on out on the yard. My mind was focused on getting out of prison, and the small thinking of some of the guys around me started to really irritate me. I found myself retreating further into myself more and more. I understood where the brothers were coming from and empathized with them, but I was tired of prison life and the gossip about what was going on out on the yard.

I had been at Riverside for a month or so when my father brought my sisters Nakia and Shamica up to see me. It was the first time I had seen them in awhile. We sat in the visiting room laughing and joking and talking about the future. It was 2006, and I was down to two years before my earliest release date. I could sense that my father was getting excited. It had been a long time coming and we agreed that the worst was behind us. Having my family visit really meant a lot to me. Their presence gave me hope and increased my desire to get out and live my life in a way that honored their sacrifices over the years. My father had stood firmly by my side and I was looking forward to showing him that his efforts hadn't been in vain. The countdown to my homecoming was underway and I couldn't have been more excited.

A few days after my family's visit, I was sitting on my bunk when the unit officer came by and handed out mail. I had received a lone letter from Ebony and immediately tossed it on the desk to read later. I had received HOPE-related letters from her before so I thought nothing of it when I saw her name. I loved the work that HOPE was doing and was eager to join the organization whenever I was released. We didn't have many advocacy groups who represented the interests of inmates. Without groups like HOPE, the State would continue to silence inmates' voices and trample on their human rights.

Our unit was first for chow so I decided I would read the letter and find out what HOPE was working on when I returned to my cell. I waited outside the unit for Anthony and headed to the chow hall. We talked about the latest trends in the publishing industry and how important it was for us to start our own companies. His insights always gave me something to think about. When I first started writing, I had no idea how I would get my stories out. All I knew was that I wanted to get my work out there and share my art with the world. The first person to talk to me about the possibility of self-publishing was my older stepbrother Will. He was someone whose opinion I valued and whose intelligence I respected. When he showed interest in my writing and started helping me work on getting my books published, I knew I was on to something.

When I got back to the unit from talking to Anthony, I went to my cell and opened Ebony's letter. I stared at the letter for a few minutes and re-read it several times before a smile creased my face. I was expecting to read something about HOPE, but instead there was a short personal letter from Ebony:

March 20, 2006

Brother Shaka,

I pray this letter finds you in good health and spirits. I have been meaning to write you for some time, but I am so forgetful (despite my youth!). I received a letter the other day from Brother Tone that made me go ahead and write. In his letter, he spoke about the need for *conscious* female correspondence, and asked me to forward his info to some of the sisters I work with (I work at an African-centered school). After reading his letter, I thought about you, probably because I met you both at the same time, and wondered if you felt the same. I assume you have sisters who you correspond with but may also want to kick it with a sister of like mind.

Yusef gave me your address. I hope that's okay. I've actually never written anyone about anything other than HOPE business. While I have received countless letters, most of which I didn't have time to reply to, I am committed to corresponding with you, even if I don't reply right away. I've gotten so used to the fast-paced world of technology that I usually communicate via e-mail or text messaging... so I will have to slow down a bit so that I can compose a letter.

I realize how important correspondence with family, friends, and supporters are to our brothers' development; this may ultimately make the difference in the choices they make once they return home. Even still, I've been neglectful in writing. Perhaps because I shoulder much weight as an active member, and now secretary, of HOPE. But I must admit that it helps knowing you are one of Yusef's comrades. That personal connection, although not necessary, makes writing consistently that much easier for someone like me who's very busy *and* forgetful to boot. I also plan to write Yusef's baba as well.

Anyway, I am writing you at work so I must close this letter. I look forward to building with you.

In struggle,

Ebony

Though her letter was short and non-committal, I knew I had to seize the moment and let her know exactly where I stood and what I was looking for. While her offer of friendship was nice, I was at a point in my life where I knew what I wanted and needed. Prison had hardened me and I knew it was going to take a special woman to help me break through the rest of the bricks that remained around my heart. There was no doubt in my mind that Ebony possessed the qualities and the determined spirit to do so. When I sat at my typewriter that evening, I wrote as though she was in my presence and we were having a conversation. I was as excited as a puppy when I received a response from Ebony a few days later. Her thought-provoking inquiries and candid responses to my thoughts and questions made me feel special. I felt like we were sharing more than our thoughts and philosophies on life; it felt like we were sharing the most intimate parts of our souls. It wasn't so much the subject, but moreso the depth and ease with which our conversations flowed. We talked about our dreams, visions, fears, setbacks, insecurities, and hopes for the future. We discussed food security, revolutionary theory, and community activism, among other things.

While Ebony has jokingly accused me of putting some serious mack down on her, it was a mutual feeling. She had a way with words that touched places inside of me that no one had before. She caressed my broken spaces with tender poetry and thought-provoking questions and helped me heal by sharing her personal frailties and life triumphs. Her thoughtfulness was second to none and I knew she was the kind of woman that I wanted to share my life with. Ebony was everything I had dreamed and imagined the woman I'd shared my life with would be. She was intelligent, compassionate, thoughtful, and committed to carrying on the legacy of our people.

After a few letters, I let Ebony know in no uncertain terms that I wanted to see her in person. She agreed to a visit, so I went to the counselor to have her added to my visiting list. Before we could schedule a visit, however, I was told I would be transferring to another joint. I knew it was only a matter of time before they sent me to another facility because I was suspected of ordering an assault on an inmate who had stolen one of my store bags. The counselor was pissed at me because this particular inmate was the laundry man for the unit and the store clerk. When the counselor called me into his office, he told me that he knew I had had the guy assaulted, but he couldn't prove it. He told me to call the goons off and I told him I didn't know what he was talking about, so he told me to get out of his office. A couple weeks later, I was transferred to Coldwater Correctional Facility, where I would finally be able to see Ebony face-to-face for the first time since we'd started corresponding.

When they called me for a visit, I had butterflies in my stomach, which died down as soon as Ebony entered the visiting room and I took her hand in mine where it fit perfectly. In the cold, cruel world of prison, I had finally found someone who was capable of loving all of me.

Chapter 25

For years, the circumstances surrounding my arrest were the focal point of my anger. Everyone who I thought of as a friend had turned their backs on me. In my naiveté, I expected them to stay true to the code of the streets. Never in my wildest dreams did I think anyone would violate the code and make statements against me. But I was a fool and had been one for a long time. Each night I hit the block to hustle, I was putting my life in someone else's hands and giving them the power to determine my future. Each time I carried a gun under the influence of alcohol, I was rolling the dice and gambling with my future. My inability to be wise in how I shared my loyalty punched me straight in the throat when the police arrived to arrest me. The friends I once had became faceless, nameless ghosts that hid in the shadows of my life.

It wasn't until I matured and evolved in my thinking that I was able to liberate myself from the anger and thoughts of revenge. I had held people to unrealistic expectations and hadn't taken into account that we were all kids, and some of us still possessed childhood fears. We acted hard and indifferent until we found ourselves shoulder deep in trouble, and the charge of accomplice to murder was as deep in trouble as a teenager could get. My undeveloped emotional side said that they should have remained silent, but I was delusional. I mean, I had just shot and killed another man over a meaningless argument, so what the hell did I know about right and wrong.

As much as it pained me to read the statements made against me, it hurt even more to know that people I thought of as friends had walked away and turned their backs on me once I was sent to prison. Not one person I thought of as a friend stood by my side beyond my first six months in prison. They proved the saying "out of sight, out of mind" to be true. It was the cruel reality of life on the streets; there truly wasn't any love.

I recall my last moments of freedom vividly. In our haste to get out of Detroit, Brenda and I fled to my sister Vanessa's house where we stayed the night. We didn't have any plans beyond the next moment. We figured we would get some dope, and then flee to Ohio. That was something else I hadn't thought all the way through. All I knew was that I needed to get out of Detroit. We stayed the night and slept on my sister's floor waiting for daybreak.

The following morning, I sold the murder weapon, then returned to Vanessa's. We sat at the dining room table and discussed buying some dope, then leaving when my sister's boyfriend Smiley returned from an errand. Brenda looked worn down and I was tired and on edge. I knew the clock was ticking so I was anxious to get on the road to anywhere other than Detroit. I recall thinking about how things would be okay once I got to Ohio.

My sister Vanessa was in the kitchen cooking when Smiley returned to the house. We talked briefly about me going to a hotel until we were ready to head out of state, but before we could finish our conversation, we heard a knock at the door. It felt like everything had frozen in time. All I remember was the look on my nephew Moota's face – he looked so innocent. All I wanted to be in that moment was an innocent baby without a care in the world.

When Smiley opened the front door and I saw the detective's stiff grey blazer, I knew my world was about to come to an end one way or another. Smiley had an AK 47 in the back room and I was ready to put it to use. I had no desire to go to prison and would rather have died than have them put me in handcuffs. When the detective approached me, I felt my legs tighten up as I prepared to rush to the back room, grab the AK, and come out blazing, but I couldn't move. I was frozen in place by the look on my nephew's face and thoughts of what his life would be like if I made any sudden moves. Instead, I tried to bluff my way out of being arrested. Instead of giving the detective my real name, I gave him a childhood friend's name who lived down the street. We had the exact same birthday, including the year. As clever as I thought I was, the detective was a lot smarter. When the officers placed the cuffs on me and ushered me out of the door to their car, my entire life flashed before my eyes. The police car may as well have been a casket because I felt cold and dead inside.

As we rode through the streets of Detroit, all I could think about was the fact that I would never cruise those blocks again. There would be no more trips to the malls, parties, cruising up and down Fenkell and Wyoming, eating whatever I wanted or laying up listening to Brenda. I had just forfeited a chance to do the things I loved or dreamed about. I had spent many days deep in thought about getting my life in order, returning to school, and living a normal teenage life, but it was all too late. I would never be a kid again.

When I reached the homicide division at 1300 Beaubien, the officers paraded one statement after another into the interrogation room. Everyone said something to the police about what they heard or what they saw. To their credit, a few tried to lie for me and did their best to get me out of trouble, but there were others who outright told everything. I hung my head in shame as the officers read each statement. I thought about each person and how we had met and what I would have done if I were in their shoes. I can't say what I would have done had I been in their shoes faced with the threat of murder charges for a murder I hadn't committed.

It was no secret in the 'hood that there were plenty of young brothers in prison serving life sentences because they refused to make a statement, even though they hadn't pulled the trigger. The police are notorious for using scare tactics against young teenagers, which can be very intimidating no matter how hard you think you are. It was this discovery as a man that helped me get over the betrayal I felt when I learned about the statements. This is also a part of the lesson that I try to impart to the young brothers and sisters I encounter. When you live a life of crime, there is no such thing as a friend or loyalty. When it comes down to it, your friends will always put themselves before you. If the judge asked them whether they wanted to do life in prison or have you do it, they'll choose you every time. It may hurt them inside and destroy a part of them forever, but it will never hurt enough for them to choose being sent to the joint. Fact of the matter is, the streets are all about self-preservation; it's every person for themself.

The days of stand up guys are nearly extinct, and there are only a few who can say they were thoroughbreds until the end. That isn't something to be proud of, but I say this because we are fixated on keeping it real and people tend to follow what they perceive as real. With that being the case or the criteria, young guys should follow the guys who go off to college or start their own businesses because these brothers are the ones keeping it real while the rest of the dudes in the streets keep it real fucked up.

When you go through each drug king pen's crew, there was always someone on the inside snitching, and sadly, these guys are celebrated. I personally find no glory in the way I lived my life on the streets. I don't value the reputation I got on the streets or on the prison yard. What I do value is what I have learned about life because of the decisions I made and how it has helped me help other young brothers and sisters. To me, the one and only lasting thing that is truly gangsta is intelligence. You can't kill it, lock it up, or deny it. Yes, intelligence is the new gangsta.

Chapter 26

When we reached our seats in the visiting room, I noticed something was different about the Ebony I had met at Carson City. A scarf replaced the long, flowing locs that at one time adorned her head, and her glowing, unblemished skin was healing from a severe bout of acne. It was a dramatic change in Ebony's appearance. I had an image of her in my head and was surprised that she hadn't mentioned the acne outbreak during our correspondence. I didn't know what to make of it, and for a brief second, I thought about conversations I had had with other inmates about women who dated prisoners. In prison, it isn't uncommon for a woman who is going through physical challenges or self-esteem issues to seek out companionship from men in prison. However, everything about Ebony spoke to her genuine interest. She asked deep, probing questions and answered my questions with sincerity and honesty. We would later discover the root cause of the outbreak and her face healed completely, returning to its unblemished beauty.

Despite the change in appearance, Ebony's warm spirit and deep, soulful eyes remained unchanged. There was a quiet sweetness that emanated from her in a way that endeared me to her immediately. She had an ease about her that allowed us to flow in and out of conversation with the fluidity of a gentle stream. We discussed a wide range of subjects about life, love and relationships. She shared with me her love for urban gardening and how she believed it was necessary for Black people to have control over their own food supply. Her passion was evident and it made me want to learn more about her work in the community. I shared with her my love of writing and goals for my life after prison. By the time our visit ended, we had discussed everything from private-owned prisons that are sold on the stock market to the abundance of liquor stores, fast food restaurants, and inferior grocery stores in Black neighborhoods.

Ebony's conversation was refreshing and fed parts of me that had been starved for years. My mind craved the mental nourishment that she provided and I could sense the feeling was mutual. When I began my transformation, I often thought about the kind of woman I desired to have in my life. I was growing as a man and my needs had grown beyond the needs of my youth. I wanted a woman in my life who challenged me to be the best man I could possibly be. I wanted a woman who would love and nurture me; who had a determined spirit and would fight the system right alongside me. I needed a woman who had a profound understanding of what it would take for me to transition back to the community and would be there to support and encourage me. Not long into our relationship, I would learn that Ebony was all of that and more.

I knew the Department of Corrections would test the fibers of our relationship in ways that would make us think we were crazy for daring to love. The system wasn't designed for inmates to cultivate healthy relationships with people on the outside. Families of loved ones were discouraged from visiting through various tactics, including invasive pat searches and disrespectful officers who talked to them like they were children. Then, there was the reality that most prisons in Michigan are far from home. While the majority of prisoners are from Detroit and southern Michigan, the majority of the prisons are in rural areas up north.

A few weeks after our first visit, I was transferred from Coldwater to a minimum security prison in Jackson, which was the first time in my incarceration that I had been transferred to a prison less than an hour from home. Ebony and I were excited when we got the news of my transfer. I had never been to a level one prison before, but I felt it was a sign that I was definitely on my way home.

When I arrived at Cooper Street Correctional Facility in Jackson, I sought out a few brothers I knew to get a rundown of the prison. They told me that Cooper Street was a transitional prison for the camp system. I was convinced that they were mistaken because I didn't think I met the requirements for the camp system. However, when I spoke to my counselor, he informed me that I had been approved for transfer into the camp system. I explained to Ebony that this approval meant that I could be sent to a camp up north. She told me to think positively and focus on staying where I was. There were guys who had found ways to stay at Cooper Street until they saw the parole board and that gave me a glimmer of hope.

The energy at Cooper Street was different from any prison I had been to because inmates were being released every morning. I ran into a few guys I had done time with at different prisons and it felt good to watch them walk out of prison after serving nearly their entire adult life behind bars. When I ran into one of my guys from the east side named E Love and saw that he was heading home, my confidence in my chances of getting out increased tenfold. E Love was far from the model prisoner, and if they were letting him go, I figured I stood at least half a chance.

Once I was settled into the flow of the prison, Ebony and I discussed visits and phone calls. At the time, phone calls were nearly eight dollars for a fifteen-minute call, so we tried to limit our calls, but it was hard. We had such good communication that we never wanted to stop talking. Visits were a great supplement because it allowed us to really connect with each other. There were days when we spent eight hours sitting and talking to each other. We played Scrabble, cards and laughed and joked with each other. There were other times when we just held hands silently, lost in our own world. Though the visiting room was always full because of the prison's close proximity to Detroit, it felt like we were in our own world. As much as I enjoyed our conversations, there were two things I always looked forward to on visits – taking pictures and our goodbye kisses.

Taking pictures with Ebony was one of my favorite things about visits. It provided me with an opportunity to sneak in feels on her booty and get extra kisses, especially when I had a cool cameraman. Looking back, my antics remind me of a junior high student getting his first kiss. Whenever I left from our visits, I would kick back on my bunk and play back every detail of our physical contact. I thought about how Ebony felt in my arms and how sweet her tongue tasted. But no matter how many kisses and feels I was able to sneak in, I was always left wanting more. It was a sweet form of torture that left me frustrated because I was ready to have all of her as a woman.

When it was time to end our visit and kiss goodbye, I was always conscious of the officers watching us kiss. Each officer had a different approach to couples kissing. Some would give us a minute, or longer if we were really lucky, and others would tell us to stop before we'd even gotten started. Whenever there was an officer who really didn't care, we took full advantage of it. The first time that happened, I experienced the deepest sense of fulfillment I had ever had. It was a sensual experience that superseded any sexual experience I had had in my life. As I held Ebony in my arms and kissed her deeply and passionately, it felt as though our souls were making love. There was a feeling of profound love being transmitted by our tongues, lips and hands. I caressed her tenderly and held her tightly for what felt like forever. When I returned to my cube, I was on cloud nine. Though we had other great kisses and moments of intimacy, nothing compared to that experience.

After a few weeks of visits, getting to know each other and laying the foundation for our relationship, I grew comfortable with the idea of staying at Cooper Street. Inmates who had been transferred in after me had already been sent up north, so I thought I was safe from taking that trip over the bridge. You can imagine my shock and disappointment when I was told – the day before my birthday – to pack up for a transfer up north. Our relationship was young and vulnerable and I knew we were about to be put to the ultimate test, a test that had destroyed many relationships.

I still had two years before my earliest release date, and I knew inmates who had been over the bridge for more than two years, so there was a possibility that I might spend the rest of my incarceration up north. There were several camps over the bridge that ranged from 6 to 12 hours in travel time from Detroit. It didn't matter, however; none of the options up north would provide us with the ability to see each other every week the way we had grown accustomed to at Cooper Street.

I hated making the call to tell Ebony I was being transferred. My fingers felt like lead as I dialed her number. In the back of my mind, I thought the transfer would be the end of our relationship. I didn't want to add any stress to Ebony's life, and I knew that regular visits made it easier for us to be together. Now we were being stripped of the one thing that made prison relationships doable.

When Ebony answered the phone, her bubbly, melodic voice made my heart ball up in a knot. I knew the news wasn't going to go over well. The words slowly crawled out of my mouth like a plump caterpillar inching its way along. "Baby, they're transferring me to a camp up north," I said with a heavy heart. That was the hardest conversation I had to have while in prison. Part of me was fearful that our relationship was too young to endure the trials and tribulations we were about to face, and the other part of me felt selfish for dragging Ebony into the crazy world of prison. I wanted to tell her to run to protect her from the madness of a system designed to break wills, crush dreams, and annihilate relationships; yet I wanted to love her, cherish her and experience her companionship.

When Ebony responded, it was through tears, which was heartbreaking to hear. She told me that she had planned to come up for a visit the following day to celebrate my birthday and sing me a birthday song. Her voice cracked a couple of times as she shared her plans for my birthday, and all I wanted to do was take her in my arms and hug away the hurt, but I couldn't. I felt helpless and vulnerable. Silently, I cursed the system and the universe for being so cruel. I mean, how could they attempt to destroy something that was so beautiful and innocent? Didn't they see the healing power of love each time Ebony walked into the visiting room? From the moment she entered my life, she had unknowingly set about tearing down the walls around my heart, and they were attempting to steal that from me.

Before we hung up the phone, Ebony sang to me the most beautiful birthday song I had ever heard, the one she had planned to sing on our visit. Parts of the song were in Kiswahili, and as I listened, I dreamed of us being on the shores of Kenya, wading in the water as she sang to me. Her voice was sweet and innocent, yet powerful and firm enough that I knew she truly cared about me. When we finally hung up, an ominous feeling came over me. I started having doubts about Ebony's ability to stay by my side. I mean, nearly everyone who had professed to love me had abandoned me, or weren't there when I needed them most, with the exception of my father. Ebony hadn't known me nearly as long as my family or childhood friends, so what would make her any different? Slowly, I began breaking up with her in my mind. I couldn't afford to be vulnerable to the winds of change that came with being sent far up north.

I had walked on eggshells before and didn't like being unable to plant my feed on solid ground.

I didn't know how far or how long I was going to be up north, and that was unsettling. The following morning, I was transferred six hours away to Camp Manistique. It was my 34th birthday, and by far one of my worst as I sat stuffed on a prison bus traveling over the infamous Mackinaw Bridge. I hated every moment of the trip because it symbolized to me the end of the best relationship and friendship I had experienced.

As soon as I could, I called Ebony to tell her where I had landed. Without hesitation, she told me that she'd be up there that weekend. I was at a loss for words. I expected her to say she'd come up at a later date once she had the time and the finances to plan a trip, but she surprised me. A few days later, just as we were getting excited about the chance to see each other, we were dealt another blow. I was being transferred again to a secure level one at the northern end of the Upper Peninsula. Camp Manistique was an unsecured level one with minimal staff, and an inmate had recently been killed at another unsecured camp by an inmate who was doing a long bid. The following week, I was transferred to Baraga Maximum Correctional Facility, which had a level one unit. Baraga was a nine-hour drive from Detroit, so I knew it would be a long time before I saw Ebony again.

Only months into our relationship, we were being tested on every level. Despite my initial doubts, Ebony proved that she was a woman of substantial tenacity who refused to be defeated by the system. Within months, she planned a trip to Baraga and drove up to visit me. She stayed for four days and we spent every second basking in the glow of each other's presence. We agreed that we could weather any storm together because our love would guide and sustain us. I had grown accustomed to fighting the system by myself, so it was a major relief to know that I had someone who possessed the fierce determination needed to overcome the obstacles that the system might place in our path, no matter how hard. Through each battle, Ebony proved that she was a force to be reckoned with.

Nine months later, I was again transferred to Marquette Branch Prison after getting into a conflict with an officer at Baraga over a job. The prison was trying to cut down on its budget and started folding two jobs into one, firing a number of inmates in the process. When I was told I would be doing two jobs for one pay, I told the officer that he had to show me in the policy where it was legal for him to force me to work two jobs. He couldn't find anything in the policy, so instead, he threatened to write me a misconduct if I refused to do the other job. Initially, I wasn't going to put up all of the supplies, but then I thought about how big of a setback it would be to lose 90 days of good time and decrease my chances of getting out of prison. So, I followed the order, then requested to be removed from my initial assignment before filing a grievance for abuse of authority. I had learned how to fight using my mind instead of my hands, and it was empowering.

I landed another job working in the library and the officer hated it. The next thing you know, I was transferred to the middle of the Upper Peninsula. When I arrived at Marquette, the officers immediately placed me in solitary confinement where I remained for seven days, incommunicado. They claimed that they didn't feel comfortable with me there because of the assault on staff case that I had caught in Muskegon in 1999. I was angry, hurt and deeply sad. I felt helpless and vulnerable to the whims of prison officials who didn't give a damn about me or my family. I had already done over four years in solitary confinement for that case and hadn't caught a misconduct in nearly ten years, so they had no grounds or reasonable explanation for putting me in the hole.

Ebony and no one in my family knew where I was, and I had no way of communicating with them. The prison staff refused to give me any of my property, I was limited to three showers a week, and I had no outside recreation. I knew right then that it was the old boy network at work; the other officers didn't take kindly to me writing a grievance on their partner. In legal terms, what they did is called double jeopardy, but in prison, we don't have a right to a fair hearing. At any given time, the administration could arbitrarily throw us in the hole and there wasn't a damn thing we could do about it. A week later, I was transferred again. This time, they increased my security level to medium security, and I was right back in the midst of the madness. Being in medium security again felt like a nightmare. Instead of being in an environment where inmates were going home, I was back in an environment where stabbings and life sentences were the norm.

When Ebony found out that they had transferred me to a level two, she went to work writing and calling the administration in Lansing. In the meantime, I was trying my best to dodge the drama on the yard. The day I arrived, there was a war raging on the yard and several guys had been stabbed over the course of a few days. A brother I knew came to me and told me that he had a shank I could use because there was a lot of beef on the yard. That was the last thing I wanted to hear, and the last thing I needed at that point in my bit. I told him that I was okay and went to my cube. For the most part, I stayed in my cube working on my third novel "Crack: Volume 2," working out or walking the yard with my cousin Chuck who happened to be there too. It was the first time I had seen him in about sixteen years. It felt good seeing a family member, but not under those conditions. We got caught up on the past before he was transferred to another facility, then it was back to business.

Shortly after I arrived, Ebony came up for a visit and we strategized on how to get my security level back down, and hopefully transferred back to the other side of the bridge. While we waited for a decision from Lansing about my transfer, I had to take care of a matter that was troubling me. There was a guy there who had molested my old bunky's son and niece. When he wrote me and told me about it, I knew what had to be done. I made the arrangements to take care of the guy, but it troubled me. I was at a point in my life where I was tired of the madness of prison and all of the street codes. I wanted to just move on with my life. However, my sense of loyalty and thoughts about what I would want done if my child had been molested was all I needed to act. That was one of the hardest decisions that I had to face because I was growing into a different phase of my life and I no longer had a desire to adhere to street or prison codes. However, my former bunky BX was like a brother to me, and by virtue, his son was like a nephew, so I had to take care of things. The matter was handled, and a few weeks later, I was transferred to another secure level one in Ojibway, which is located in the Upper Peninsula so far northwest that it's in the Central Time Zone.

Ojibway was better known to inmates as O-stab-a-way because of all the stabbings that took place there. Despite its designation as a level one, it was run like a level two. A lot of the inmates there had done long stretches in prison and still had a few more years to go, so they were easily provoked. They had grown up in prison during the era when stabbings and violence were a regular occurrence. The racial tension between inmates and officers was intense because of a recent riot that had erupted in response to a White officer who allowed a White inmate to stab a Black inmate. Adding insult to injury, Ojibway was more than ten hours from Detroit, which meant visits were rare.

Once I settled in, I went to yard to see if there was anyone there I knew. I ran into one of my guys from the east side named Mo Bounce and he gave me a rundown on the joint. We walked the yard and got caught up on what was going on in each other's lives. It had been over ten years since we'd been at the same prison, but we maintained contact through letters. Mo Bounce had over twenty years in and had been denied parole multiple times. He told me about the parole process and we talked about my chances of getting out. We both knew it was going to be a battle, but I told him that I was going to make it as hard as possible for them to keep me hostage.

Unlike most level one facilities, Ojibway had 8-man cubes and cells. I was lucky to get a cell with one bunky instead of a cube with seven other guys, so I took advantage of the time in the cell and did some writing and studying. Mentally, I was preparing for my future, so the fewer distractions I had, the better. I called Ebony whenever I could, but it was difficult to talk as much as we wanted or needed because the unit had limited phone access. Plus, calls were still more than $8 for a 15-minute phone call.

Though I was over ten hours away, we did what was necessary to maintain our visits. Although not ideal, Ebony made that long trek with complete strangers in an effort to share travel expenses. She trusted me to find a solid brother whose girl was interested in a visit and would be able to split the cost of gas and a few nights in a hotel. Once I made the connection, Ebony would coordinate everything else. Within my first seven months at Ojibway, we had three visits, which helped us grow tremendously as a couple. During our visits, we talked about my upcoming parole hearing, we argued, we laughed, and most importantly, we dreamed of our future together. Instead of allowing the system to break us, we grew stronger and more committed in our love for each other. Ebony's letters and our weekly phone calls became my lifeline and inspiration in between visits. On my roughest days, I thought about the dreams we shared and the future we aspired toward, and that kept me grounded.

As the months wore on, I started growing anxious. I was getting closer and closer to seeing the parole board, but there was a class that I needed and hadn't been placed in yet. Even still, we started asking our family, friends and members of the community to write letters to the parole board on my behalf, and I continued working on my business plan.

As my earliest release date grew near, we started sending requests to the prison administration to get into the Assaultive Offender Program (AOP), a group therapy class required for all inmates with an assaultive case. It was the last of my recommendations that needed to be completed before I saw the parole board, but the waiting list was longer than my arm. Although I had seen many brothers go to the parole board without completing AOP, I didn't want to be in their situation. It was through no fault of their own, and that was the tragedy of it all. The parole board refused to let anyone go who hadn't completed the one-year program yet the state didn't have enough slots to accommodate the number of inmates that were required to complete AOP. Ebony and I went to work trying to get me into AOP, but to no avail. As the year wound down and it was time for my counselor to do my Parole Eligibility Report, I still hadn't been added to the list to take AOP. I was concerned, but tried to remain optimistic.

A few months into 2008, I was added to the waiting list and told I would be taking the class at Ojibway. I was excited to get the news about AOP because I knew that completing it would be one less excuse the parole board could use to deny my release; however, I dreaded spending another year at Ojibway, ten hours away from Ebony. But just when I was ready to settle into the idea of taking AOP at Ojibway, the group was cancelled. That was a devastating blow, and at that point, my only hope was to get transferred to another facility that had a new group starting before I saw the parole board, but it never happened. Like many of the brothers before me, I was forced to go to the parole board without completing AOP.

A couple months before it was time for me to see the parole board, Ebony and I discussed my strategy for the interview. I knew the changes I had made in my heart and in my life, but I was also conscious of my reputation in prison. In seventeen years, I had accumulated thirty-six misconducts, caught a case, and spent 7 years total in solitary confinement. Though my file reflected the rebelliousness of my early prison years, I knew how unforgiving the system would be.

While I knew my early behavior in prison might be an issue, I was still optimistic about my chances of getting out of prison. I had taken the necessary steps to become an asset to my community instead of a liability and knew that if I were released, I would go to work immediately mentoring young men and women who were on the path that I took in my youth. In the two years we had been together, Ebony and I had started Drop A Gem Publishing and released our first novel. We had also helped publish a book for children with incarcerated parents through HOPE. My writing was being published in other outlets and a number of people in the community were supportive of my work and efforts. I had no doubt that I would successfully complete parole if given a chance and make a difference in some young man or woman's life once I was released. It was this spirit that I carried forth as we prepared for the biggest moment of my incarceration.

Ebony garnered a great deal of support from the community and had people write letters to the parole board on my behalf. Men and women like the Detroit Black Community Food Security Network's Executive Director Malik Yakini, who was then Executive Director of Nsoroma Institute and owner of Black Star Community Bookstore, where he offered me employment. Dr. Gloria House wrote and offered transitional assistance, Dr. Ashley Lucas wrote of my transformation and my creative abilities. Community activist and founder of Pioneers for

Peace Weusi Olusola wrote about the importance of the work I planned to do. My father wrote of the growth he had seen in me over the years along with my sister Nakia and stepbrother Will. There were a few others who also wrote on my behalf, so I was excited about the support I would have when I was released.

In August 2008, Ebony accompanied my father, stepmother and son Jay on a visit a couple days before my parole hearing. It had been a few years since I'd seen my son because of the distance and I was beyond excited to see the young man he had grown into. I also missed my father and stepmother because it had been a minute since I had seen them as well. When they entered the visiting room, they wrapped me in the warmest hugs. They were the Black family version of a Snuggie, providing me the love and warmth that was needed to survive the cold world of prison.

Our visit started off cool and relaxed despite the heavy cloud of my parole hearing hanging above our heads. After we settled in, my father started talking about my freedom and what it meant to him and the family. As he shared his thoughts, my eyes welled up with tears. I had not cried in the seventeen years of my incarceration, but I could no longer hold back the tears. I felt the overwhelming pressure to free Ebony and my family from the shackles of prison. It had taken years for me to realize that I was not locked up alone; my incarceration had impacted my family as though they were sitting in a cell with me. Indeed, no one goes to prison alone. Incarceration impacts the entire family and community. My father hugged me as I allowed the tears to flow freely. As the tears ran down my face, it felt like all of the pain and sadness from my incarceration was leaving my body.

It was refreshing to hear my father tell me that no matter what happened with the parole board, they would never leave my side. I explained to them that the worst-case scenario was a two-year continuation of my prison sentence. They told me that they were ready to stand by my side no matter what the decision. My family's words strengthened and emboldened me with the courage to face the parole board the following morning. I knew I would have a sleepless night, but it was a night of peaceful contemplation, meditation and prayer. The time had come for me to come face-to-face with my destiny.

When the officer called me to report to the control center for my parole interview, I took a deep breath, said a last minute prayer, and walked bravely to the control center. It was time, and I was ready to put prison behind me. However, the State had other things in mind, things that made me nearly lose my mind.

Chapter 27

Never in my wildest imagination would I have thought the parole board would treat my father with the utter disrespect displayed by Enid Livingston, the parole board member who conducted my interview. When I entered the small, cramped room with my father, an ominous feeling came over me. Though Livingston wasn't in the room physically, I could feel her negative energy coming through the monitor where she conducted the interview via teleconference. Her voice was dry and her expression stoic when she asked me to say my name and inmate number for the record. When the formalities were done, she asked me why I had murdered a man. I began explaining the events that led up to the murder, and before I could get a complete sentence out, she lit into me. She was very combative and blatantly disrespectful. She wasn't trying to hear anything I said and cut me off every chance she got. She didn't want to hear anything about the man I had evolved into or the things I had accomplished during the last five years of my incarceration. I did my best to represent my case with integrity and objectivity, but none of it mattered. When she was finished interviewing me, she asked my father if he had anything to add. My father started speaking, and within thirty seconds, she cut him off, saying that she had heard enough. She told me to have a good day and said that I would hear something soon. She also told me that I needed to get into AOP before I was released from prison.

When I walked out of the control center and headed back to the cellblock, I was full of mixed emotions. Part of me wanted to believe that I had a genuine chance of getting parole, but the more logical side of me knew that I didn't stand a chance. I tried to remain optimistic, but the more I thought about Livingston's brashness, the harder it was to think about things positively. When Ebony and I talked later that day, I told her how things had gone and she encouraged me to think positive and stay focused on coming home. I trusted Ebony with my life and her words were the comfort that I needed.

Over the next few weeks, we contacted Lansing again in an effort to get me placed into AOP, but kept getting conflicting information. Just when I was wearing down, I was told to pack up because I was being transferred to another prison to take AOP. The following day, I was shipped back downstate to Gus Harrison Correctional Facility in Adrian. It was south of Detroit and only an hour or so away. I could barely contain my excitement. It had been a long two years over the bridge for Ebony and I. The long drives for her to see me and the long droughts between visits were finally over.

We still hadn't received a decision back from the parole board, and I was holding out hope that they would give me a deferral instead of flatly deny me until I finished AOP. It meant that I would not make it home on my earliest release date, but upon completing the program, I would be immediately considered for release.

My focus was as sharp as an eagle's eyesight as I looked toward the future. When I got to Adrian, I spent most of my time in my cube writing and studying things I knew I'd need to know when I was released. I kept my interactions limited to a few people I had met while there and a few people I had known over the years. They were all focused on going home and I wanted to be around that kind of energy. I also took advantage of unaccredited classes offered by Project Community and the Prison Creative Arts Project (PCAP), both sponsored by the University of Michigan. The classes gave me a creative outlet that challenged me as a writer and artist.

I was fortunate to meet and develop some genuine friendships that have endured to this day. I met young men and women like Alex Ochoa, Laura Rosbrow, Chris Rapisarda, and Nicole Hugget who were all student volunteers that came in and did workshops once a week. We challenged each other as artists, and eventually put on a show for the prison. That was my first time acting and writing for the stage, and I loved it. It was also there that I met Dr. Ashley Lucas, who is an incredible writer and theater instructor. She taught me a lot about acting and sharing my voice in different mediums. Ashley and the students gave me honest critiques of my work, which boosted my confidence as a writer.

Unfortunately, the administration terminated our classes for no apparent reason, but I had built such a great relationship with the students that we kept it touch through letters. They reached out to me via snail mail and we continued to share our work and life experiences. They asked deep, probing questions about my life, and I asked them to send me updated information about the free world. It was a mutual exchange of information and experiences that made the last leg of my incarceration more bearable.

A month or so after I arrived at Adrian, I received a letter from the parole board indicating that I had been denied parole for another twelve months. The impersonal letter said that I would be a menace to society, and therefore, could not be released. When I read their decision, I was crushed, but I refused to give up or give in. I knew that no matter what their decision, I would still have to complete AOP, which consisted of weekly sessions with a psychotherapist for ten months.

It was a let down for Ebony and I, but we felt that the worst was behind us; there was always a chance to be called back early and see the parole board before the twelve month continuation was up. In the meantime, I focused all of my energy on completing the requirements of AOP. When we got our date to begin the group, I learned that the therapist who would be facilitating our group was a psych named Mark Skinner. I was a bit nervous because I had heard a lot of negative things about him, namely that he kicked people out of the group for trivial matters and held some racist beliefs. The last thing I needed was to be kicked out of a group that took forever to get into.

On the first day of the group, I took time to feel out Skinner and realized that he was just a straight shooter. His biggest thing was taking accountability and taking all excuses off of the table. He came across brash and insensitive, but he had a point that I agreed with. I was tired of listening to guys make excuses for their actions. When I began taking responsibility for the decisions I had made in my past, I learned the difference between excuses and explanations.

Things were going great in the group until one day Skinner told me that he didn't think they would ever release me from prison. His statement came out of the blue and rubbed the other inmates the wrong way. A few of them jumped to my defense and asked him why he would say such a thing. He said it was just his personal opinion based on what he had seen happen to other inmates. His words stung and took me aback. I was aware of the games that Skinner played to see if he could throw a person off of their center. Instead of expressing anger, I told him that I was confident I would be released at some point and would do something with my life. He nodded with a smirk that told me he either didn't believe me, or he did, but would never admit it.

Once I transferred to Adrian, the months began flying by. Ebony came up for a visit every week, sometimes twice a week. Despite the parole board's denial, we continued to plan for the future because we knew there was a strong chance that I would be called back early to see the board again. In the meantime, we took advantage of each visit. No matter what the weather was like or what her workweek was like, Ebony came up to see me faithfully. Our bond deepened with each hug, kiss and conversation. I knew it was taking a lot for her to stick in there and that increased my desire to be home, sharing life with her.

One visit we'll never forget was the day Ebony came to see me in the middle of a snowstorm. Neither of us knew that the weather would get as bad as it did, or that the back roads leading to the prison would not be plowed until late in the evening. About twenty miles outside of the prison, she got stuck in a ditch on the side of the road. Although she managed to get her car out of the ditch, a few more yards down the road, her car got stuck again. Stuck in the middle of nowhere with no cell phone reception, it took about 15 minutes before someone stopped to help her.

When Ebony came into the visiting room, she was visibly shaken, and I felt like a piece of shit. I was tired of seeing her suffer for our love, but there was nothing I could do. Though we never said anything about it, we knew that they could continue to deny my parole until I had served my entire forty-year sentence. We tried to remain optimistic and continued preparing for life after prison, and as AOP began winding down, I started feeling better about my chances for release. When they called me back for an early parole consideration, I just knew that I was going to be released. I was given a date of May 20, which was my father's birthday and me and Ebony's anniversary. The symbolic date was confirmation that things were lining up in the universe for my release.

We researched the parole board member – a woman – who would be interviewing me. From what we learned, she was very fair across the board so I expected to have a better hearing than the first one. The weather that day was perfect, which we saw as another good sign of things to come. When I entered the room with my father, the energy was different from the first hearing. We went through the preliminaries before we got down to business talking about my past. I started off using the language I had learned in AOP like thinking errors and empathetic roleplaying, and she stopped me mid-sentence. She told me that she knew the language of AOP, but wanted to know what was going on in my mind as a nineteen-year-old with a pistol. She was sincere and wanted me to give her the real story.

I told her how I felt after I got shot at the age of seventeen and how I reacted to that experience by carrying a gun everyday. I let her know how deeply sorry I was for taking my victim's life and what my plans were for the future. I showed her the work I had been doing to help other inmates, and the work I had done to prepare for life after prison. She said she was impressed and had yet to encounter an inmate who was as prepared for life after prison as I was. She said she admired me for my honesty and ability to take responsibility for my actions. As we wrapped up, she said I would hear something from the board in the next few weeks.

When I left the interview, I was on cloud nine. I felt like I had a great chance of getting out and couldn't wait to talk to Ebony so that I could share the good news. Ebony came up to see me that afternoon and we basked in the good news as though we already had our decision in hand. Over the next few weeks, we started planning my homecoming and discussing things that we needed to do. First on our agenda was finding me employment considering the bookstore where I had planned to work was forced to close. We talked about my needs in terms of clothing and the paperwork needed to get an ID. We were so ready to experience the world of normal living that we could taste it.

Whenever Ebony came to see me, there was a glow to her that I hadn't seen in a while. When she entered the building, her radiant glow lit the room, and my heart, up. She was truly my joy, my rock, and I wanted nothing more than to make her the happiest woman in the world.

I spoke to my counselor weekly to see if she had gotten word from the parole board. She also believed that I would be released because the State was in a budget crunch and they had to start letting more guys go home. The way she saw it, how could they deny me considering how much I had accomplished and how prepared I was. All of the positive energy coming my way had me way more excited than I was comfortable with. I couldn't sleep, and when the yard was open, I walked the track non-stop with my homeboy Terry who was also preparing to go home. We talked about what we would do when we were released. I couldn't wait to get out and sell books and talk to young men and women who were living on the edge and needed a lifeline.

About a month or so after I had seen the board, my counselor came to my cube and said she needed to speak with me when count cleared. The expression on her face told me that something was wrong. She was normally upbeat and cheerful, but her expression held a sadness that I hadn't seen before. I immediately thought of my father as he had been through a few recent surgeries. I couldn't imagine life without him, so I prayed that there wasn't anything wrong at home. When count cleared, I walked slowly to the counselor's office with all kinds of thoughts racing through my head.

As soon as I stepped into her office, she looked up at me and delivered the words that threatened to destroy my sanity. "They denied your release again," she said softly. I couldn't believe the words coming out of her mouth. I had done everything I could, but they had shot me down again. At that point, Skinner's comment began bouncing around in my head like jumping beans. "They're never going to let you out," his words said, mocking me. As I thought about that possibility, the anger began boiling up inside of me. I was so pissed and hurt that I didn't know what to do. I wanted to curl up and die because I knew how devastating the news would be to my family. I was tired of seeing them get their hopes up only to have them dashed, so I decided right there in that moment that I wasn't going to see the parole board again. I could no longer be a tool in the destruction and devastation of my family.

Shortly thereafter, the unit was called for chow, but I didn't have an appetite. The thought of the smell of the chow hall made me nauseous. I was tired of everything about prison and felt like I couldn't take another day without going completely crazy. I felt like I was nearing my breaking point when I picked up the phone and called Ebony.

The sound of Ebony's voice coming through the receiver nearly caused my knees to buckle. I told her about their decision and she told me that she was on her way up to see me. In my head, it felt like it was going to be our last visit. I couldn't see her going through another year of torture. Besides, I had always dealt with my incarceration best when I felt like it was just me with my back against the wall. Though I was tired of life in prison, I had been inside long enough to know that I could do the entire forty years if I had to, but I couldn't do another year knowing that her happiness was hinging on me coming home so that we could pursue our dreams. Ebony wanted a family of her own and I wanted her to have that, even if it didn't include me.

As I took my shower, I thought about what I would say to break up with Ebony. She had invested her everything into our relationship, which made it even harder to break up with her. However, I knew she deserved to have a man who was free to share life with her fully, without restrictions. Yes, Ebony deserved to have a partner who could hold her at night, kiss her in the morning, take her out to nice restaurants, and dance with her whenever the mood struck. She was worthy of having a man to be a father to her children, who would be there to put toys together, fix bikes and do the things that fathers did, but I could give her none of these things.

I sat silently in the visiting room waiting for her to enter. I replayed what I would say to her in my head and made peace with my decision. It had been an incredible experience loving and being loved by her, but my heart would no longer allow me to carry on. She deserved to be free even if I wasn't.

When I looked up, Ebony was standing on the other side of the security doors being processed into the visiting room. As she entered the room, I could feel the tears bubbling to the surface, and as soon as she reached me and took me into her embrace, I broke down. Once we got to our seats, tears poured from my eyes as we held hands and I talked through sobs of despair. As much as I hated to admit it, the system was winning. It was taking away the love of my life and I was devastated. I looked Ebony in her eyes and told her that I could no longer allow her to suffer alongside me. She held my hand and stroked it tenderly as I poured out my soul to her. She wiped away my tears and listened intently as I told her that I wasn't going to the parole board again because I refused to play their game. When I finished venting, Ebony looked me in my eyes and told me that there was no way in hell I was giving up and letting them win. She reminded me that we were "in it to win it," and she would never give up on me. No, giving up or giving in was not an option.

She reminded me of everything we had gone through and how we had overcome every obstacle placed in our path. She reminded me of how strong my spirit was to have endured four and a half years in solitary confinement and how I had done the hard emotional work that others ran from. Her words emboldened me with a surge of strength that made me feel as if I could physically lift the prison with one hand and leave at will. Her reminders of what I was made of gave me the boost that I needed to fight like hell for a freedom I had earned. For the rest of the visit, we strategized and planned our next steps. In my weakest moment, Ebony was there to lift me up and I knew then that our bond was unbreakable.

A few months later, I was transferred back to Cooper Street in Jackson. I had completed AOP and was afraid that they were about to send me back up north, but when I spoke to the counselor, she told me that she had no idea why they had sent me there. One thing she was sure of, they weren't going to send me back up north to a camp. It was a relief, but there was still a great deal of uncertainty. I figured it was best for me to settle into a routine and continue to work on my plans for release.

I spent my days working out with my brother-in-law Smiley and my guy Derek Ford. They were positive lights and told me that they believed I would be getting called back early to see the parole board and finally released from prison.   Their words were comforting and it felt good being around men who knew me. I shared with them the books I had written and they told me how much they loved my writing and were proud of me.

Ebony and I spent as much time as we could on visits and on the telephone dreaming of our future together. We agreed to speak into existence what we wanted and keep our thoughts on the positive experiences we would have when I was released. We created vision boards that included a picture of her and I in front of our home in Detroit. She even went out and shopped for my coming home outfit and started preparing the house for my homecoming. It felt good being in tune with someone who believed in all of who I was.

A few months later, I was called back early to see the parole board for the third time. It had been nearly two years since that first interview with Livingston and I felt like this was the shot I had been waiting for. Once again, my father accompanied me to the board, and this time, the parole board member who interviewed me was an older Black man who was known to be tough and no nonsense. After the preliminaries, he asked me what I would do if I were released. I felt like I was giving the speech of my life. I told him of my plans as a writer and mentor and how much support I had in the community. He probed to see if he could punch holes in my plans, but there were none. The things I planned to do had nothing to do with getting out of prison. I had plans to right the wrongs of my past.

Within a few weeks, I was informed that I had received my parole and would be getting transferred to a prison in Detroit for a re-entry program. I called my father and he rejoiced with the good news. When I talked to Ebony, I could feel her smile beaming through the phone. We had done it, and now it was time for us to experience the true joys of being at one with your soul mate. When I finally got the paperwork, I couldn't believe it. I slept that night with it safely in my hand and looked at it everyday until I was transferred to Mound Correctional Facility, one of two prisons in Detroit, for the last sixty days of my incarceration.

I spent those last sixty days working out, reading, and talking to or visiting with Ebony. We were so excited that we smiled for the entire visit whenever she came to see me. Our love had endured four years of ups and downs and it was finally time for us to share life as a man and woman should. On June 21, 2010, Ebony came to visit me for the last time inside of a prison facility. It was my 38th birthday, and the following day I would walk out of prison after serving 19 years in prison.

When I inhaled my first free breath, it was like a baby taking in air for the first time. The free air tickled my lungs and caused me to smile from deep within. I was officially a free man, and this time, I planned to do it the right way.

Afterword

During the last two years of my incarceration, I was bombarded with story after story of what life on the other side of the prison wall would be like. The stories ranged from wild coming home parties to tragic stories of untimely deaths or multiple returns to prison. It was all subjective, but each person spoke their truth as though it was the only way a homecoming could go. As much as I wanted to say with finality what my homecoming and transition would be like, I knew I couldn't. I had big plans, however I knew that I was entering into foreign territory and returning to a world that was vastly different from the one I had left behind 19 years earlier. When I went to prison in 1991, there were no sleek Apple Mac Books or iPhones and gas was only $1.05 a gallon. There were no social networking sites and people either called and talked to their friends or met them face-to-face instead of texting and emailing. I was essentially being tossed head first into a new society with a whole new way of communicating.

When the days finally wound down and I sat in the visiting room with Ebony for the last time, it still felt like a dream. It was my 38th birthday and there was so much going through my mind. As much as Ebony and I had talked about our life together after prison, it was still hard for me to comprehend the fullness of the moment. As calm as I was on the outside, on the inside I was overwhelmed with thoughts and emotions; I had finally come face-to-face with starting life anew. The thought of all I'd have to learn and unlearn weighed heavily on my mind. I tried to conceal what I was feeling because I wanted to focus on the joy of the moment with Ebony.

When Ebony left the visiting room at Mound Correctional Facility on June 21, 2010, I went back to my unit with the biggest smile on my face. In less then 24 hours, Ebony and I would be starting a new phase of our journey together. There would be no more bars holding us back, no more kisses and hugs overscrutinized by overzealous guards, and no more damn prison blues.

The following morning as I walked toward the control center, the last 19 years of my life floated through my head. I had walked in a young manchild, and was now walking out as a grown man, at least that's what I thought. What I hadn't accounted for was my arrested development when it came to adult interaction and behaviors in the free world. I had never had a real job, a mortgage, car note, insurance or a mature adult relationship, and within the first year, I found myself struggling to catch up with the rest of the adults who had lived regular lives.

It would be a struggle juggling the various phases of my transition. The challenges would include rebuilding relationships with my family, catching up to modern technology, getting used to being around a lot of people, trying to find employment, and navigating the ups and downs that come with relationships.

When I walked out of the parole office on the day of my release, I took in Ebony's beauty like a man dying of thirst taking his first sip of water. She was radiant and dressed sexier than I had ever seen her. On visits, she was forced to dress modestly so as not to be denied entrance, but she more than made up for all the years of having her sex appeal restricted. She had her beautiful locs twisted to the side and her dress rode dangerously high on her thighs. It took all of my discipline not to ravage her in the parking lot. She had brought my oldest son Lil' Jay with her to pick me up, and I hugged my son for the first time as a free man, then shared my first kiss of freedom with Ebony. I then turned to a brother named Red Montgomery who had also just been released. He had promised to be the first person I sold a book to when we got out, and he remained true to his word. Ebony had brought copies of my first novel "Crack Volume 1" with her, allowing me to make my first official sale. When we finished our transaction, I hopped in the car with Ebony and Lil' Jay and headed to get something to eat. We had planned on eating at a fancy restaurant, but when we arrived, they had closed. Instead of the gourmet meal Ebony had planned, my first meal was a chicken sub from Subway, and then it was time to reconnect with the family.

The first couple of days of my release are a blur and were filled with a number of memorable experiences. The first day, all of my siblings, cousins and friends came by with the exception of my sister Tamica who was living in Seattle. We ate the lasagna that my stepmother had made at my request and had a few celebratory drinks as I got caught up on what was going on in the family. I got a chance to meet my nieces Toot and Nu Nu in person for the first time along with my nephews Oshea, TJ, and all of my younger cousins who had been born while I was away. My daughter Lakeisha came over with her son, and it was amazing seeing her for the first time in person since she was a baby. It was a great feeling to see the woman she had grown into, and I was looking forward to learning more about her. By the end of the day, I was filled with emotions at the outpouring of love and support from my family.

The festivities continued into the weekend. My father held a barbeque in my honor and more family members came over. It felt great catching up with my cousins, grandmother, aunts and uncles. Some of our friends from our old neighborhood on the east side came by along with some of my guys from the joint who had gotten out before me. The familiarity of their faces warmed my heart and soul and I drunk in every moment, conversation, hug and kiss. As much as I enjoyed the warmth and love of my family, it was the smile on Ebony's face that touched me the most. After four years, we finally had our time together.

Ebony doted on me, pampered and spoiled me from the first day I came home. She cooked me loving meals and drove me around Detroit as I took in the reality of my freedom. Each moment we spent together was sacred and helped cement our unbreakable bond. I don't think we slept much the first week I was home. We stayed up talking and making up for all of the loving we had missed out on. Hey, we grown! LOL

With all of the love, there were still battles to be waged against the system. We had to fight my parole agent to get approval for Ebony and I to live together and would later battle with them to get approval for me to travel out of town for business. Though I was free, the system was still in control of a lot of areas in my life.

After all of the excitement of coming home died down, I started settling into a routine building our publishing business. The first week home, I spoke at the US Social Forum and sold a few books. Ebony took me to a few local bookstores including Harlem World, which is owned by a guy named Ice who is now a good friend. It was exciting planning book signings and selling and signing books for strangers in the D. Each day felt like a new adventure and I felt myself slowly stretching my wings.

I had never had a legal license so I had to study for my driving test. It took me about three months before I was confident enough to take the test and I aced it. Being locked up for so long made it difficult for me to gauge how far or close things were, so it took a minute for me to adjust, but I once I got the hang of things, I was good. There were many other things I had to adjust to, including learning to roller skate again. Skating was something I loved doing, so to celebrate my homecoming and make a few dollars, I organized my first skating party. I hadn't skated in nearly 20 years, but I was determined to skate again. One of my friends who had come home before me gave me a pair of skates and I went with him a week before my event to practice. When I hit the floor, I thought I was going to kill myself – my rhythm was off and I almost fell several times. Instead of being defeated, I took the skates home and started skating around the basement until I got my rhythm back. The following week at my party, I was back in stride like I had never stopped skating.

I spent a great deal of time on the Blackberry that Ebony had purchased for me rebuilding and repairing relationships with my family. My phone was basically glued to my hands most of the day. I had missed out on so much over the years that I felt like I could get it all back by staying connected. However, there was no getting back what I missed out on.

As the weeks went by, I found myself getting into the groove of things and experiencing a great deal of firsts. I went to my first Tigers game and had a ball, and then caught my first flight ever to Wisconsin, where I was invited to speak at the University of Wisconsin-Platteville. It was an amazing experience and I enjoyed every moment of the flight, including the turbulence I had heard so much about. Professor Karen Gagne, who I had met while in prison, introduced me to the Black Student Union and they paid for Yusef Shakur and me to do a keynote address for their annual Ebony Weekend event.

Within a few short months of my release, I landed a part-time job writing for The Michigan Citizen, which I enjoyed immensely. I reviewed CD's and wrote feature-length stories on writer and director dream hampton and the Floacist of the famed group Floetry. When I interviewed the Floacist, I had to pinch myself. She had the sexiest accent and the sweetest spirit. The things I had dreamed of doing were beginning to manifest, but nothing came without a fight. As much as I enjoyed working for the paper, when they had to let me go due to budget constraints, I had to make some tough decisions. They agreed to give me a few assignments a week, but it was too much of a financial strain on me. I had just purchased my first car, a 1996 Caprice Classic, which guzzled gas, so by the time I drove around the city gathering information for a story, I was nearly breaking even. I was thankful for the experience, but knew that I had to start investing in my own talent and finding ways to make it happen as an entrepreneur.

2011 ushered in a great deal of change and excitement for Ebony and I. I had met a local filmmaker named Ian Harris who agreed to make a documentary about my life. I had also landed my first acting gig playing a single father named Darren in the Mocha Monologues, which was written by a team of writers that call themselves the Live Ladies of Literature – Adra Robbins, Tracie Christian and Dawn Wisdom.

After a month or so of searching, Ebony and I moved into a new townhouse, and shortly thereafter discovered she was pregnant. It was the greatest news in the world. I was so excited for us, but moreso for Ebony. She had dreamed of being a mommy and I knew she would be the best mommy in the world. As we celebrated the great news with our family and loved ones, my desire to succeed increased. Ebony had been holding us down for the most part, and I wanted to put myself in a position to contribute as much as I could and help relieve her of the financial burden of caring for our family. Though I was selling books, it wasn't enough to earn a real living so I started putting in resumes and seeking out employment, but nothing came up. It was very frustrating and demoralizing because I realized how my felony was impacting my employment opportunities. The economy was tough and it didn't help that I had the stigma of incarceration clinging to me.

Ebony encouraged me to keep my spirits up and not give up or give in. Even though I was struggling emotionally and financially, I continued to work hard in the community volunteering and selling my books wherever I could. Whenever I was invited, I spoke at local high schools and returned to the University of Wisconsin-Platteville to do a workshop on prison reform. While in Wisconsin, I got a chance to meet Dr. Cornel West and have a great dialogue, but none of these things compared to the excitement I was experiencing as a father-to-be. With each doctor's visit, our excitement grew, and when we learned we were having a boy, we were overjoyed. We chose the name Sekou Akili Senghor and began preparing for our son's entrance into the world. I knew I could never make up for the time I had missed with my two oldest children, but I was determined to be the best father I could be to Sekou. I knew I would love him with everything I had inside of me.

During this time, I had begun discussing the possibility of opening my own bookstore in the city and sought out potential locations. As luck would have it, I ended up reconnecting with a designer named Clement Fame Brown, Jr., who I had met while working for The Michigan Citizen. He had a design and branding shop called FAME SHOP and extended me the opportunity to put my book boutique in his shop. We discussed how working together would not only help us, but help the neighborhood surrounding the store, which was located on Joy Road and Meyers. We focused our energy on promoting and marketing the shop as a one-stop spot for fashion, arts, music and entertainment. During the summer, we hosted a grand opening and gave away food and backpacks to the community at an event we called Joy Day. We had barbers cutting boys' hair for free, bounce houses for the children to jump and play in, and a host of entertainment from local poets and musicians. Even though we were struggling financially to provide for ourselves, we knew that our work was having an impact. As the year wore down, I continued my mentoring efforts at Cody High School and Tri County Educational Center in Southfield. Around this same time, the Knight Foundation rolled out a pilot project called BMe (Black Male Engagement) Challenge to recognize Black men doing positive things in the community.

I was nominated by several people in the community for the BMe Leadership Award. I created a video profile and people in my social network promoted it among their friends and family, which put me on the grantmaker's radar. Those who submitted a video were told to submit a proposal for any project that we wanted to do. I discussed my thoughts with Ebony and we agreed to write a proposal based on an idea I had for a program I named Heart of the Matter. I believed writing was a way for mentors like me to get to the heart of the matter when it came to working with our youth. When we discussed it further, we decided to change the name of the program to Live In Peace Digital and Literary Arts Project, which was inspired by two separate incidents in my family. Over the previous summer, two of my nephews had been shot and one of our childhood friends murdered. Our goal with the program was to inspire children to pick up pens and pads instead of guns and bullets to help them process their emotions and get at the root of their anger and frustration.

When it was announced that I was one of the winners of the BMe Challenge, I was overwhelmed with joy. I couldn't wait to implement the project at Cody and Tri County. I had a fondness for the students and faculty at both schools, and I knew that they would be just as excited. It was an amazing moment for me on several levels. It felt like everything was coming together perfectly for Ebony and I.

The fall ushered in more excitement as we began counting down the days to Sekou's birth. Throughout Ebony's pregnancy, Sekou was snuggly nestled sideways in her womb. The doctor warned that if he didn't turn around, he would have to be delivered by cesarean section, something Ebony dreaded. We grew more and more concerned as his due date neared and he still hadn't turned. We had gone to birthing classes and did everything we could to prepare for a natural birth, but Sekou didn't want to cooperate. During one of the final ultrasounds a few weeks before Sekou's due date, the doctor confirmed that Sekou hadn't turned and Ebony would have to have a C-section. Ebony was heartbroken because she wanted to experience natural childbirth, and I was heartbroken because I knew how much it meant to her. I tried to do my best to cheer her up and help her see the blessing that was before us. The doctor scheduled a date for the C-section and we were prepared for Sekou to enter the world on December 1, 2011. But just before Ebony was due to have the C-section, the doctor did one last ultrasound, and miraculously, Sekou had turned around at the last minute.

On December 12, 2011, we checked into the hospital. Sekou's official due date was December 6, and Ebony's still hadn't started contractions so the doctor decided to induce Ebony's labor. For eight hours, I watched my best friend, fiancée and mother of my child undergo extreme labor pains. It was so hard watching her suffer. We had agreed to do the birth naturally and Ebony was determined not to give in to the pain. I coached her the best that I could and encouraged her to hold on in those moments when she was ready to give in. I knew Ebony was a strong and determined woman, but watching her go through the process of giving birth deepened my love and respect for her. After eight hours of labor, Ebony gave birth on December 13, 2011 to the most amazing baby in the world. Sekou came out with his eyes wide open and showcased a loving, alert personality from day one.

Sekou had some struggles urinating when he was first born so we had to stay another day in the hospital. We were both beat and hadn't slept much over the last few months, but our excitement overshadowed our weariness. When we were released from the hospital, we were overjoyed to take our baby boy home. The first few months were a challenge for us as we adjusted to parenthood, but I wouldn't change those moments for anything. Sekou's presence in our lives has been the most amazing part of our journey. From day one, I knew Sekou and I would have a special bond. Sekou made me start thinking about my life differently, and as I watched him grow over the first few months, I thought about my role as a father. More than anything, I realized that I wanted our son to grow up in a very different environment than we had grown up in. I think the role of parents in general is to ensure that our children inherit a world better than the one we inherited. It is toward this goal that Ebony and I work as parents. In my eyes, I couldn't have chosen a better co-parent. Watching Ebony dote on Sekou is one of the highlights of my life. Her tenderness, thoughtfulness, and motherly instinct keeps Sekou covered in a blanket of pure maternal love. The joyful experience of being new parents was a great way to bring the year to an end.

When 2012 got underway, the BMe Challenge winners were invited to the Charles H. Wright Museum to receive our leadership awards. It was a great day for me and my family. It was also a great moment for Yusef and I. We had brought our lives full circle from our days at the Michigan Reformatory. As much as I loved having my family come out to the awards ceremony, the ultimate was sharing the experience with my father. For years I had longed to show my father that I was serious about changing my life and working to make a difference, so even though I had won the award, it was really an award for him because he had taught me what it meant to be engaged in the community as a Black man.

The year got off to a great start, and over the course of a few months, I made a trip to Wisconsin, and finally to New York. I had longed to go to the Big Apple since I was a child listening to hip hop music, so when I was given an opportunity to speak at the Left Forum, which was held at Pace University, and to a group of students at Fordham University, I couldn't have been happier. The cherry on top was being able to meet my dear friend Zhana face-to-face for the first time. We had met nearly ten years earlier when I was in solitary confinement and she was a student at Binghamton University. We corresponded for a couple years before we eventually lost contact. Through the miraculous world of social networking, we reconnected and she invited me to speak at Fordham University where she was teaching. Ebony and I packed Sekou up and drove to New York where we stayed for a few days taking in the sights and sounds of Harlem, the Bronx and Times Square. We also hung out with Professor Gagne who there visiting as well and a few other amazing people. It was a great trip for us all.

The Live In Peace project was in full swing as spring rolled in and I continued my work throughout the community. The students were enjoying the class and I was growing with each session. Watching once shy, introverted street-toughened kids blossom into brilliant writers and expressive word artists kept me inspired. With each story, poem, or Haiku they shared with me, I found myself learning the true meaning of a mentor. There was something profound about listening to the youth I worked with without interrupting them. Once they knew that I was willing to listen with empathy and without judgment, their stories began to delve into the harsher issues that no one wants to discuss. They shared stories of sexual and child abuse that were both horrifying and heart-wrenching at the same time. However, there was an element of hope in every line that they wrote. It is this hope that keeps me advocating on their behalf and working to raise awareness about the issues they face.

I knew when the grant that I received as winner of the BMe Leadership Award ran out, it would be difficult for me to keep up my work at the school. I was still technically unemployed and finding a job became a full-time job. Whenever I wasn't working with the students, I was researching job opportunities or networking with others to create job opportunities. I went to whatever meetings the Knight Foundation invited me to, and that kept me hopeful. There were a lot of great things going on in the city of Detroit and I wanted to be a part of them all.

When May arrived, my focus shifted to walking down my last month of parole. It had been nearly two years since I walked out of prison and I couldn't wait until June to be able to say that it was finally over. A lot had changed since I'd been home. I was battle-fatigued, but Sekou and Ebony kept me hopeful. Finally, on June 28, 2012, I was released from parole and all of the restrictions that came with it. When I exited the parole office for the final time with my discharge papers in hand, I had a bop in my step infused with joy and optimism. For the first time in over twenty years, I was able to live the majority of my life as a normal human being. I no longer had to pee in a cup while strange men stood beside me staring at my penis to ensure that it was actually my urine drizzling in the cup, or seek permission to travel out of state. Overall, I felt free until I ran into some areas of my life that my felony impacted, and would continue to impact for the rest of my life if I didn't fight for justice.

I celebrated my release from parole with Ebony and our family as we watched Detroit's annual fireworks display. As overjoyed as I was with being released from prison, I was a bit stressed out and depressed. I had been trying to find steady employment and things weren't working out for me. In the midst of a tough stretch, I was invited to attend the Steve Harvey's Hoodie Awards with Yusef Shakur. When we arrived in Las Vegas, I didn't realize how profoundly I would be impacted by my experience. The first night we attended a white party and the following night we went to the awards ceremony, which featured a concert that included Stevie Wonder who performed the Grand Finale. The thing that resonated with me the most about the entire experience was how professional and classy the event was orchestrated. It reminded me of the men I had worked with since coming home. I felt like we had the potential to work on a high level and do some amazing things together. When I returned to Detroit, I spoke with my partner Fame about my desire to be singularly focused. The thing was, I had to figure out what the focus of my work would be. It was a difficult thing to do because I had the immediate need of cash flow and that was blurring my vision a bit, however I was hopeful that a breakthrough was coming and I'd finally be able to tap into my inherent potential.

Despite my skillset, finding employment proved to be a challenge in ways that threatened my sanity. Book sales were nominal and speaking engagements were sporadic. There were days when I did great and days when I spent countless hours trying to hustle books, only to walk away with two or three sales. I wasn't sure how much longer I would be able to hold on to the idea of finding a job or making it as an author. However, I refused to give up or turn to the streets. I knew there was a divine purpose for what was happening in my life. I talked to Ebony at night and vented my frustrations. She listened and did her part to encourage me to keep pushing forward. One of the things she told me to think about was how having a regular job would impact my work with youth. Ebony knew enough about me to know that a regular nine-to--five would drive me as crazy as not finding employment. We were both firm believers in the idea that some opportunities were missed in order for us to have a better opportunity open up. I continued putting in resumes, attending networking events, and sitting in on business meetings that I was invited to, however my heart was not in it. The desire to write was strong, and the thought of writing my memoir began to tug at my conscience. I had planned to get it done, but couldn't focus due to my quest to find employment and make money. However, the urge was growing stronger by the day.

In July, a few amazing things happened. I was given a call back for a part-time position that I had applied for working with the Knight Foundation to establish a sustainable version of BMe. I was overjoyed because I knew the work would allow me to continue doing some of the things I was already doing in the community. It would also allow me to make a few dollars and some great connections. Our job wasn't to begin until September, however we had training in Baltimore before the official launch. When I returned home, I went to a meeting that the Knight Foundation had invited me to and met a group of people who would change my life.

When I got the invitation from Rishi Jaitly, who was working for the Knight Foundation at the time, I was undecided on whether I would attend the meeting or not. I had gone to a few meetings and I was growing tired of walking into these meetings with hope and optimism, only to leave feeling uninspired and empty. I had met a few well-meaning people at some of these meetings, but none ever followed through on conversations or emails that we exchanged. There were a few people who said that they were interested in working with me and helping me get my life on track, but all I got was empty rhetoric. I was growing cynical, however I wasn't quite ready to throw in the towel.

I decided the meeting was worth attending, and figured I could at least add my voice to the conversation. When I arrived, I was told that the director of the MIT Media Lab Joi Ito and Colin Rainey of a Boston-based firm named IDEO would be giving a presentation about work that they were interested in doing in Detroit. I had no idea who either of them was, and when I looked at the front of the room where they stood, I was convinced that they were no different than the rest of the outsiders who saw Detroit as a charity case. I figured they would come in and give some syrupy spiel on how they would make a garden or paint flowers all over neighborhood buildings to make the natives feel positive about the blight and high levels of gun violence that they were subjected to daily.

I listened intently as Joi and Colin talked about the ways that they were interested in working with Detroit. Their ideas sounded exciting and heroic. Instead of religious missionaries, it felt like they were tech missionaries. However, I knew their plans were based on what they had been told about Detroit. They had been sold the distorted, romanticized version of Detroit, and the gallery where the meeting was held reinforced this version. I felt this was unfair to them and the Detroiters who worked feverishly to make a difference. I never want to see anyone fail at an endeavor that has great potential and that was what drove me to speak up. There was a calm, intentional presence about Joi that told me he was sincere, so I decided to share my thoughts when he was done with his presentation.

I spoke about the importance of including the real Detroit in the conversation if they really wanted their work to make a difference. I told them that I would take them around Detroit and introduce them to some people who were doing amazing work. Colin and Joi looked at each other, then told me that they were down to come back to Detroit. We shook hands, and when they left, I felt like something special had occurred. When I got home, I told Ebony that I felt good about the meeting, however I really couldn't give her anything more in-depth. There was just something about Joi that told me he was sincere.

Within 15 minutes of leaving the meeting, Joi emailed me and told me that it was great meeting. A couple days later, I got an invitation to visit the MIT Media Lab. I had never been to Boston, so I was excited to check out the lab. Over the next week, I did some research on the lab and was blown away by their work. However, the research paled in comparison to actually going to the lab. During our tour, we saw cars that fold in half to make parking in cities easier and an interesting gadget called Makey Makey that allows you to make music with bananas or anything else you plugged it into. I was completely blown away by the high levels of innovation and the interesting people that I met while there. When we sat down for dinner that evening, I knew something magical was happening. Colin, Jess Sousa, Jess Goldfin and Joi made me feel at ease. We enjoyed a great meal, a few drinks and some good conversation. I wasn't sure what to expect moving forward, however it was very clear that we would be working together in the near future.

Not long after our meeting in Boston, Colin, Jess Sousa, Jess Goldfin and Sean Bonner made a trip out to Detroit. I was honored when they asked me to be their tour guide. There was no pretentiousness on their end and I could sense that they really wanted to learn more about Detroit. As an ambassador for Detroit, I wanted them to see the complexities, contradictions, beauty and ugliness of our battle-scarred city.

We piled into two cars, headed up Grand River from downtown, and drove through several neighborhoods. As we drove, I offered commentary about the different neighborhoods we were traveling through. We travelled through a neighborhood known as Zone 8 where Yusef had grown up gangbanging, and then continued traveling west toward Brightmoor where I had grown up selling drugs. In between, we stopped in Rosedale Park, which is a nice middle class enclave with big, beautiful brick homes. It was one of the many contradictions about the city that I highlighted. A few blocks west of Rosedale Park, we entered the neighborhood known as Brightmoor. It was one of the many neighborhoods that had suffered decades of neglect.

Brightmoor had earned a reputation for high levels of gun violence and drug trafficking, but it was also an area full of promise and hope. Amidst the burned-out houses and vast stretches of empty, overgrown lots there is an artistic and entrepreneurial movement on the rise spearheaded by the owners of Sweet Potato Sensations, the Artist Village, and Motor City Java House. It's also an area where urban gardens are being used to counter the culture of drug trafficking. It was also important for me to show the team the areas where well-meaning folks had dropped the ball.

While in Brightmoor, we got out of the car and walked around and talked with people from the community to get a sense of their needs and challenges. The more time we spent together, the more I began to believe in their sincerity. Over the course of the next couple of days, we visited D-Town Farm and interviewed its director Malik Yakini. We also sat and talked with Yusef at his café and bookstore called the Urban Network. Malik and Yusef were two people who I felt would provide a deeper understanding of Detroit's landscape and I was glad to be able to share their perspectives with the team from the Media Lab.

After several of weeks of traveling back and forth to the lab, we came up with a plan to launch an innovators' guild called IG Detroit. The guild would consist of design challenges that reflected some of the innovation already going on in Detroit as well as other ideas that hadn't been considered. In a matter of a few months, we were able to build solid relationships, assemble teams, and come up with a plan to tackle the challenges we outlined. Finally, on October 5, 2012, we embarked on a life-changing journey filled with innovative ideas and engaging discussions. Along with the original team that I met through MIT Media Lab and IDEO, there were a host of students, faculty members, fashion designers, writers and comedians, both professional and amateur, who came together for the IG Detroit weekend. We assembled in groups and headed back out into the streets to explore our ideas. I was excited when my team members assembled and we headed out for the day.

Our team looked more like a rock band than a band of innovators as we hustled into the large, black SUV. White, Black, Asian, short, tall, casually dressed, it was all there – the only things missing were guitars, amps, a bass, and a dope lead vocalist. But we were no band. In fact, we had yet to band together around the task at hand, and in essence, this ride through the gritty streets of Detroit would be our feeling-out period. We were getting to know each other against the backdrop of a city that had been labeled the rust belt capital and the murder capital of the world, depending on who was telling the story.

We drove block after burned-out block and I watched the varied expressions of my passengers through the rear-view mirror. The expressions ranged from disbelief and sadness to intrigue and hopefulness. In my own eyes, I saw a tinge of embarrassment for our city, for the people who call Detroit home, including myself. For the first time in a long time, I looked at Detroit objectively and it was painful to digest what was happening to my beloved city. However, the pain was soothed by thoughts of what was underway.

As we traveled around Detroit, I felt compelled to give a voice to the societal fractures all around us, but where was I to begin? How could I sum up the tearing asunder of a city that at one time was a place of pride and joy? There was no easy answer and the gravity of it bore down on me. So instead, I simply said there is so much hope and potential here, and it was these simple words that set the tone for what I hoped IG

Detroit would mean for that weekend. Though we had yet to sit down in our workspace, I could see the wheels of innovation starting to spin.

Personally, this was one of the most exciting and rewarding experiences I've had. Being able to work with such humble, giving, thoughtful, and highly motivated people turned out to be the highlight of my weekend. The synergy of urban dwellers, tech geeks, authors, and design innovators proved my long-held belief that you see the best of humanity when artificial barriers are replaced by real life experiences. The creative energy and inspiring spirits were contagious and brought our projects full circle.

Over the course of what turned out to be a four-day weekend, we tackled five challenges: DIY lighting, digital community, air monitoring, DIY soil safety, and compost rotation. We worked in small groups dispersed throughout OmniCorp, a maker space located in the heart of Detroit's Eastern Market. Each group had its own space to iterate on ideas that were shared at the inception of IG Detroit, but we all checked in on each other from time to time. We genuinely enjoyed each other's company and had a blast each night when we wound down from our workday.

When it was time to conclude our weekend and share our projects, I had mixed feelings. On the one hand, I was very excited to see what innovations the other teams had come up with, but on the other hand, I was a bit saddened that our weekend was coming to an end. I had made friends with people who I believe will be a part of my life for years to come. I had laughed and joked with designer Christopher Bevans, comedian Baratunde Thurston, and shared soul food with Haiyan Zhang, Christina Xu, Tara Brown and Erhardt Graeff. In addition to innovating, we were creating a human experience that will have a lasting impact for years to come.

After we presented in front of the other groups and invited guests from different groups in Detroit, I talked to those in attendance to get a feel for what they thought. From what I gathered, there is a great deal of hope and optimism about the future of IG Detroit. I could even sense from those who were cynical in the beginning that they were impressed by what we were able to accomplish in a relatively short amount of time. They were excited by our work and showed interest in working with us moving forward. It was a good sign that we are on the right path, and I am looking forward to the next phase of IG Detroit.

As I approach my third year home, I am looking forward to the next phase of my journey challenging others to right the wrongs that exist in our world.